ELEPHANTS
in My Room

TRUE STORIES BY
Christie Nicholls

For Weasel.

CONTENTS

ACKNOWLEDGEMENT

It would be impossible to share this book without thanking my writing partner of 12 glorious years, Magnum.

In every possible way, Magnum has been a true companion. He's stood by me in the dark, helped me find my way through the haze, and reveled with me in the ravishing light.

I would not be, without Magnum.

Thank you, "Maggie." Thank you, "Bobo."

I take great comfort in knowing that you are everywhere.

INTRODUCTION

H i. Welcome to my room. You're probably wondering who I am and why you are reading this book. I don't know what to tell you. I'm not famous. Not even close. *Famous* people write books, I know. Charlie Sheen wrote a book of poetry. Snooki wrote a memoir/lifestyle guide called *Confessions of a Guidette.* Kendall and Kylie Jenner wrote a sci-fi novel. *A sci-fi novel?!* So, who am I? You might have seen me on commercials, or a poorly attended stand-up comedy show, or maybe you caught one of the cringeworthy TV shows I've been in. Why read this book? It's funny and it's honest. Just like Charlie, Snooki, and the Jenner gals.

Before I tell you about what you'll read in this pithy memoir from a nobody, let me just tell you (before I forget) that I have the short-term memory of an amoeba. Every day is an Easter egg hunt for me—searching high and low for misplaced glasses, keys, and a cell phone that is perpetually on silent. The glasses are usually on my head, the keys are still in the front door, and the cell phone is fifteen minutes into the speed wash cycle in the washing machine. What I lack in short-term memory, however, has been cruelly made up for by a long-term memory so vivid I can recall all the awkward details of my childhood. Wahoo!

In this book, you'll find a nice little collection of honest, if not humiliating, true stories (a.k.a. "elephants") from my past. In some cases, I've added photos to enhance your experience. With each story, I've reached some moral or "lesson learned," though many of my mistakes (or "elephants") recur in subsequent chapters. Oh well. Me and Charlie Sheen – human beings after all.

My hope is that by reading these stories you'll be inspired to share your own "elephants" and from those we can all laugh, or cry, or cry-laugh, or laugh-cry, or just order a delicious, juicy cheese pizza. Sounds good, doesn't it?

The stories in this book are separated into four sections:

"A Broad Abroad" tells four different stories about my experiences living and traveling abroad. It's about sticking out as a family and somehow sticking together because of this.

"Odd Jobs" tells four more stories (I love symmetry), about some of my spectacular failures in the workforce. In all these stories, you'll see it's quite obvious that I suck at my job, but I don't suck as much as my bosses!

"Dearly Departed" is all about lessons learned from dead grandparents (and a grandparent figure). If you are one of those people who enjoys laughing *and* crying at the same time, you'll appreciate this section.

"Boys to Man" is a section for mature audiences only! It tells four stories of boys I dated in college and graduate school. The accounts shared here are genuinely humiliating and will certainly make you feel better about your own dating track record.

Okay. That's it.

Let's get started, kiddos.

Feeling confident AF before my dance recital in May of 1994.

PART 1

A Broad Abroad

CHAPTER 1
Nein, Ferdinand

Casa de Bischoff, in all her glory.

In 1989, my immediate family spent the first of two summers in Belém, Brazil, joining my dad (a nerdy *and* fierce oceanographer) on his research appointment at the Universidade Federal do Pará. We stayed at the home of a German scientist who offered up his beautiful (and vacant) bungalow, a place so grand we called it Casa de Bischoff. It wasn't an ideal bungalow by any stretch. It was effectively a one-bedroom loft that stood on lanky stilts amidst a jungle of thick trees and even thicker insects. Casa de Bischoff was shaped so much like a bug that I was sure at any moment the home would spin a web or up and run away with all our things. Dad told my brother Beluga[1] and me the "good news" the moment we arrived—that we'd get the chance to sleep outside on real, authentic *redes* (hammocks). We were just seven (me) and eight years old (Beluga), and we were to spend a summer dangling on flimsy hammocks, inches from a dense soup of Amazonian critters. Were we concerned? *Nope.* Why? Because Casa de Bischoff had an un-chlorinated pool, an ample assortment of tarantulas to tango with, and a transnational German shepherd who went by the name of Ferdinand.

Ferdinand was the permanent resident of Casa de Bischoff, and he made his status known by threatening a limb removal from anyone who didn't pass his TSA security clearance. Ferdinand was the first purebred German anything (canine or otherwise) that I'd met in my life, and *boy-oh-boy* did I have a crush. He was inquisitive, had an ample snout, and everything about him was German-intense. Perhaps the most entertaining of his intense personality traits were his ears, which were constantly swiveling as they responded to sounds and stimuli (in the same fashion and type-A-ness as a deer).

I liked the fact that you had to prove yourself to Ferdinand; it felt as if I were spending the summer with Simon Cowell of *America's Got Talent.* Much like Simon, Ferdinand was a tough pooch to win over, but we developed a system of communication that was mildly telepathic. Ferdinand would look at me with eyes that said: *All right, I see that you have a treat for me, but tell me, why shouldn't I just pluck out your femur instead?*

---

1   Please note that "Beluga" is a childhood nickname given to my brother by yours truly. As odd as my parents might be, they did not name their firstborn after a whale.

And as a seven-year-old, I'd have to tell him, *"Ferdinand, no matter what you say or do, I'm still going to hug you around your neck for a solid count of ten Mississippi because I am very much in love with you."*

We had very few responsibilities at the Casa de Bischoff. However, those we did have, my father took very seriously. First responsibility: the pool. It was unchlorinated, so Dad needed to simply empty it before it grew frogs. Second responsibility: make sure that the "ducks were safe." By that I mean, keep an eye on the heterosexual duck couple living on the pond that was a pleasant showpiece. Their wings were clipped, probably to make it seem as if they chose to live at the quaint little pond and dine on the finest of Brazilian duck food, Fogo de Quack (this cringe-worthy joke is for the three of you who know Fogo de Chao). My dad lived up to his supposed German descent by being at one minute intensely terrifying and the next intensely gay; so, he took on both chores as if they were direct commands from the Führer, and delighted in their completion with a super fruity caipirinha by the pool. Even though to Ferdinand, the ducks were literally *sitting ducks,* Dad made sure to use his one lowly semester of college German to communicate the rules to the *hund.*

Dad cleaning the pool with a broom. Ferdinand standing dangerously close to a waterless deep end.

That's me, winding up to pitch some stale bread to Mr. and Mrs. Duck.

The first night we arrived in Belém, we didn't yet have our hammocks. So, Beluga and I slept on couches in the living room, located in a section of the loft closest to my parents' bedroom. We were situated on the equator, which meant it was hot enough on the second story of the spider (house) to forgo bed sheets (and this worked out well, because we had no sheets to use). I couldn't sleep that first night, which was (and still is) common for me. There is something about not having bed sheets that made it seem as if I were just lying on a couch, not really serious about sleeping—just hanging out at a furniture showroom. When I remembered our German host was outside probably just licking his balls (yep, he still had them), I thought I'd invite him up to see how Americans slept.

I crept outside and found Ferdinand taking in the night sky. I caught him just as he was picking up something on his radar - his ears pushed forward and ingested distant sounds. I led him to the front door of the house, a threshold he wasn't allowed to pass. He paused and telepathically beamed his concern to me.

You sure about this, kinder (kid). . .?

I nodded. Together, Ferdinand and I gingerly walked up the dark mahogany stairs. I watched his face change as he crossed a threshold that was, to him, strictly prohibited.

So, this is what this place looks like. Wow!(Giddy tail wag.)

Not a beat later, he was back to his serious shepherd self.

Well, I better run surveillance. (Tail settles down and takes a stiff posture.)

Ferdinand took a walk around the loft, beginning near the kitchen.

He moved on to the door leading to my parents' room. I held my breath—his circular canine breathing was a little too loud. Thankfully, he made less noise than my parents' own snoring snouts, and did not wake them. Ferdinand turned, and as he made his way past the living room, he paused to take a look down at Beluga, whose face was planted on the thick white rug, his fins (arms) sprawled out.

Ferdinand browsed the bookshelf, dampening the bindings of untouched texts with his wet nose before hitting up the formal dining room. Past the dining room was the wraparound deck, with all its doors open. Once outside, he crouched down low, preparing to fight a curtain that picked up a breeze and became animated. With the wave of fresh air, Ferdinand held his nose high to file this one last scent.

Being a hospitable seven-year-old, I led him to a loveseat where I thought he'd want to lie down. He ignored the invite and turned his back to me so he could face the entrance at the top of the stairs, alert and ready to de-limb. With Ferdinand inside the house, I found it easier for me to drift into a heavy sleep that was interrupted six hours later by my father screaming.

"*Nein,* Ferdinand! *Nein!*"

Immediately following the sound, I smelled it: a giant pile of shepherd schnitzel. I opened my eyes to find that Ferdinand had dropped a load on Herr Bischoff's white rug.

"Who in the *hell* let him in?" Dad barked.

I pinched my eyes shut. I would pretend to sleep through the schnitzel inquisition, until it was all good and cleaned up. Dad stomped his way back from the kitchen to the load of shit and commenced scrubbing and cursing.

"Nein, Ferdinand. Nein *du scheiße ut—ut-side! Scheiße* outside!"

With the final command, Ferdinand ran ut-side, and Beluga, being just inches from the shit pile, stirred. As soon as Beluga's nose registered the smell, he blasted off the rug.

"What the *heck* is that?!" he yelped.

"*Someone* let the damn dog up," Dad responded.

But before Beluga could declare his innocence, he discovered he was *covered* in mosquito bites. Everywhere—his face, armpits, the soles of his feet, his eyeballs. *Wait a minute,* so was I. I popped up—*what the hell?!* I went to bed in white skin and woke up in hot-pink polka dots. Beluga started in on a wail. Our shared discomfort distracted us from the dog shit; my parents, on the other hand, were relatively bug-free in the master bedroom. Though I eventually admitted it years later, it was obvious that I had been the one to invite the German shepherd upstairs. They assumed this not just because I was the resident night owl, but also because it was common knowledge that I was a fan of the canines. (In my free time, I created a very clumsy superhero/alter-ego known as "Dog Woman." Years later, Beluga would shorten my superhero name to...you guessed it... "bitch.")

Ferdinand's shit smelled especially bad because he was served two meals every day: cooked rice, meat, and a light gravy that smelled like a cup of aged zombie blood. Dr. Bischoff, whom I never did meet, had two Brazilian caretakers who were home most of the day to feed Ferdinand and maintain the grounds. They didn't speak any English, but we found ways to communicate. There was the time I unknowingly stood in a fire-ant hill and started screaming, and one of the ladies shook her head as if to say, "Don't stand in the fire-ant pit, and put some damn shoes on." I shadowed the caretakers because they were teenagers, and by seven-year-old law that made them impossibly cool. They put up with me for the most part, but knew that if they brought out the sack of rice for Ferdinand's food, I was long gone.

About to fly a kite (and get eaten alive by ants).

You could say Ferdinand's dump on the carpet got his and Dad's relationship off on the wrong paw. My father's take on dogs was summed up when I told him (many years later) at age twenty-three that I had gotten a dog of my own. "Why would you go and do that? All they do is eat, shit, and die." I didn't have the heart to tell Dad that his own bedtime routine, which he always announced as "time to shit, shower, and sleep," was nearly the same. Dad would continue to wonder what contributions Ferdinand made to our quality of life—not just to us Nittrouers, but to the human race as well. His position on dogs was so opposite of mine that I thought I was adopted. I vehemently defended Ferdinand from all of Dad's insults, but especially those insults given in Dad's pretend German. "Nein more *Nein Ferdinand,* Dad!"

For most of our time in Belém, we'd stay around the pool or the fire-ant-ridden grounds of Casa de Bischoff. It was gated for safety and only a few times did we venture off to explore the neighborhood.

If we went into Belém, it was to grab groceries, or sometimes we'd stop by the university and see the monkeys that lived in a small cage on campus. It was fine enough; but even as a kid I could tell that the monkeys were miserable— just furry humans trapped in a cage without antidepressants or alcohol. Another activity was eating at a truck-stop "restaurant," which I enjoyed only because at age seven they let me drink my weight in iced coffees without judging me.

Truth is, I never really wanted to leave Casa de Bichoff. It was a nice sanctuary from a level of poverty that I had difficulty processing as a child, and still struggle to process today. We'd drive away in our rented narrow van, a jerky stick shift that smelled like the ethanol it was fueled on, leaving behind our gated casa and entering a much crueler space. You couldn't get into Belém without passing the communities of people living in cardboard huts, where kids my age adjusted their rooflines after the daily downpour of rain known as "three o'clock showers." Even at age seven, I understood that Brazil was in the southern hemisphere, and that fact meant it was technically 'winter'. Winter meant school. It was a hard pill to swallow, that these kids living in the cardboard communities didn't go to school. Sure, I *hated* school but somewhere in me, I knew that it should be a right of every child to have a school to hate.

When we left Casa de Bischoff, we left behind a manicured tropical landscape, thick heavy palms, parrots, a pool, a hip duck couple. To then go and experience the city was like seeing a beautiful piece of theatre and happening to meet the sound, stage, and lighting technicians who made it possible. Like the theatre crew, the people of Belém were unfairly overworked, unhappy, and full of pungent smells. Poverty in Brazil was far worse than what I'd seen in the seediest parts of Manhattan in the 80s. There were children that begged and pickpocketed; there were paralyzed or dismembered people desperate for anything. Once I saw a woman who had no arms and no legs painting with a brush in her mouth. She was working next to a festive café where my parents had bottles of cold beer and I had an icy Guaraná. What happens to you when you see something like that and know that you can only leave behind a piece of paper money or a coin? Regardless of leaving or not leaving money, how callously unsophisticated must our brains be, if we can see another human in pain and simply walk away?

Whenever we returned from our trips into town, we received Ferdinand's mandated TSA-like snout inspection, which, at the time, made me feel rather important. In all of our pictures from Belém, you'd always find Ferdinand's tail somewhere—it was like a *Where's Waldo?* puzzle. Ferdinand was always around, and proved it by stamping photos with a big, bushy tail covered in tie-dyed colors of dark chocolate and coffee.

Photobombed by Ferdinand's tail, and yes, I'm anxiously tracking the ants that had made a meal out of my feet the previous day.

*Ferdinand just barely moves out of frame as I redefine
the meaning of a "shit-eating grin."*

Ferdinand loved watching us by the pool; and by this I mean he
loved grabbing ahold of a foot as you jumped off the ledge, or gnaw-
ing at your hand when you were clinging to the edge (as I often did).
He'd get especially barky on weekends or partying weekdays when
Dad introduced his signature game of "Melon Ball." During Melon
Ball tournaments, fifteen or so *hammered* humans would face off in a
water polo match that used a gargantuan watermelon as a ball. Anyone
under 180 pounds made for the lanai when Melon Ball got under way,
except for Ferdinand. He'd nip at hands and counted down the seconds until the "ball" got tossed out of the pool and would crack open.
There he'd stand over his watermelon carcass, chewing thick pieces of
pink watermelon meat like they were handfuls of Big League Chew.

"Ferdinand! Nein!" my dad would yell, assuming that we'd all want
to eat the waterlogged melon during the closing ceremonies, as if it
were the Neanderthal ritual.

Just like any good 'buddy cop' flick (think *Turner and Hooch*), the
more time Dad and Ferdinand had together, the more they delighted in teasing each other. My favorite exchange to watch was when
Ferdinand followed Dad to the edge of the pool and waited as Dad

performed a dramatic dismount for one of his dives (a.k.a. the unintentional belly flop). As soon as Dad had liftoff, Ferdinand sunk his teeth into Dad's heels. Another great show was when Ferdinand would steal paper plates during dinner, only to eat them in their entirety and later deposit shit-paper piles (think "shit spit balls") on the walkway. Sometimes Ferdinand would crawl under the floating mahogany stairs and nip Dad's feet as he went up to the main story of the house. Ferdinand *loved* to fuck with Dad, and who could blame him? It was *his* house, after all, and *we* were the guests.

Ferdinand also loved to shadow Beluga and me when we took to torturing substantially sized insects. Ours was a match made in *hund*-heaven; naturally children and German shepherds were perfect partners in persecution. We found the biggest termite mounds and took them out with some makeshift torpedoes and rockets. *Wunderbar,* Ferdinand would say as the mound erupted into dust clouds. A local Brazilian boy/genius showed us where scorpions hung out (under logs) and how to poke them so much that they bitch-slapped a stick with their tails. Also fun was the creek behind the house that had a powerful flow of water that looked to be chocolate milk, but tasted, as I found out, like liquid piranha farts. Ferdinand always accompanied us on our explorations, standing with his head cocked, and his signature German shepherd eyebrows arched in a fashion that suggested his mind was *effing* blown.

Once, when we returned from a three-day research trip, the swimming pool had grown frogs. For my dad, who had a responsibility to clean it, this was disgusting. For Beluga and me, this was magic - a giant cauldron of pets. Before Dad flushed the frogs, we took two tadpoles and put them in a liter-sized water bottle, watching every second to chart their growth. When they outgrew the water bottle, we poured them into a big bowl, with enough room to get fully froggy. When they reached a size large enough to be photographed for their high school yearbook photo, Ferdinand ate them. He couldn't help it; I mean, they were growing in dog bowls. Surely to Ferdinand, frog was the equivalent of lobster. I'm sure he approached the frogs the same way a patron at a fancy restaurant might eye the lobster tank in the foyer. He was a classy dog, after all.

If Ferdinand was rowdy during Dad's Melon Ball tournaments, he was even rowdier at Dad's fortieth birthday party thrown by the Amazonian scientists. Dad's intentions for the party were all too clear: to pulverize any and all memories of his thirties. To accomplish this, Beluga and I were given a job: to juice as many limes as humanly possible so that the adults could and would bleed caipirinha. The caipirinha is the more down-to-earth cousin of the margarita, with simpler ingredients: sugar, lime, and a *lifetime* of cachaça. Always wanting to make money, I took to my job seriously. I cut the limes—and incidentally my hands. I bled on the lime, had lime juice bleed into my wounds, and I really howled when I found out there was no money involved in my free labor as a seven-year-old barback. Remembering the cardboard huts I could be living in, I decided to call my bar prep a birthday gift. Yes, I gave a gift that got my parents, their friends, and most of Belém utterly *wasted.*

Dad's 40ᵗʰ – countless caipirinhas at Casa de Bischoff.

After a full day of caipirinhas and Melon Ball tournaments, a funny thing happened: Dad invited his old pal Ferdinand to come upstairs. This was the turning point in their relationship, both of them breaking protocol for the love of a good celebration. Or, as my dad put it in his butchered Portuguese, "Come on, Ferrrrrrrrrrrrrrrrrrrdinarddd. Let's *celebrar!*"

And thus, both Ferdinand and Dad finally figured out a language they shared: drunken Portuguese. By the end of Dad's 40ᵗʰ birthday party, he was in a face-plant on the master bed, groaning into the sheets as if he were crying.

"Dad? Dad, what happened?" It was Beluga, always a Sherlock Holmes of sorts.

"Buhhhhhhhhhhhhhhhh duhhhhhhhhhhhh buhhhhhhhhhhhhh," Dad replied.

"Are you okay?" Beluga asked, seriously concerned.

And then he said it, the best Dad line in the best deadbeat Dad delivery.

"No. *I'm dying.*"

Beluga, not understanding the hyperbole resulting from an early-onset hangover, threw himself on the bed and cried.

"But you can't die, Dad. Dad, no!" he sobbed.

Dad rose above the occasion and gurgled out, "Guhhhhhhhhhhhhhhhhhhhhhhhhh."

I decided that since Dad was dying and Ferdinand was sleeping like a human upstairs, I'd leave my hammock behind and do the same that night. My legs and arms were already so coated with mosquito bites that there was literally no fresh blood left in me. Since the couches were taken, I found a spot next to Ferdinand. He fell asleep before me this time, tuckered out after a long day of partying. I watched him. He took in air from flexible nostrils that delicately dented in and out with each breath. His nose wasn't just smelling; it was thinking. What a perfect creature he was.

The next morning, when there wasn't a shepherd pie in the house, Ferdinand strutted down the stairs like a new dog.

A few settled and happy days later, Ferdinand took it upon himself to walk up the stairs to see why we weren't by the pool or near the creek. Once up the stairs he saw that we were packing things into our suitcases. He got closer, like all hunds do, checking to see if we were putting things in or taking things out. His nose followed the clothes as they went in, his tail lowered and slumped between his legs. He backed up slowly, deliberately, as if he'd just walked in on an extramarital affair. We continued to pack, somewhat giddily. I was excited to get back to Long Island, to my friends and less aggressive mosquitos (where bites would only cover 33 percent of my arms and legs).

Not long after Ferdinand had walked upstairs, we heard it: a *shrieking* quack. I ran out to the pond to see what happened. I went right to Mrs. Duck, who was going on and on about someone who'd done something that she didn't like. "Uh uh UHHH uh UH UH," she screamed to me. I looked around, but couldn't find Mr. Duck. . . He must be . . .

"No, no, no, no . . ." Dad yelled as his feet thundered down every step of the stairs. "No, no, no, no," he yelled in a building crescendo. Then he saw it; we all saw it.

Ferdinand emerged from the trees behind Mrs. Duck, carrying her beloved husband of four years, Mr. Duck, in his jaw. The look on Ferdinand's face was that quintessential dog look of "what's the big deal, guys?"

And just like Marlon Brando's infamous "*Stella!*" in *Streetcar*, Dad clutched his face, dropped to his knees, and let it rip: "*Nein, Ferdinand!*"

Ferdinand finally heard him this time. He dropped the duck, gave Dad a look, and retreated behind a tree, where he likely took stiff shots of Bärenjäger. He spent the whole day there, too, not bothering to eat Mr. Duck. He left the body sitting there—a cold duck. Beluga and I were grossed out by the attack, but not because we had any loyalties to Mr. and Mrs. Duck. I suppose it was sad seeing Mrs. Duck without her partner, even if she and her husband were always so pretentious. We were now afraid of Ferdinand—he had killed something that was part of *his* family. He had ended a life, and for what reason? Would he do this to us? Was that *really* why he nipped at our feet in the pool?

The next morning, we were up at five a.m. for our journey home. Beluga and I rolled up our hammocks as Dad huffed our bags out of the spider-house and into the research van. Ferdinand walked in from the darkness and took a look around the outside of the van. He was cold, moody, and all business. Very formally, Ferdinand gave our suitcases a final once-over.

So, you're going on a trip. I better make sure you don't leave with any of my things.

As Beluga, Mom, and I were standing around watching Ferdinand's practice, Dad returned with a suitcase the size of a Kodiak bear and dropped it to the ground. What he didn't realize is that he dropped it on top of Ferdinand's paw. Ferdinand made a sound we had never heard before—it wasn't quite a yelp, or a cry, but mostly it sounded like "Naaah-hun!" We instantly grabbed the pup around the neck, crying "Oh no, poor Ferdinand!" Even my mom admonished my dad for what we all thought was a strategic attack on the convicted duck murderer. Ferdinand sat with one paw outstretched and dangling, as if he were drying his nails after a juicy manicure. We hugged him until he put the paw down on the ground, walked around, and cheerfully shook off our human affections.

"What was that sound?" Beluga asked.

"He just said, 'Naaah-hun,'" I said, still amazed that the dog could speak.

Amidst the exciting discovery of Ferdinand's "Nah-hun" language, we said our good-byes to the hund, not certain if we'd ever see him again. I hugged his neck as long as I possibly could. Beluga shook his paw like a businessman. My mom gave him a hardy pat down. When Dad got to him, we held our breath, hoping he wouldn't add insult to (paw) injury. Dad looked down at the pup, petted the top of his head, and said, in his best German yet, "*Gut hund*, Ferdinand."

Our car slowly pulled away from the house, with barely enough dawn light to illuminate Ferdinand's panting tongue. We watched as Ferdinand walked to the pond, turned in a few tight circles, and lay down on the exact spot where he'd left Mr. Duck. He lay like a sphinx; perfectly poised and serious. Suddenly it dawned on me. From Ferdinand's point of view, the ducks were the most valuable thing on his property. Ferdinand didn't kill Mr. Duck just to kill something; he did it so we could take something of his with us. Ferdinand saw that we were leaving and he wanted to give us something—an offering, a gift.

As we left the gates of Casa de Bischoff, it all made sense. I turned to Beluga.

"Naaah-hun," I imitated as best I could. Beluga laughed.

"Naaaaaah-*hun!*" he retorted.

"*Nah* hun hun . . . or nah HUN *HUN?*" I asked, now adding some inflection.

To anyone else in the car, our conversation was further evidence that Beluga and I were "special" kids, but somewhere inside us we knew what gift Ferdinand had actually given us. That first conversation in the car, in an odd combination of *nah* and *huns*, would become a new language for Beluga and me, and one that we'd continue to speak for the rest of our lives. We'd create stuffed animal characters that spoke explicitly in Nah-Hun language, a dialect that only he and I could decode and give meaning. What was even better was how, as we grew older, we used the phrase "nah-hun" to stand in for anytime we had a misunderstanding, or we had hurt each other. Just like Ferdinand, we'd drag a "paw" on the other person's closed bedroom door and say, very kindly, "Nah-hun?" Or, as we got older, if a compromise just couldn't be reached and insults were being thrown this way and that, a "nah-hun" simply meant "you're hurting my feelings." It could be said in person or on the phone, written in a text message or an e-mail, but the sentiment was always the same: "just like Ferdinand, I'm vulnerable too."

CHAPTER 2
Bowling Bologna

We tagged along on another one of Dad's summer sabbaticals, this time to Bologna, Italy; the birthplace of salami's less attractive cousin, baloney. We began our summer in Italy with a red-eye flight to France, where the frogs in front of me smoked the entire flight (this being 1991, mind you). At age nine, I didn't drink, smoke, or sleep on flights, so I spent most of the time folding my legs into a tight pretzel and watching for signs of life below me. *What the fuck was actually down there?* Even as the child of an oceanographer, I'm still not sure I believe in the vastness of oceans. What if the Atlantic Ocean was actually a sea of seahorses—not those gross tiny aquatic creatures, but ponies who swam, spoke English, and adored little girls?

Italy and apparently all of Europe were devastatingly expensive, and we were on my dad's stipend, which didn't even cover one human—it covered one *scientist*. When we arrived post red-eye to the airport in Nice, we met our spunky little rental car. It was roughly the size of an airplane restroom, smelled like hot barf, and handled like a jackhammer.

Dad, a.k.a. Clark W. Griswold, proudly posing with our Italian rental car.

In Bologna, we rented a three-bedroom apartment from an Italian woman who, unbeknownst to us, also sublet one of the rooms to a very wealthy Japanese woman. Our roommate was wonderfully organized and beautiful, and she didn't use her bedroom all the time (I now realize she was probably out screwin' an Italian or two - *get it, girl*). Luckily, her rock star life outside the apartment meant I occasionally had my very own room, away from Beluga.

The apartment was on the fifth floor and had a long, narrow balcony that I spent a lot of time on—when I could handle the heat. Summer in Bologna was much like it sounds —it was like living inside a sticky, hot baloney log. Our weekdays were really boring; looking back on it now, I'm jealous of my nine-year-old self, but when you're nine the last thing you want to do is stay inside an Italian apartment for the entire day. My mom would read steamy novels in her room, and Beluga and I were left to entertain ourselves indoors.

A typical day looked like this: I would wake up and take a trip to the bakery, where I'd buy one loaf of bread, bring it home, cut it, spread Nutella on it, and take all the flakey crumbs out to an interior courtyard for a gang of hungry pigeons. They'd nod as they ate the crumbs, I'd appreciate this gesture, and we all killed a little time on planet Earth. A few mornings I took it upon myself to pack my dad's lunch, which was something like a five-course meal with Nutella spread across every course. You might say I developed a Nutella addiction that summer... and you would be entirely correct in saying so.

Because everything was so damn expensive, my mom refused to buy us any kind of games or souvenirs. We couldn't pack much in the way of toys because we had to fit in two months' worth of clothing, scientific gear, and hard liquor. These last two ingredients, scientific gear and liquor, were always stowaways that were found in our luggage. At every arrival, I'd unpack and find that all my elephant t-shirts smelled like the leaky MacNaughton's whiskey that Dad had snuck into our bags. Our return trips were no better on the nose; in this instance, all my clothing smelled sulfuric and salty, a result of Dad's oceanographic samples from the bottom of the seafloor. Once home and unpacking, I'd inevitably come across some dark gray/brown sludge tucked away in my bag and I would complain to Dad. He'd look at me and say flatly "Dolly, that (sea) mud is money."

Mom's solution to the "no toys in Bologna" policy was to make toys out of free hotel shampoo bottles and soap boxes by drawing faces on them with an Italian Sharpie (a *Sharpio!*). I took my shampoo, conditioner, and soap people and created what I called a "soap opera." I combined them with my stuffed elephant, Dumbo, and was able to perform a decent range of rough and tumble characters. It helped that my brother was desperate for any form of entertainment, so I had a small audience. Much like Tom Hanks's volleyball bestie, Wilson, in *Castaway*, we created a crazy colony of confidants. Our soap stars were good company, for the most part, though during one episode I accidentally chipped off a piece of Mr. Sal Soapstein, absentmindedly inhaled it, and found that his flesh burned the inside of my nostril for three solid days.

I found another source of entertainment—writing a happy little short story about two best friends torn apart by death. Admittedly, it was a rip-off of *Bridge to Terabithia*, but I added my own marks—my protagonist was part Native American and happened to look like the American Girl doll, Kirsten. Yes, life in Bologna was all very Victorian; being locked up in an Italian apartment without much to eat or drink, while writing dark and sad stories about death on the plains of Montana (where my story was set).

Beluga took up his own hobby, too: wine making. Using emptied wine bottles collected from my parents, he'd pour in packets of imported Crystal Light lemonade, mix them with Italian tap water, and recork the bottles for us to enjoy at our evening meals. The concoction tasted like something you'd puke up after an aggressive white-wine tasting, but it was entertaining enough to hear him describe a four-day-old bottle as "vintage."

Preparing a meal at our apartment in Bologna. Beluga uncorks a crisp bottle of Crystal Light, aged one day. The expression on my face accurately captures how I feel about cooking with family.

Beluga's other pastime was watching Italian television. It was pretty painful to see him suffer through the language barrier, but he stuck with it, like a good ol' TV-lovin' American expat. Always seated next to him, in the living room, was the strangest feature of the apartment: a giant wedding cake that was preserved in a glass display case. Most of the apartment had bizarre props like these, but the cake had a peculiar energy to it. I'm not saying I believe in cake ghosts, but were a scientist to come out with a paper on it, I would certainly read that paper. Throughout our entire stay at the apartment, I wondered when Beluga and I would have a knock-down, cake-out fight and demolish it, but our father warned us as only he could: "Don't fuck with the cake."

On the occasions when we left our apartment in Bologna on weekdays, I never felt comfortable out and about, because we were so easily identified as outsiders. Even though I was only nine years old, the other kids seemed to run circles around my fashion sense. I still have PTSD flashbacks of Italian kids looking at me in the eyes and then directly at my shoes, and back up to my face to convey their repulsion. One time, a little Italian girl nearly upchucked after she saw my American feet in sandals. Her disgust and other reactions like it marked the beginning of what would become a lifelong insecurity about my feet.

After six weeks in Bologna, my dad came home with a brilliant proposition: "Why don't we try out *Bowling Bologna?*"

Bowling Bologna?!

Now this was not a typical thing for my family—to partake in anything that might be credited with the label "family friendly." Bowling Bologna was just down the alley from us but it was never within our budget to venture inside. Beluga and I were beckoned by the chimes of the electric pinball machines and arcade games—or "money suckers," as Mom called them. When Dad said the words Bowling Bologna, we dropped our Nutella and Crystal Light wine, and ran to the door.

As soon as we walked through the doors, I felt like a kid in a bowling alley. My biggest relief came when I discovered the mandatory shoe rental. Ah, bowling shoes – the great leveler of foot-fashion insecurity. Any newfound footwear confidence was smacked down when I realized that I'd never in fact bowled before.

We entered our names on a clunky keyboard and they appeared on a computer screen with edgy green font (*THE FUTURE*, I thought). My name, or the first six letters that were allotted, was displayed on TV for all of Bologna to see — "CHRIST." *No pressure to bowl like a messiah or anything.* I found the smallest ball in Bologna and cradled it in my string-cheese arms. As the smallest in the family, I was last to take a roll. This gave me time to study my parents, who were campy in their performance; Dad would imitate a professional and Mom would lift a leg, like a graceful dog urinating.

The screen alerted us that it was time for CHRIST to bowl. With both hands on my ball, I swung it around to my right side, and chucked it forward with all my might. The ball made it about five feet and stopped in the middle of the lane. Assuming that bowling was like any other sport, where the entire court was fair game, I walked out on the (very slippery) lane and gave it a wobbly kick.

"No! No, no, no, aye, NO!" screamed an Italian man in a shirt that exposed enough chest hair to hide a family of badgers. He hurried over to the walkway next to our lane and took a step out to pick up the ball. Knowing I didn't speak Italian, he waved a finger at me and returned my ball.

I panned around the room to see who had witnessed the ordeal. Yep. Everyone had seen it. They saw my failure to move the ball more than five feet, my runway walk to the ball, and my roundhouse kick. Mostly, they saw me get in trouble, and "they" were (yet again) Italian kids. I took a seat on a row of plastic orange chairs, hanging my head to watch my feet dangle above the ground. Even with the right shoes on, I was giving them more fodder to find me different, stupid, weird. *Ugh.*

When it was my turn again, I tried a similar approach, though my ball only made it five feet and three inches. My dad sent another ball toward the one stuck in the lane. He sent it maybe halfway down the aisle, after his ball wiped out and rolled to a stop in the gutter. The bowling manager, again seeing us, said something to the effect of "mamma mia" and rescued both balls.

With more looks from the Italian kids, it became all too clear: I was really not cut out for Bowling Bologna.

The next few rounds, I volunteered to be an observer. There was just no way of getting around it; I was bad with balls. Even the giant TV had registered my failures and broadcasted them for all the Italians to see.

CHRIST: 0. 0.

After a few turns and a few bowling beers, Dad had an idea.

"I'll help you bowl. Just stand over here." He motioned to a spot in front of him.

"No thank you," I countered politely.

"D-D-D-Dolly," he said, which was his stutter for dramatic effect, "do you want to knock some pins down?"

"Yeah."

"I can promise. D-D-Dolly, no, I *guarantee* you will knock pins over."

Destruction of any perfectly organized arrangement has always been a huge passion of mine.

And so, I stood in front of my dad, as we assumed a co-bowling stance that is best described by picture:

We sent the bowling ball flying into the formation, knocking not just one, but three whole pins to the ground. I was ecstatic. I soaked up the clamor of noisy pins falling to the floor, crying out for the loss of their perfect assembly. I had to have more. On our second round, we took out two more; that made for five whole pins, conquered by none other than CHRIST herself.

My dad and I continued our signature technique for every frame of that game and the one that followed. We were calling more attention to ourselves as outsiders, bowling in a position that would be frowned upon even in West Virginia. With each frame, we got more serious and more celebratory when a pin gave up ground. We taunted and insulted the pins, loudly, outrageously, and enough that I completely forgot to notice the Italian children and parents staring at us.

Sure, bowling gets labeled as a distinctly American "sport"—with the beer and the balls and the destruction of things without concern for cleaning it up. The truth is that bowling is universal. No matter where in the world you bowl, it's always the same thing: it's clumsy, stupid, and unhygienic. Ultimately though, it's just an excuse to stand around together in the same shoes. So, when I caught the Italian kids laughing, I turned to face them and chose that time not to look down at my feet. Even if our form was different (and it *really* was), we were all there for the same reason; to break balls (on some pins).

CHAPTER 3
I Love English

*My family of "Brilliant Assholes" at the All Saints Church
in Lanchester, England (the adorable blonde child in the front
is not a Nittrouer, and hence, not an asshole).*

If my dad's side of the family had a family crest, it would be a light-bulb, a middle finger, and an Entenmann's Danish. As my grand-mother so eloquently put it: "The Nittrouer family? We're assholes. Brilliant assholes." I imagine this phrase "assholes, brilliant assholes" would also line our crest, written in pig Latin with the finest crayon available.

The moment we got word that my aunt Karen, who we suitably nicknamed "AK-47," was engaged to marry an English gentleman, we booked our tickets across the pond that very same day. The trip began for my immediate family, arriving from different cities into Chicago's O'Hare Airport, kicked off in style at the Chili's *Too* bar. Following several Sam Adams pints, we were ready to keep all of our fellow passengers up with incessant conversation.

I figured out at a young age that my brother Beluga was an excellent, if not the best, person to have seated next to you on a flight. Beluga has always had a way with flight attendants—a trait he inherited from my mom's side, whose family crest reads, "Will Charm for Alcohol." Beluga always got extra pours of complimentary wine, free headphones, potent life advice. My favorite was when he was twenty years old and he pressed the call button to order his scotch for "an emergency nightcap." Only Beluga could deliver the cheesiest lines with an earnestness that *always* won over the flight attendants. "What a tight little French twist," he'd remark drunkenly, always with one eye closing and his twisty bar-fight nose extra red and glowing. He'd continue oozing such compliments like, "I mean, how *do* you get it *soooo* smooth and tight?"

After about six hours of mid-Atlantic partying, we decided to sleep the last forty-five minutes of the flight, arriving in Heathrow like hell on earth. We found our luggage and our rental car and made it to our hotel in Windsor, angry that we were ready for our check-in at six thirty a.m. but our hotel was not. Our solution was to wander around Windsor in search of anything that was open and willing to feed us caffeine. Our first stop was an Italian café. The joint was primed for asshole tourists who wore sweatshirts and baseball hats that advertised not just that they were American, but from what state they hailed. For Beluga, it was spelled out in collegiate lettering that he was from "WASHINGTON." As such, it was only appropriate that he order the eight-pound "authentic-o cappuccino" in Windsor. The steep price was one my mother was not happy about – and a common theme for them to bicker about. Mom hates spending money, but Beluga loves spending Mom's money.

Mom shot passive-aggressive stares at Beluga until she'd had enough of his audacity. She sashayed up to Beluga, clenched her jaw and very slowly and dramatically asked: "Who. Do. You. Think. You. Are?"

The cappuccino maker glanced up from his foam job and banged the nozzle like it was his head against a brick wall. Beluga did not whisper his response, nor did he hide his stew of dehydrated post red-eye morning breath.

"It's *fucking* seven a.m. I've been drinking for seventeen hours. If you expect me to walk around castles and shit without puking in the queen's—" Beluga was interrupted by Dad, who stepped in between them.

"Woah, woah . . . *dahhhb* . . . *dahbbb*, let's just cool our jets," Dad said, ever paranoid about fitting in with whatever culture we were supposed to be fitting in with—British, Italian? He motioned for Beluga and Mom to move toward the door before adding a tip and voicing "arrivederci" in a cringe-worthy American accent.

So far, so good. We were *caffeinated assholes*, off to pose in front of the palace with our teeth bared. Knowing that my dad hates posing for pictures, I purposely held out my camera for an extended stay when snapping photos of him, especially when he was within earshot of several pleasant-looking Japanese tourists. I knew he'd give them a good show.

"Just take the *fucking* picture," he repeated through gritted teeth, like a ventriloquist at the end of his rope.

Dad, advising me to "take the fucking picture."

That night in the hotel room, with our doors and windows wide open for all our neighbors to hear, we had warm gin and tonics and decided that we better find an Indian restaurant because British food was "so fucking shitty." We stopped by a pub first and had a few pints; I'm not sure exactly how many, but enough that when we arrived at the Indian restaurant, we felt emboldened to ask why they charged for "bread" (naan). Despite all this, we were at our best in Windsor. There's just something about knowing that Queen Elizabeth weekends in a castle across the street that will make you think twice before dropping trou and peeing street-side.

The next morning, we were up early, trying to squeeze as much out of England in the four days we had to get up to Lanchester. We made a stop in Stratford-upon-Avon, where we saw Shakespeare's so-called grave (if you believe he was actually human and not a robot) and a production of *A New Way to Please You* at the Globe Theatre. Even with my "I'm a thespian" scarf, we stood out at the theatre, probably because we spoofed actors' accents with our own impressions, which were straight up knock-offs of Robin Williams' insurmountable performance in *Mrs. Doubtfire*. When my family wasn't insulting the sacred art of theatre, they'd ask mildly intelligible questions like "where are the curtains?"

After my cultural experience, Beluga was raring up for his: smoking hash. To score some hash was no easy feat, because for one thing we reeked of "tourist" (I blame the Nike running shoes) and it just so happened to be July 4th, a day to celebrate our *independence* from (not our *dependency* on) England (to give us hash). I'm not really a pot smoker and I certainly wasn't at that point in my life, but the thought of following up our evening of shitting all over Shakespeare with some hash...it just felt *bloody* right.

The plan was simple: find the shittiest looking bar and the drunkest, most toothless patron, buy him or her a pint, and tell him or her in our best cockney impression to "make with the hash, please." The first part of the plan worked: we found several patrons sans teeth, one we even bought a pint, or two, and things were real chummy *until* it was leaked that it was our Independence Day. The entire bar, upon hearing the news, turned their stools in unison, making an awful screech. They stared and we waited.

In the thickest accent, as if he'd pounded a jar of marbles and hadn't yet swallowed, our toothless pal yelled:

"Well bloody 'ell, what is we waitin' for? We've bett'er celebrate, then!"

And with that, he ordered us pint, after pint, after pint, as the entire bar sang our national anthem. This tradition, when one person starts singing and the others join in, was a trick that would come in handy a few days later with Aunt Karen's in-laws.

After our bellies were full of John Smith's Extra Smooth, we stumbled out of the pub with our toothless host. We took seven or eight pictures outside a red phone booth, and started to part ways, until Beluga got a look in his drunken eye.

"Jehh-Jeff, Jeff^2. *No.*" My mom tried asserting control over Beluga, which she knew was a waste of words and air at this point.

From our position, we could see Beluga hand our guy a wad of cash, following which the guy gave him a thank-you nod, and that was it. Beluga didn't know it at the time, but that would *be* it. The next day as we waited for a wad of hash to arrive, we learned that our independence came at a price. Beluga's payment to our toothless friend was just an overdue tax for all that tea we dumped in Boston Harbor many moons ago.

Hash-less and hungover, we headed northbound the next day and found a hotel in Skipton that was about as American as you can get: it had a parking lot, an ice machine, and you could do a full turn in your room without having to open a door. Because ice was "abundant," as my dad declared, we prefaced dinner with a few gin and tonics. After our dinner, Dad reviewed the meal for all the restaurant guests to hear, "it was a big bowl of bland."

We took to the backyard hills of our hotel to taunt livestock in our equally bland British impressions. One cow, as it turns out, took offense and charged after Dad, who got away but shortly after doing so slipped, landed on his ass, and slid far enough that he destroyed his pants. After a reasonable amount of doubled-over laughter and hyena-like cackling at Dad's expense, we decided to retire to our hotel rooms for more G&Ts.

---

2   Jeff is my brother Beluga's formal name.

I was several G&Ts deep when I took this oddly pleasant photo.

I'll admit, the "brilliance" my grandmother speaks of about our family is most readily seen in our ability to turn any and every budget hotel room into a full-blown cocktail lounge. Every ounce of our brilliant, boozy creativity is put to use. Mom will end up with a swiped candle from a restaurant, place it in a plastic cup, and *presto!* Mood lighting! She'll throw down a scratchy bathroom towel and cover it with a hearty arrangement of three-day-aged leftovers. *Hors d'oeuvres!* If it's an extra fancy rager, Dad will fill the bathtub with ice, creating a massive cool pool for all the alcohol. Forget the iPhones for music, because we use the motel alarm-clock radio as a fuzzy (sometimes incomprehensible) soundscape with extra-long commercial breaks. After all this setup is in place, we get absolutely *shit-canned* and talk for hours on end.

At around ten p.m. the phone rang and as drunk as I was, I assumed it was the queen of England thanking us for our visit.

"Cheerio," I greeted her.

"Yes, I'm *terribly sorry to bother you* . . . but the neighbors have . . . they have complained that it's a bit too loud. Would you mind terribly to keep it down just a bit?" The request came from a wiry man who was stationed at the front desk.

"You have my word, good sir," I replied after pounding my gin and tonic and slamming it on the bedside table.

"Thank you *so* very much." He emphasized the 'so' like a real prince.

"*Indeed.*"

The next part of our "nightcap" escalated in volume due to multiple disagreements. My mom and Beluga were arguing about a girl Beluga was interested in dating, while my dad and I were even more loudly arguing about toilet-seat etiquette. It's common knowledge that my father and I are the loudest of the group, especially if our discussions have anything to do with gender or feminism. Though Dad claims to be a feminist, he's also been known to mistake feminism for a brand of budget tampons.

"I think the woman should put the toilet seat up, out of respect for the men," my dad grumbled through the side of his mouth.

"That's horse shit!" I said.

"What about men's rights?"

"Both genders need to sit when they shit. Men shit all the time. That means like seventy percent of toilet usage happens with the seat down. Therefore, majority rules."

"Well, I"—Dad paused for a hiccup and then stuck his landing— "I shit standing up."

"Liar! Big, fat, fuckin' *liar!*" I was officially yelling.

At this point the phone rang again, and, somewhere in the back of my mind, I wondered if this time it actually was the queen weighing in on the debate.

"Good day, mate." *Shit,* the gin produced the wrong accent.

"Terribly sorry, this is reception again, and the noise is too loud for this late of an hour. Please, if you don't mind just keeping it down a bit . . ."

"You got it, old chap," I said in a voice that came out more like a wasted John Wayne than British.

Like all good drunks, we tempered our conversations to a lulled whisper-*scream*, and maintained this level until we found a topic that we all *agreed* upon. For some unexplained reason, a Nittrouer in agreement is even louder than a Nittrouer in disagreement. Also, because our number of F-bombs quadruples in agreement conversations, our "getting along" is deemed more offensive to those people within earshot.

A knock at the door stopped our conversations. *Ruh-roh.* My dad, having just confessed to shitting standing up, answered the door, as if he had no idea what the problem could be. The weaselly British man took a tone that was best described as "nearly perturbed."

"Sir, I have called twice and after we received our third complaint, I stood outside your doorway and I must say"—I was secretly waiting for him to validate my point about toilet-seat etiquette— "the noise is *quite* considerable."

The way he emphasized *quite* was so quintessentially British that I grabbed my notebook and wrote down the entire phrase, muffling a rolling giggle. "We're going to have to break up your party," he continued, as he stuck his head around the doorway to see my mom, brother, and me sitting in our respective corners of the ring, with a bottle of duty-free Bombay whimpering near the windowsill, nearly killed.

"Sure," Dad agreed. Then, turning to us, he spoke loudly enough so our neighbors could hear him as he said in the itchiest American accent: "All right, guys, time to hit the sack."

Meeting the Extended Assholes

The following day, we left behind our soiled reputation in Skipton, and made it to the bustling metropolis of Lanchester, England, population: 1367 ¾.

We checked into our hotel, The Kings Head. Beluga and I shared a room that was about as large as a handicapped bathroom stall, and was sandwiched by rooms filled with family members of our soon-to-be uncle, John.

"Remember," Mom said, stopping off in our room to loan Beluga an iron before we met everyone, "be on your best behavior." Her eyes darted around the room like a paranoid spy looking for bugs. She continued, hunching low, bugging her eyes out and whispering, "*They can hear us.*"

"Yes, in fact, it's true. . . The walls are quite thin," replied a chirpy British woman from behind the wall.

My grandmother once told me, in what I call a thick Philly twang: "I can't think sumthin' and nawt say it." She graciously passed on this chip to all of her progeny, and has never thought twice about calling us out for being an asshole, or if she was in a better mood (a few glasses deep in 'blush' wine), a "son of a gun." All three of my grandmother's husbands died, and while she jokingly called herself a "black widow," I think most of us wondered if she had actually insulted them to death. Three of her four children made it to the wedding in England: her oldest, "Chuckie" (my dad), her second youngest, "AK-47" (my aunt Karen), and her "baby" (my aunt Patty). I am closest to Aunt Karen's kids in terms of age and temperament. My cousins Todd and Julie like to think, drink, and fight. Much like Beluga and me, they truly lived up to the crest. My aunt Patty's much younger kids, Kelly and Jenny, grew up in Canada and subsequently disguised their asshole qualities through French immersion classes and culture.

We met our extended family at the other hotel in town, the Queens Head. All thirteen of us experienced a lesson we'd continue to talk about over the next four nights: British people take all of their suppressed feelings out on their cuisine. In short, British food is far more offensive than any "obnoxious" American's personality. I ordered a pizza and gritted my teeth as every single family member asked the same question, upon seeing the "pizza," "Why is there mayonnaise instead of cheese?" A few others ordered shepherd's pie, which came out looking like a white hockey puck covered in a shepherd's diarrhea. We were left with no choice; we had to be assholes to our meal. We animated our food, making it talk and move; we even made it eat itself and then throw itself up.

This first night was certainly a strategic move on our soon-to-be Uncle John's part – he'd let us get our 'fucks and shits' out of our system before he introduced us to his family. After we'd drained the taps of draught beer at the Queens Head, we made way for more drinking at Uncle John's row-home. Once inside his picturesque place, which was sandwiched between other darling Easter-egg-colored homes, we played a cutthroat version of charades.

In our family's version of charades, it wasn't so much about guessing the clues as it was about insulting the quality of your teammate's performance. After a performer failed to get their teammates to guess correctly, there was an earnest pause and a question of "*What the fuck is wrong with your brain? How in the shit is this (act-out with offensive impression of player) Frosty the fucking Snowman?*" Any confrontation like this was forgiven if the rest of the group laughed loudly enough. If the insult wasn't forgiven, it was "Fuck you, you're crazy, I'm done with this shit." Throughout the game, which went until 4 a.m., anyone with Nittrouer blood dramatically quit at some point and rejoined only to spite the opposing team.

The following day was the rehearsal dinner at, of all places, a Chinese restaurant. This was where we met Uncle John's deceased first wife's brother and his wife, a wonderfully British-classy woman who had a 'fancy for Shakespeare.' We spoke politely about Shakespeare's genius (though between us, I don't really give a rip about his writing, aside from *Julius Caesar* and *Hamlet*). Still, I wanted to make a transatlantic connection, and it turned out that the woman and I bonded so much that she told me she would mail me materials from her Shakespeare collection. It was a generous gesture and a great step toward merging the American and British sides of the family. Perhaps I wasn't such an asshole after all; maybe I was . . . the other side of the crest?

Right on cue to this promising moment was the sound of aggressive glass clanking. *Ding. Ding. Ding.* Oh no. It was my dad, of course, who was several drinks in and standing to give a toast. We waited for him to speak, but he didn't speak; he began singing for all the restaurant to hear, the most uncomfortable solo piece of all time, Auld Lang Syne. Now, before I continue, it should be noted that my father's singing voice is so foul that he was required to mouth the words in his high school's glee club. Worse than this were his lyrics – astoundingly incorrect:

"My all the maintenance be forgot . . ."

After he'd made it through a bar or two, something incredible happened, the entire restaurant stood and started singing along. They interlocked crossed arms and swayed to and fro, outsinging our made-up American lyrics with the real deal. The song ended and though the dining room dynamic was awkward (like a morning walk-of-shame *awkward*), we couldn't help but wonder if we'd made a cultural connection.

Uncle John leaned over to explain to Dad that it wasn't magic; it was tradition to stand and sing whenever someone began singing "Auld Lang Syne."

AK-47 and Dad aggressively sandwich Uncle John.

I watched from across the table as my Dad digested this new information. He took a beat and did what I knew he'd do. He stood up and held his glass high.

"To John and his bride."

The crowd clinked and echoed him: "to John and his bride." We drank and settled in. Unfortunately, however, the kraken did not sit.

He cleared his throat, a delirious giggle leaked out, and he began, "Mayyyyyyy. Mayyyyyyyyyyy . . . may all the quaint things be a lot . . ."

Feeling a sense of familial obligation, I joined in, followed by my cousins, followed by our other family, and finally the entire restaurant sang again—excited only for some vague hope that it would be a single encore.

Before tea and dessert came out, Dad went up about three more times, with each time the restaurant patrons exuding less and less passion in their singing. By the tenth time, he was laughing so hard he couldn't form the words, and mostly slurred the melody, especially as he watched the oldest of blue hairs stand to sing. On Dad's thirteenth or fourteenth stand, the manager approached John with a request that we leave. Uncle John handled it like a gentleman, considering he was kicked out of his own rehearsal dinner.

This about sums up our collective reactions to Dad's incessant singing.

"The party bus," as we renamed it, dropped us at the Kings Head pub, where we ordered "pints of anything." Shortly after our order came, the bartender spoke in an accent so thick I thought he might pass out after rolling his R's.

"All rrrrrrrrright, I'm lockin' up the dewwwrrrrrs."

"We *just* ordered these pints here," my brother protested drunkenly. We all waited, jaws clenched and fists balled, ready to rage at the injustice that we were told to leave the bar.

"Well guuud fuhhhr uuuuuuu," said the bartender through a bristly beard.

"Wait a minute now. . . we just got our drinks," Dad, suddenly a diplomat, started up with the bartender.

"You don't have to leave; they just can't let anyone else in," Uncle John noted, desperately trying to deescalate.

"What? For how long?" Dad asked, bitterly confused.

The room stood still as the bartender uttered the most *perrrrfect* words we'd ever hear:

"You can stayyyy awlll nighhhht," he threatened like a punchy pirate ghost.

We scratched our heads. We were locked in a British pub for the entire night? After the bartender saw that we'd fully digested the offer, he added:

"Though I'm not too shuwwwrrrrrr you can handle it."

"Chuck," John chirped in his signature birdlike enthusiasm, "there is a law in certain Commonwealth territories that requires bars to shut down at ten p.m. so the drinkers don't drink so much they can't get to work the next day. The bar is technically closed to those on the outside, but for us on the inside . . . we can drink as long as we stay upright."

HO-LY SHIT.

An odd thing happens when you find out you're locked in an eighteenth-century pub with your extended family.

*If you look carefully, you can see my grandmother
smooshed between her two grandsons.*

Once the news that we could stay all night sunk in, we all pretty much lost our shit. My brother took over the role of bartender and tried his hand at properly pouring Guinness. If his beer didn't settle *just so*, he'd pound the pint and start all over. Locals spent a good deal of time hitting on my grandmother, while my aunt Patty smoked a thick cigar in the corner and acted like she was Tony Soprano. My cousin Todd danced with Julie's boyfriend, Jeremy. At one point, Julie and I were planting deodorant around the bar to see if we could get the locals (who definitely did *not* use it) to give it a try. The night took on a movie-montage shape—the jukebox played giddy Beatles songs, and any word uttered produced long, loud laughs. We slipped in and out of accents and made bizarre discoveries of shared genetic traits. We partied like there was no tomorrow.

Jeff finally figures out how to properly pour a Guinness.

Zombies

When tomorrow finally arrived, we all felt like we had been bitten by a flesh-eating hangover. In an attempt to be good tourists, we took the long and windy road to Durham to see "fuckin' castles and shit." We walked around beautiful architecture groaning and complaining about our heads, backs, and balls. Some a-hole thought it'd be a good idea to hike to the top of the Durham Cathedral. Though the historical environs were all very rustic and Hogwartsy, I made it to the top stair of the tower only to puke a mixture of Guinness and lo mein. It was a haunting combination of flavors that I'm afraid I'll never shake from my memory.

At the top of the effing castle, attempting to smile and not barf

Wedding Bliss

Though we had a day off between the rehearsal and the wedding, we again got ourselves locked into the pub the night before the wedding and exercised no self-control. If we felt bad climbing around on the castles in Durham, we felt worse on wedding day.

All right, fine. I'll go ahead and say it: I don't like going to weddings sober. I find them to be redundant, overly dramatic and mildly creepy. Why the heck do I need to watch you sign a contract that binds you together until death? *And* you expect me to watch that shit sober? *BOR-ING.*

My family shared this sentiment regarding weddings and so before the wedding we polished off a couple of bottles of sweet, sweet, *oh-fuck-me-it's-so-disgustingly-sweet* British sparkling wine. Taking our cues from the bride, we drank and talked and talked and drank, because it's not like we had anywhere to be. Luckily Aunt Patty, wearing the stupidest hat I've ever seen (and I've seen some dummies, *trust me*), was at the church before us and able to explain why the bride was so tardy. "She's drinking."

Meanwhile, AK-47's wedding was happening.

AK-47 and Uncle John were married at the All Saints Parish Church, which was built in the twelfth century, and though it is an architectural masterpiece, it is also mildly terrifying. I believe my exact words upon entering the space were *holy shit.* Aunt Karen walked down the aisle, the pastor did his thing, vows were exchanged, and we were almost done. The final part of the ceremony involved both families witnessing the signing of the marriage license. We were led into a very small room, chock-full of hungover assholes. We stood carefully, our lips sealed, knowing any wisecrack could ruin the happiest day of someone's life. To all of our combined shock, all assholes kept their brilliant mouths shut, and pressed into nice, big American smiles.

Once outside the church for wedding pictures, the locals noticed something strange: a big, bright ball in the sky. In fact, it was over eighty degrees Fahrenheit, which as it turns out, is the exact boiling temperature for people of the British Isles. The wedding party of Williams and Nittrouer was to have a formal dinner at the Queens Head, where we'd be served our choice of shepherd's pie or quiche. Beluga, Jeremy, and I were seated apart from our parents and cousins and were angry about that and the looming reality of more British cuisine. And that, my dear friends, is when Jeremy (now my cousin-in-law) introduced me and Beluga to his fail-safe wedding go-to beverage, the Jack and Ginger (Jack Daniels and ginger ale). It's strictly against our family policy to order hard liquor overseas, except for what we'd brought over in our checked baggage or had bought at the duty-free store. An exception to this rule is made, however, if someone else (Uncle John!) is footing the tab.

The combination of no air-conditioning and an unusually large number of Americans meant that the kitchen took at least two hours to produce our Shepherd's pucks. That was not a problem for us, because we were making a steady dent in our first course, which I called "cold soup" (Jack and Ginger). As I enjoyed my soup, my father gave a speech that was milder than the rounds of "Auld Lang Syne." My aunt Patty, still wearing that stupid hat, spent her speech discussing the differences between American and British toilets. It was a clever use of symbolism; it's just that the shepherd's pie, in its shade of deep shitty brown, was finally delivered at the precise moment Aunt Patty launched into the extensive toilet talk.

Seeing that his aunt was flailing, and fueled by a few bowls of soup, Beluga pulled British and American flags from our centerpiece and stood behind her to demonstrate the merging of both cultures. It was performance art at its very worst. The Brits were not amused.

Beluga's intercultural performance art.

After I'd drank *all the soup* at the Queens Head, it was time for act three of the wedding celebration — an American-style reception that was held at the local senior center in Lanchester.

We entered the old folks' club to the sweet vocal stylings of a Neil Diamond impersonator, who opened with a miraculous performance of "America" (with that deliciously cheesy chorus of: "we're coming to America"). I hit the dance floor with my mom and cousin only to find that our enthusiasm garnered participation from Americans only (Aunt Patty and Aunt Karen). It was common knowledge that all the American guys were off smoking hash in the woods, but the rest of the British guests were just watching us, unenthusiastically. I channeled my frustration at this by heading to the bar and ordering more soup.

For the first half of the reception, I was a crazed wedding-dance shark—unable to cease choreography for fear that my stomach would burst. Occasionally I'd catch the eye of a British person over sixty and attempt to summon them to the dance floor with intense eye contact, broad smile, and spastic arm movements. In retrospect, I must have looked like a *shit-canned* Cheshire cat. Though there were a few mandated British dances that got more people on the floor, there was a painfully clear division between the British and the Americans. We were far outnumbered too; it didn't seem right that we were hogging the stage.

During Neil Diamond's slow dance, I had a "drunk-piphany." My eyes narrowed and I stared off at a British flag, stewing up an internal monologue that was delivered to me directly from the lips of Jack Daniels himself. It went, and please imagine the most slurred internal monologue you can, like this:

Is this it?

Are Americans . . . bad? Are we Americans just stealing all the dance-dancey times? Are we just invaders? Iraq, man. Iraq. I mean, we all saw a very beautiful wedding between a woman who survived breast cancer and the Uncle Gromit who lost his first wife to cancer. They had second chances. Can't we? Americans, British. Brimericans? Ameritish? Sure, we won the war and got all the good teeth, but they got The Rolling Stones and The Beatles. But all you need is love. Yeahhhhh. Love. L-O-V-E. If nothing else, we have love. And you know what? I love England. I love this place with its ugly food and inedible people. I love England. Wait, no . . . I am actually in love with England.

It was at this point that I marched onto the stage and took the microphone directly from the claws of Neil "Dyemond" (or however he differentiated himself). It was rude, but I was drunk and I needed to save the world.

"Listen up, everyone, I have something to say." The crowd paused their conversations and turned to look at the *plastered* American. "I just wanna say . . . this is such a beautiful day, in such a beautiful country. England is great. Really great and John and Karen, am I right? *Soooooooo* beautiful. And I know we're the Americans dancing big and stuff, but you know we want to share the floor with you . . . because . . .this is a beautiful...and because..."

I paused to look at the crowd of British faces staring back at me. If looks could talk, theirs would have said, 'we hate you.' I had to do something. Something *big*. . .

"Because . . . *I love English!*"

Oops. I didn't stick the landing, so naturally I kept going...

"I love English, you love English, and we all speak it, so you better . . . dance. You. Better. Dance."

I wasn't getting the response I wanted, so I went full Mel Gibson-hostile on the Brits. Still on stage and clutching a cup of soup, I yelled at one blue-haired woman in particular. She tried to look away, but I didn't let her.

"*You.* You have *no* excuse for not being up here. *None. Zero. No excuses.* So, get up here. Cause I love your country and *I love you.*"

What happened next? Well, let's just say the blue hair didn't say it back and Neil "Dyemond" grabbed the microphone from my hand.

I was played off to "Song Sung Blue." I waited for a few British ducks to waddle on stage. They didn't. My next move? Hit up the bar for more advice from Jack.

"I'll have a Jack and Ginger, please," I told the trolls behind the cafeteria-style window that served as the bar.

"I'm sorry," said Troll #1, a teenager with teeth the same size, color, and shape as a Shetland sheepdog.

"A Jack Daniels whiskey mixed with a ginger ale," I repeated, like a condescending ESL teacher.

"I'm afraid we're all out."

"But . . ." I looked right at Jack Daniels, sitting upside down in one of the freaky European liquor dispensaries. Fine. They wanted to play hardball, so would I. "I'll just have a White Russian."

"So sorry," Troll #1 said as she looked down at the ground.

"A White Russian is just, it's vodka and milk," I tried.

"Sorry . . ." She continued to draw out her apology as if it would stop me.

"Fine. Black Russian, please."

"No, terribly sorry. . ."

"A Russian? Literally just a cup of vodka," I said, kind of kidding, kind of serious.

Troll #1 walked away to help another guest and Troll #2 stepped up to play the game and shake his head.

"Hi there. Scotch, please." I tried, thinking I had the right answer.

Nope, he shook his head.

"Newcastle?"

My mom approached me at the bar on my ninth attempt at a drink order.

"Chris, what are you doing?"

"I'm looking at the booze, Mom, *but it's not going into any cups.*" The trolls gave a look to Mom. "That's right, you guys," I continued, "I can *see* Jack Daniels over there, but I don't see him in my mouth."

"Uh, Chris...they're cutting you off," Mom revealed.

"*What?* I've only had . . . like . . . like . . . five-teen drinks."

"Let's go," she urged.

"Wait a minute, wait a minute, wait a minute." I addressed the trolls, "Can you see what I'm doing out there...on the front lines?" I looked at a nametag, which, at that point, was a cup of alphabet soup with no meaning. I grabbed for any name I could cook up. "*Daphne,* can you *see* what I'm doing on the dance floor? I'm making them dance." I looked out on the dance floor. There were a few Nittrouers thrashing their arms around to make that *terrible* fake trumpet gesture for "Sweet Caroline."

"Let's sit for a minute," Mom said, secretly loving the entertainment I was providing her.

"Fine. Fine," I said through a hiccup. "You know what, Daphne? I *lied*. I *don't* love English."

At the bitter end of the wedding reception. I was officially cut-off and royally pissed off at "English."

Partying Is Such Sweet Sorrow

The day after the wedding, I was about as hungover as is humanly possible, and I was about to embark on a potentially nauseating travelling experience with my brother. Though our time together in England went inexplicably well, at that point in our life Beluga and I did not exactly get along. Still, for some reason I felt compelled to take a trip with the *king* of the assholes. We said our goodbyes to family, got into an airport-bound taxi, went through security, and headed to our gate.

In the waiting area for our Ryanair flight, there was a group of thick, meaty men, clearly plastered and screaming songs in husky, hoarse voices. It was a drinking song that they were all chanting in a fashion similar to our family's version of "Auld Lang Syne." Waiting passengers glared at them in a way that I had been glared at the night before. Like me and like my family, these airport assholes didn't stop. In fact, they kept going, and grew even louder while picking each other up, squealing, shrieking, and thundering down the sky bridge.

"Who *are* those guys?" I asked the ticketing agent who took my boarding pass.

"Oh, I'm terribly sorry for the noise," he said, while looking at my ticket. "They're just heading home. They're *Irish.*" He exhaled as he said it, as if he'd just received a parking ticket.

As we boarded the plane, I watched the drunken group take their seats. They somersaulted into their row and gave each other juicy smacks on their heads.

"Well," I said to Beluga as we made our way to our seats, "it looks like we're headed in the right direction."

CHAPTER 4
Stand-Up Sweden

"*Dahhbbb dahhbbb*," my dad said, which was his angrier equivalent of *ummm*. "Damn it, Dolly, I told you this would happen. *Damn*." To my Dad, nothing was as heinous and unforgivable as not planning for the language requirement during your senior year of college. "You should have taken that *dang* French placement test. This is bad. *Real* bad."

"It's not the end of the world; it's just a choice between Swedish, Chinese, and Russian," I told him, holding the phone away from my ear so his yelling wouldn't do permanent damage.

"I told you what happened to me, I . . . I *warned you*," he said. "I thought I could handle college German, and you know what happened? I couldn't pass. I. COULDN'T. PASS." He waited for a reaction from me and when I didn't give him one, he upped his intensity: "It was a very *sad* thing." He took a deep breath. "*Fine*. You should learn Swedish. You'll have to learn a whole new alphabet with Russian and Chinese, and your aunt Julie is Norwegian. You could talk Swedish to her at family dinners," Dad added, stupidly.

"Dad, that's not how it works. I'm going with Chinese."

"*Dahhbbb Dahhbbb* . . . those students aren't beginners! They've been talking to Grandma Chin for twenty years; you think they're gonna cut you any slack? *Bù, bù, bù!*"

"Dad, you sound racist."

"Oh come now. Chinese is a complex language that deserves more than your twenty-one-year-old attention span."

He was right about the attention span thing. Mid conversation, I had wandered off somewhere and found myself wondering if bees ever sleep. *Do they sleep?* Does anyone have an answer to this? Anyways, back to the question at hand. I needed to get into a language class quickly and get out with a pass. The next week at eight thirty in the morgon (morning), I was sitting with a class of twenty-five students, while our teacher, who had lightning blonde hair, spoke exclusively in Swedish. It was part of an immersion practice, but I felt as if I had fallen into a terrible acid trip where my teacher was in fact the Swedish chef from *The Muppets.* I spent that first day and many days following with a continual thought of *what the fuck are you singing about?* We were given dittos and worksheets with busty women who were labeled "hon" and mustached men labeled "han." "I" was a "jag," which is pronounced "yog," but for me it always just came out like "*JAHGG.*" For three quarters of my senior year, I suffered through written exams, oral exams, and the worst of all these – the fucking pancake parties, all because I was sure that I could pass the language credit and move to China.

The joke was on me, because Swedish became an STD I couldn't shake. In graduate school at the University of Wisconsin, my area of "expertise" (which was the result of a love-hate relationship with the woman-hating Swedish playwright August Strindberg) became Scandinavian theatre. I'll admit, what the Swedes don't say to your face (nearly everything) they save for the stage, which makes for tremendous theatre. So, I stumbled along in grad school, researching Swedish writers and directors, earning my necessary graduate school patches.

As my Swedish STD grew, it became more aggressive and difficult to hide. Somehow, I was accepted into the theatre PhD program at UCLA with the understanding that I was the resident "Scandinavianist," a title that sounds an awful lot like a growth resulting from an aggressive STD. As it turned out, I ended up teaching a Scandinavian literature course for twelve quarters in a row. I tried to veer off from the Swedish/Scandinavian track when I submitted my preliminary proposal for my dissertation to analyze American stand-up comedy. The prospectus was accepted under the condition that I include a chapter on Swedish stand-up comedians. *Vad fan!* (translation: *what the hell!*)

So, that brings us to the title of *this* chapter, where I took my mother to Stockholm for the explicit purpose of researching stand-up comedy by women.

Getting There

We met at Newark Airport, where I found Mom wandering outside a Sbarro in her typical flying gear: a seventeen-year-old MCM denim jacket, self-hemmed jeans, and four-inch black-patent wedges. I've *never* understood my mom's airplane ensemble. For someone who travels internationally about fourteen times per year, working alongside my oceanographer father in filthy contexts (cutting up samples of ocean sediment), she opts to fly in five-inch heels that turn her body into a teetering scale. Atop this scale, she *barely* balances a carry-on bag that is the size of a fat golden retriever. Her air-travel traditions are bizarre on every front. She is adamant about not purchasing a drink or a snack—why would she when she has a Ziploc bag full of mixed sunflower seeds and shells (and by mixed I mean she has the shells of former spit-covered seeds mixed with fresh seeds). To avoid the drying and thus wrinkling effect of altitude, Mom perpetually applies thick globs of face cream that leave behind a greasy, perfumed dew that makes its way onto everything she touches. It's true that my dog Magnum can smell when Mom's plane touches down at LAX.

After briefly reconvening, we boarded our plane to Sweden, Mom slamming her golden-retriever-sized carry-ons into the sharpened cheekbones of the sandy-haired Swedes heading home. As our plane taxied on the runway, I "saw the sign"—the boldly situated IKEA right off the runway in Newark. Something about that bright yellow shit-can of a store seemed to offer a great omen for our trip. I leaned over to Mom with a suggestion,

"Mom, let's order some wine!"

"What? I'm not paying eight dollars for Nakedtoes," she said, flipping through her *Oprah* magazine to fold off a corner of a recipe she'd never make.

"Barefoot? They don't even sell that wine. It's better wine than Barefoot." I was fluent in *Deb* as we call it, the language my mother speaks (wherein incorrect names and identities are used 87% of the time).

"Oh, right, *Barefoot*. No thank you."

"Well, we need something to have a 'toast' to our transatlantic trip!" I said, knowing that the use of the word "toast" would get her.

'Toast' was an oft-used family buzzword that tactfully allowed alcohol into a situation that didn't necessarily warrant it. Why, we couldn't just have a Bloody Mary at ten a.m. on any given Sunday, but we could certainly stand on the deck and have a toast to the new crop of squash growing in Dad's garden.

"That's sixteen dollars for two glasses of wine," Mom continued, turning to me, just as her glasses slid down the bridge of her overly moisturized nose.

"I'll pay," I offered. We paused for a minute—probably the longest moment of silence we'd share that week.

"I'll buy this round, you buy the next," she added.

Like most of my Mom's analogies, celebrity name mix-ups, or airplane apparel choices, I didn't understand the logic, but boy was I entertained by it. As we toasted, we got caught up on the latest news in our life, pausing briefly to discuss the coolness of the flight attendants, only to get back to the hot stories of the day.

"How about George Clooney? That 'I'm winning' business? What a *weirdo*."

"Oh, I know, Charlie Sheen. He's clearly done too many drugs and now it's starting to show."

"That's right, Charlie Sheen. . . *Oh, brother*." She took a pause *not* to reflect on how/why she confused Clooney and Sheen, but to take a look at my feet. "Those shoes you're wearing, are those the John McFaddens you told me about?"

"Yeah, Steve Maddens. I got them at Marshalls for fourteen ninety-nine."

"What was the 'compare at'?" Mom asked, on the edge of her God-damned seat.

"Forty-nine ninety-nine."

"Yeah, I like those," she said, impressed.

According to our Marshalls credo, the real value of any clothing/shoes/accessory was determined by the difference between the "suggested retail" and the final purchase price. Technically speaking, my John McFadden's were worth $35.00—a very "likable" value.

We arrived in Arlanda Airport early in the morning, and as soon as we got our bags I made a beeline to the tourist bureau to purchase train tickets to get into central Stockholm. I rehearsed a handful of transactional Swedish lines in my head, hoping the other lady also stuck to the script from my college textbooks. Instead, as Swedes often do, she heard my grammar/accent/vocabulary and as a "courtesy" began speaking in English. Well, this was music to mother's cheap ears and she swooped in with her own mastery of English. The next thing I knew, we were on the bus into Stockholm. It wasn't how I wanted us to begin our first trip together—just the two of us—but I decided to stuff my feelings on the subject, as is the Scandinavian way. As they say, when in Stockholm . . .

Our bus was especially narrow and it teetered out of the parking lot and drove off into a gray, desolate landscape. Sweden in March was not as magical as I had imagined—it somehow managed to have both the sting of winter and the emptiness of early spring. Mom looked out the window, clutching her miniature black backpack that she reserved only for travel. It was one of those practical carry-ons that was a close cousin to the fanny pack and would have fit better back in 1993. Despite this, she loved the bag and it was one of those props that annoyingly defined my mom, and for that reason I kind of loved it. It already had a history, like the empty aloe vera jug she recycled and used as a water bottle for a good part of the 80s.

Our first steps out of the bus and onto the sidewalk caused an embarrassing slip-'n'-slide, made possible thanks to cobblestones, snow, hidden ice, and unpredictable roller suitcases. I followed a map I'd printed that led us to our hotel, the Birger Jarl, or "Yo Burger" as my mom insisted on calling it. As we wobbled along to the hotel, our teeth chattered, as our bodies were still surprised by the cold, heavy Stockholm spring.

"Well, I need to put my panties on, I'll tell you that," Mom said. After many years of knowing her, I understood that Mother was in fact wearing underwear, and that "panties" were her oddly X-rated abbreviation for "long underwear."

The kind people at Yo Burger let us check in early but warned us that we were not permitted to eat the breakfast buffet, as that would be a violation of the rules (and Swedes love nothing if they don't love their rules). We got into our room and took a much-needed two-hour nap, waking up a little before the lunch hour.

After properly layering with "panties," we were ready to tackle the walk to Stockholm's Dansmuseet (dance museum), which was probably not the first stop for most visitors, but was a must-see for my mom. As a dancer and a dance teacher, my mom couldn't be kept away from anything that had any semblance of dancing; any glimpse of coordinated movement and she was right there watching and thinking. All throughout my childhood, my dad, who always had the TV on for background noise, would call out, "Buddy, they're dancing" when anyone on TV was showing a shred of choreography. Mom would run in and stand in front of the television and watch the dancing in a chewing-gum commercial.

After I had my fill of the dance museum's exhibits, I sat in the café with a beautiful cup of Swedish *kaffe* and went over my notes for the stand-up show I was performing the next day. I was terribly nervous to perform in Sweden. My parents were not very happy about my decision to do stand-up, or as they put it. to "stand on stage and say disgusting things." I was just months away from having a PhD in performance studies, and by their logic I didn't actually need to *do* comedy; I just had to criticize others for how *they* did comedy. The only time my mom saw me do stand-up before Sweden was when she flew down to LA with my dad, Aunt Julie, and Uncle Pat for a show at the Downtown Comedy Club. They were seated in the front row and were literally bled on by the host, Garrett Morris (of *SNL* fame), after he popped a sizable nosebleed just moments before he brought me up on stage. The crowd was slim, and during my entire ten-minute set, my parents sat inches from me, making a face that suggested they were passing a rather jagged kidney stone. Needless to say, I bombed, and it was (and still is) the only time I've cried immediately after walking off stage.

After several hours of poring over the few exhibits in the museum, Mom entered the café with *exhilarating* news.

"I got us tickets to see Victim! He's performing in an hour, right here, right in the museum!" she said, beaming.

"Victim? Mom, what are you talking about?"

"I talked to the woman who works here and one of the most famous principal dancers from the Swedish ballet is performing right here! His name is Victim." Mom handed me two tickets with the name Wikström printed in large font.

"Ah, you mean Vick-Strum," I pronounced correctly. "Mom, it's not *victim*."

"Well, you get the point. It's going to be so great, Chris. He's doing a solo!" Mom's enthusiasm was powerful but not contagious. Sure, I could enjoy some dance here or there, but I just didn't find watching bodies as entertaining or unpredictable as listening to the comedy made with language. We were just different that way. She loved bodies; I loved words.

Nevertheless, we were first in line to choose our seats for the "Victim" show, which was a pretty impressive feat, considering how oddly aggressive Swedes are when it comes to forming lines. Inside the museum, they had carved out a long and narrow catwalk for Wikström to perform, with seats surrounding him on all four sides. It gave the effect that we had created a cage for him to prance around in, something that made me feel voyeuristic and gross. The lack of space between him and us made me uncomfortable, especially coming from the stand-up stage, which keeps intimacy at bay by requiring a microphone. Maybe Mom was right — maybe "Victim" was a better way to describe this dancer.

When Wikström took the stage, he was topless, with small, black spandex pants on, and he stood at military attention. It took every ounce of my self-restraint not to make a joke about how silly it all was.

It was just all too serious, and it dawned on me that it had been many moons since I had sat for a dance solo. The hint of a single spotlight signaled the beginning of the piece; after that, we heard the faint rattle of a snare drum that matched Wikström's militaristic posture. My mom leaned over to me and whispered. "I love *Boléro*," she said, never moving her eyes off Wikström.

Boléro is an orchestral piece that you've probably heard before—maybe you were flipping through stations in your car and you caught it on public radio, maybe you saw it in a film (the famous scene with Bo Derek from *10*), or maybe you just remember it from your past life. It's not something you can forget. *Boléro* is far and away the most haunting composition I can think of, which makes sense, because it was created explicitly for a dancer (it was commissioned by Ida Rubinstein in 1928). It is an ode to a crescendo, and by this I mean it is a perfectly calculated build from the very beginning. It starts with the delicate rhythm of a snare drum, and suddenly a flute enters, followed by a clarinet, and as the song progresses so do the size, shape, and contributions of every character in the orchestra. Each instrument has its solo and its moment to say something within a repetitive and regal beat. With more time, the sound grows more powerful; it becomes threatening and hypnotic, like a mob gathering to do something *really* big. But the composition is also like witnessing someone's life unfold—hearing them gain knowledge, but knowing that the louder it gets, the closer it is to the end. Or maybe the song just tells of the evolution of our planet and all the pieces that fit together, or perhaps it is evolution told in reverse, as Boléro ends with a big bang.

Wikström gave a performance so equally haunting as the score that I was sure he had been possessed and so had the audience. We couldn't take our eyes off his movement. If the score of *Boléro* was an ode to a crescendo, Wikström's dancing was an ode to the complexity of the human body. Every inch of his body was controlled and disciplined, down to his very fingernails. When the tempo picked up, so did Wikström's sweat, and we sat so close that as he turned he sprayed us. It was a bizarre mix of baptism and SeaWorld show, but we were too transfixed to dodge it.

It was, hands down, the most incredible piece of performance I've ever witnessed. Before the show, I couldn't fathom how just one wordless body could hold my attention for twenty minutes. Wikström's performance made it so I wasn't sure if I had actually been dancing too; it was entirely possible that there was no line between us at all. We were all part of the cage; we were all *Boléro* dancers. It took me 28 years, but I finally saw what Mom saw in dance.

(Trying to) Stand-Up

To go from the brilliance of *Boléro* to the shitty, seedy scene of stand-up comedy the following day was not the easiest of transitions (especially when I was trying to convince my mother of stand-up comedy's credibility). The show took place in southern Stockholm and was produced by a goofy and lovable Swedish man in his late seventies. By American stand-up standards, it was an incredibly well-appointed and classy venue, a point I talked about for the first minute or so. Mom had sat through maybe three or four comedians before me who spoke explicitly in Swedish, and we both laughed, though we had *no fucking clue* what they were talking about. My mom knew two terms in Swedish: *mor* (mom) and *tack* (thank you). Despite this, she sat through two hours of comedy from Swedes, even when one stopped midsentence and said in cool, effortless English (knowing she was a visiting American), "You have no idea what we're saying *and yet* you laugh." Something about being in that small space with low ceilings and lots of blond people and hearing "and yet you laugh" as if it's an accusation—it definitely felt a little Holocausty.

As far as my language skills were concerned, I could sort of make out a premise, but it sounded something like "I like think not very shower me bad. But . . . school I want to have to go to underwear in the metro station." The stand-up comedians often used the expression "Eller hur?" which is a close enough translation to the Midwestern go-to of "Ya know?!" Anytime they said "Eller hur?" I'd laugh because it indicated in some way that there was a punch line, and it reminded me of all the jolly characters I met in the Midwest (*and* William H. Macy in *Fargo*).

I performed in English at the show—my set was about twelve minutes and it was difficult to tell if the audience was laughing or just groaning. My set was relatively clean (no dirty jokes) and I tried to offer some commentary on Swedish culture. The truth was, having to follow the dancing "Victim" with my Mom there, proved too difficult. The performance we witnessed stuck out in my mind and made comedy seem so . . . unmoving.

Despite being called out for our fake laughing, the comedians we met were all very friendly and they appreciated when we sat around following the show to have a drink of *fatöl* (draft beer). When you order a beer in Sweden, you have a choice of alcohol content and size, so if you love beer like I do, you get to order like you're fucking Wonder Woman. There's no better feeling than having a mediocre show and saying "Ge mig en stor stark öl" ("Give me a big, strong beer"). We sat around an empty café talking with young Swedish comedians about comedy, my mom kindly giving the only feedback she could to the Swedes: "Your stage presence was really something—the way you hold the microphone, wow!"

It wasn't that the first show was bad—it certainly was better than the show my mom saw in LA; it's just that it didn't live up to what I imagined it might be. The thing about stand-up, which I knew at that time and wanted my parents to understand, is that it can actually change people. It's no coincidence that comedians and magicians are paired together in the performance world. It doesn't always work with comedy, but when it's good—when all the elements are right there—it's an alchemy that turns your pain into bliss. You can actually recycle painful energy into something as inexplicably brilliant as a big, full-bodied belly laugh. I've always been a fan of music because it communicates the emotion we don't have the capacity to express in words. Comedy actually *changes* one's emotional state. It's transformative.

Mom and I continued about our adventure in Stockholm, beginning each day with the breakfast buffet, where we stuck out like American thumbs because we had conversations (rather than sit silently). We made our own comedies - one instance being a metro mishap where Mom didn't get on the train with me before the doors closed. The train jerked forward without the conductor batting an eye over her screaming and waving from the platform. "I'll get off at the next stop," I yelled and signed to Mom from inside the train, as I crossed my legs and doubled over to keep from pissing my "panties" from laughing so hard.

Mom with the incredibly phallic hot dog poster.

Mom tagged along for two nights of the Bara Brudar (Just Chicks) stand-up shows, which featured diverse female stand-up comedians performing at a gorgeous theatre near the Yo Burger. Mom sat through five shows while we were in Stockholm, not having a clue what they were saying but "reading their body language." It was a trick she learned as a dancer, I'm sure.

Mother Has a Fondness for Cats

After my first go at stand-up in Sweden, I rewrote my jokes to better suit the bigger crowd at the Big Ben comedy club. These rewrites included a rather ballsy and *Boléro*-inspired decision to use my college Swedish on stage. After we arrived at Big Ben and about ten minutes before the show began, I took a look inside to see the stage and house—it was packed to the gills with a lutfisk-loving audience. All the seats were full, and people were standing on the sides crowding in. It was already hot and sweaty, which was such a sharp contrast from the temperature outside. The large crowd was as terrifying as it was perfect. My mom and I didn't have space to watch the other performers, but we came in to watch the comedian who went on before me. As we stood off to the side of the stage, my heart pounded. It was such a big audience, it was so full, and I wasn't sure if I would puke or die first.

The host took the stage and I knew my time had come. *Oh fuck*, I thought.

"This next comedian has come to us all the way from the United States. You're gonna love her. . . . *Christie Neat-chower.*" (This was before I used my grandmother's maiden name 'Nicholls' as my stage name.)

I left my mom and walked toward the microphone, in a three-second transaction that felt like three years. All I wanted was for her to see why I couldn't just *write* about stand-up as a crusty academic, and why I *had* to be a part of it. I took the microphone and proceeded with the new set.

***

My mom heard the following:

"Jag heter Christie Nittrouer. Jag kommer från Canada. . . . No no, fuck it, I can't even say it. Jag har rest till Sverige från USA med min mor. Hon heter Debbie. Säg hej till henne!"

(I point to Mom, and the entire audience turns and waves to her.)

"Hon tycker att Sverige är mycket vackra. Hon tycker att Svenska killar är mycket varmt."

(Audience members giggle.)

"Och hon är . . . kåt."

(Audiences members roar with laughter, covering their faces, and looking back at her. Mom smiles and gives them a classic American thumbs-up.)

***

The Swedish audience heard the following (translated to English by yours truly):

"My name is Christie Nittrouer. I come from Canada . . . no, no, fuck I can't even say it. I have come to Sweden from the USA with my mother. Her name is Debbie. Say hi to her!

"She thinks that Sweden is very beautiful. She believes Swedish men are very warm.

"And she is . . . horny."

***

Once the audience had stopped laughing about me outing my mother as horny, I turned again to her and translated what had happened.

"Mom, I told them that you think Sweden is a very beautiful country and that you have a fondness for cats. *Kåt* means cat, Mom."

"Yep," she said, nodding and smiling, again, like a quintessential "happy American."

The rest of the set, mostly in English, came off swimmingly. Oddly enough, it felt like Swedes understood me better than Americans, and because of that my mom seemed to understand it, too. I was pretty smitten with the experience and fell in love with everyone in that room—they were perfect humans, and just like Wikström it was hard to tell if they were me or if I was them. Like all good performance, we weren't really sure who was responsible for it.

On the way upstairs, Mom grabbed my forearm.

"You were incredible, best I've ever seen you," she stated.

Interrupting this very special moment was a drunk Swedish man who'd seen the show. He came up to my "horny" mom and immediately hit on her. She explained that she was happily married to my father, but she enjoyed some playful banter with the Swede, throwing in a few made-up Swedish words of her own. We asked the guy if he would take a picture, which he did. A millisecond before snapping a photo of us he asked my mom if she thought he was "warm."

Smiling extra big for the "mycket varm" (very warm)
Swedish man who snapped this photo.

Mom and I took the T-Bana home. Once we got to our stop, we skated over ice patches in the bitter cold, recapping the show like we do after any performance we see together. We were giddy and charged from the show—exactly like we felt after seeing Wikström.

"So, when that shorter blond guy said, 'Irky derk, irky berk derk, ya icky tycky tack,'" and he tapped his head, what did he mean?" Mom asked, dodging a big slick of black ice.

"Mom, I have no fucking clue. I was running through that Systembolaget joke, the new one I did about their liquor stores," I said, grabbing her arm so I didn't hit the black ice myself.

"Oh yeah . . . how they lock up their alcohol like a prisoner, that one was good. Why do they do that system-boloney stuff, anyway?"

Once we were back at Yo Burger, we had a rye and ginger and sat on our twin beds, talking about comedy until four in the morning. Mom went through butchered routines of her favorites: Ron White, Ellen DeGeneres, and Chris Rock. We talked about comedy's highs and its lows. I described the many open mikes I attended, which are probably the closest thing to hanging out in a mental institution, except that at the open mikes they charge you five bucks to enter. Mom asked her fair share of questions, too.

"But why in the hell would you go to an open microphone?"

"*Open mikes*, Mom; they're called open mikes. They're just like going to high school—no one really wants to go but you just *have* to go," I told her.

I went on to explain that just like high school, there were cool cliques at open mikes, and silly arguments, food fights, breakthroughs, but mostly they just blew. Mom listened about the good in comedy, too—the show I created, *Good Humor*, and the unique friends I made.

As gross and undependable as it had once seemed, Mom had finally given my relationship with comedy a chance. That trip to Stockholm was the first time I saw comedy performance as a relationship, too. By "relationship," I mean the understanding that it isn't always perfect or pretty, but you know you have a *very* long road together and you just trust that. Like any relationship, there are milestones that mark a new dis-covery, or a setback, or maybe even a surprising redirection. If I hadn't been moved by dance, in the way I was with Wikström and *Boléro,* I wouldn't have had the same experience standing up in front of all those Swedes.

Sure, it might be a stretch to make a parallel between a classically trained principal ballet dancer and my stand-up set, where I declared that my mother was horny for "warm" Swedish men, but to me the sim-ilarity is pretty clear. Ultimately, performance is about making people feel things—sometimes it's goosebumps and tears, but sometimes it's the *best* kind of tears, the silly ones you get when you're laughing so hard you confuse your own body. I think that kind of laughter is the closest thing we get to an out-of-body experience; we leave for a few minutes, we get outside ourselves, and we enter something much bigger. We forget everything that isn't laughter. I mean, how lucky are we humans to have that gift? To know that we can share an experience like that with a room full of strangers in Stockholm, or anywhere we might venture on the planet. To know that there is always a possibility for laughter across cultures . . . I don't know; it just makes the planet seem a whole lot smaller and a little bit "varmer."

Huddled together on the balcony of the Intiman Theatre,
moments before the start of the Bara Brudar (Just Chicks) comedy
show in honor of International Women's Day.

PART II

ODD JOBS

CHAPTER 5
Cinderella Sitting

T he glorious practice of "back-to-school shopping" is a yearly
ritual my family never practiced. Unfortunately, my mother's
logic of "why would you get *gifts* for returning to school?" did not take
into account the fashion-dependent social hierarchies that develop
around age nine. In 1993, our social elites were established based on
their ownership of Converse sneakers, or any article of clothing from
Gap Kids or the Limited Too. Also popular were loafers or boat shoes,
which were proudly displayed at the Bass Outlet at our town's shopping
center, in the Stony Brook Village. The loafers cheerily sat in the Bass
window display and I stopped to admire them many times—imagining how different of a person I'd be if they were on my feet.

*Yep, all the pieces would just kinda come together if I had a pair of brown
loafers from the Bass Outlet,* I routinely thought.

As it turns out, it was outside the Bass Outlet when I had a busi-
ness-related epiphany in the spring of 1993. Much like the main
character, Kristy, in Ann Martin's preteen cult classic *The Baby-Sitters
Club,* I (Christie) had a "great idea." I was just like Kristy, who lived in a
town "across the pond" (and by "the pond," I mean Long Island Sound)

in Stoneybrook, Connecticut. I also lived in Stony Brook (New York) and, as far as I could tell, I was just a sloppier Long Island version of Ann Martin's star. The parallels were uncanny. All I needed was a nerdy Mary Anne (my best friend Becky covered this with her Coke-bottle glasses), a hip Japanese friend named Claudia (my other best friend Dorothy was quite hip and born in Colombia), and a slut from California named Stacey (this would be my biggest challenge—none of my friends were cool enough to get that title).

With a vision of brown loafers dancing in a bubble above my over-sized ten-year-old head, I began advertising at my mom's dance studio:

CBS: Christie's BABYSITTING Services

Cheap, Fun, Flexible

689-8931

I got my first call from a client, the Tempsey family, when I was ten years old, just a month shy of eleven. Though in my mind I was already eleven, physically I looked like I was eight-going-on-nine. Why any parent would choose to leave their three daughters aged six, five, and three with me is beyond my comprehension. The truth was, the three Tempsey sisters were not well behaved; in fact, they were quite rowdy, especially if it involved sharing anything in the color pink. They lived in a fancy early-90s house with lots of mirrors and angles—it looked like a Long Island version of Kelly Taylor's home in *Beverly Hills, 90210*. Sure, my rate was only three dollars per hour, effectively one whole US dollar per child, but I offered as much protection as a parrot (my voice was shrill enough to alarm other humans of *Intruder! Danger! Polly wants a cracker!*)

To give you an idea of my small size, here is a portrait of me, taken several months after I began my babysitting career — clearly weighed down by the fake rose I am clutching.

On my first night of babysitting, the instant the sun went down, I remembered I was afraid of the dark. I coped with my fear by raiding the Tempsey's fancy pantry and by eating about twenty Fruit Roll-Ups while watching reruns of *The Dick Van Dyke Show*, *The Mary Tyler Moore Show*, and *I Love Lucy* on Nick at Nite. Though the Tempseys came home late, I never fell asleep because I was sure the second I did the murderers would show up. Despite this, I felt bizarrely comforted by the silly voices of Dick, Mary, and Lucy. I was also comforted by the money I was earning. On my first night, while taking a hearty late-night Fruit Roll-Up-inspired shit, I figured I'd made seventy-five cents for the fifteen minutes I spent on the can. *Not bad.* At that rate, if I took 26.6666667 Fruit Roll-Up dumps, I could pay for the $20 Bass loafers.

The empowerment I got from the promise of cold hard cash to buy things that would make me cool (like *LOAFERS!!!*) was enough to sustain my overwhelming anxiety about being a ten-year-old responsible for three small children in a home that was not mine. My first night of babysitting was such a hit that I was asked back the very next night. *Yep, I was that cheap.*

On night number two, all three kids had already eaten dinner, and my job was as simple as watching a Disney movie on a fancy big-screen TV that was the size of our living room rug. While I never bought into Cinderella's bullshit rags-to-riches story, I still appreciated her love of good shoes.

About thirty minutes into the movie, the youngest Tempsey sister grunted for another bottle of milk, so I left the basement to fetch it. As I was pouring the milk, I heard a sound that only a six-year-old clad in Belle's *Beauty and the Beast* ball gown is capable of making. Jaime, the oldest, was not crying about one of *her* evil sisters either—it was something much worse.

"What, what, what?" I thundered down the stairs, as only an anxiety-ridden, flat-footed ten-year-old could.

There was no response, just a mind-altering shriek. Then, finally, as I rounded the corner of the basement stairs, Jaime howled: "My foot exploded!" She frantically waved her hands over her right foot, which was extended in front of her and covered with glass and blood.

" *What happened?*" I was genuinely flabbergasted. Was this a new disease? I watched *Dateline* religiously and they'd never warned me of this new disease called SFEIC (spontaneous foot explosions in children)!

"I was trying on the slipper," Jaime said, motioning to a drinking glass that she had shoved onto (and broken with) her right foot "because I'm—"

"No, I am!" her middle and oft-forgot sister interrupted.

They continued on in a tone so shrill it made me contemplate grabbing a shard of slipper and sending it into my femoral artery. The pool of blood underneath her foot was steady, but it didn't seem to bother her if she continued to focus on proving her identity.

"If you were *Cinderella*, then why did your *fat foot* break the glass?" asked her middle sister, going in for the blow like only a middle sister can.

It never dawned on me that I should have interjected and explained that glass cups are not designed to double as footwear. I was too busy thinking about whether or not I'd have to call her parents and end up on the cover of *Newsday*, headline: BAD BABYSITTER EXPLODES KID'S FOOT. Could I stitch Jaime up myself? I mean, I'd sewn some pretty bitchin' outfits for my collection of Boyds Bears stuffed moose. The visual took me down a gruesome path—pink thread, a six-year-old screaming, and the inevitable moment when her parents came home to find their oldest daughter had a pastel Frankenfoot.

Nope, I had to call her parents. *Bass loafers be damned!* Fine, babysitting didn't work out. I could always find work doing manual labor—at sixty-two pounds, I could probably get hired by a family of ferrets.

"Jaime, I'm going to get you some ice and call your parents. Don't move."

She heaved several intense sobs and eyed her sister, who was eying her own glass cup. I snatched it quickly, fearing that she, too, would fail the Cinderella test. I ran upstairs and rehearsed lines as I prepared an ice pack.

"Mr. and Mrs. Tempsey? I hope you're enjoying the one hour you've had away from your three children. I was wondering if you could come home and fix the foot of your eldest child, Cinderella, because it seems to have spontaneously exploded."

Nope. They'd can me for sure. I had to buy some time to see if Cinderella was simply being melodramatic. I ran downstairs and distributed a fresh ice pack to Jaime, who howled at the chill. Sure, I had no clue what I was doing, but if ever we were injured as kids, my parents always said, in a tone so cool and unaffected, "just put some ice on it." We could be holding out a severed finger to them and it was "*yep,* ice will do the trick." I had to think. . . . WWKD? What Would Kristy (of *The Baby-Sitters Club*) Do? Eat a Fruit Roll-Up? *No! C'mon Christie! How can you be thinking of delicious Fruit Roll-Ups at a time like this?* I grabbed the phone, found the list of emergency contacts, and a Fruit Roll-Up for backup.

"Mrs. Tempsey, it's Christie." My voice quivered like I was Stuart Little, standing on a stool and yelling into the receiver.

"Yeah?"

"Jaime had . . . a foot accident."

"What do you mean *accident?*" Mrs. Tempsey responded, assuming by "accident" I meant bedwetting and by following such logic, assumed her eldest daughter had pissed on her own foot.

I responded with the most cryptic Stuart Little line ever: "She's bleeding a lot and I think you might need to come home."

Not fifteen minutes later the Tempseys were home and tending to Cinderella. I cowered by the stairs like a dog who'd just gotten in the trash and was awaiting a scolding.

"Christie, Tom's going to take Jaime to the ER and I'll drive you home."

"What?" Jaime said.

"We're taking you to get your foot fixed," Mrs. Tempsey explained, still dreaming of that glass of oaky chardonnay she'd left at the restaurant.

"I want Christie to come, too," Jaime begged. It was a line that single-handedly undid her action of throwing me under the bus by cramming her sausage toes into glassware.

"No, Christie needs to go home."

This sent Cinderella into more hysterics, but her fit had suggested that ol' Fruit Roll-Up eatin' Stuart Little had some value after all. Her father picked her up and carried her up the stairs as she wailed like a hammered sorority girl: "I'M CINDERELLA. I'M CINDERELLLLLLAHHHHHH!"

I was dropped home without payment and with great anxiety about explaining the outcome of my second day of work to my parents. As it turned out, my parents found the whole thing to be hysterical. They were likely relieved that for all the weird shit I did, I never imitated my idol by jumping off our roof with a feather, screaming "I'm Dumbo!"

The next morning, Mrs. Tempsey called to tell us that Jaime was successfully stitched up by a medical professional and they wanted me to come back so they could finish their dinner. *Wait, they want me to babysit the very next night after their daughter was sent to the ER while in my care?* Now I don't know if this made them bad parents or *incredibly* bad parents, but it meant my good name was redeemed. *Newsday* headline now read: 10-YEAR-OLD BREAKS RECORD FOR FRUIT ROLL-UP CONSUMPTION.

Returning to the scene of the crime was not easy, especially when Jaime hobbled in with her wounded foot bound in an oversized (and very un-pink) boot. For some inexplicable reason, she was very happy to see me and seemed to flaunt her injury as a rite of passage. Our routine was nearly identical to our routine twenty-four hours earlier. We went down to the basement with a collection of dolls and costumes in various shades of pink. We sat in front of the giant TV and discussed what cartoon feature we should watch. Jaime began the discussion.

"I will *not* be watching *Cinderella*," Jaime said, as if she were Zsa Zsa Gábor.

"No, of course not. We don't have to watch that!" I said, nervous as shit.

"Good, because I hate *Cinderella*," Jaime clarified.

"Me, too," chimed in the middle kid.

"Me me, too, yeah," said the youngest, not the sharpest tool in the shed.

"You know, I never liked it either," I said, relieved I could finally speak frankly about my distaste for princesses. "I just don't buy it either. Cinderella never tried to get a different job, or go to school. She just hit the lottery with some fairy godmother. The stuff with the sisters too—sisters don't always have to fight."

The Tempsey sisters nodded at me. Could it be? *They understood?!* Why, in just two days with me, they'd gotten over a crippling case of princess worship! Well, I must be a genius! I could start a religion, a cult, a rehab for other princess addicts!

"I don't wanna watch Cinderella cause Mommy said glass slippers are just make-believe. I want to watch something *real*, like *The Little Mermaid.*"

The Little Mermaid? Where a slutty redhead in a bikini cuts off her tail, her tongue, and can only lure her prince with a personality that is best described as Hilary Duff-like? *That's* real? I stood up and walked over to the collection of VHS tapes; I removed *The Little Mermaid* and read the back of it.

Runs eighty-three minutes.

Eighty-three minutes equals roughly $4.50...nearly a quarter of the way to my $20.00 Bass loafers.

I turned to the three amigos and smiled widely. "Okay. I can live with that."

CHAPTER 6
Selling Out

My parents had a deal worked out where they'd cover two-thirds of the cost for my college tuition, so long as I paid for the other third. I'd been saving up money since I began babysitting at age ten (see previous chapter) and I had a good chunk of it already saved. Still, I loved to pore over the classified ads in our shitty little college newspaper at U-Dub (the University of Washington) with the hope that there would be a lottery-ticket job hidden somewhere in those classifieds, just waiting for me to discover it and change my young life. Every week the job postings were the same, leaving me a choice between babysitting gigs that required "light housework" (it's *never* "light") or selling my eggs. One year I told my mom I was thinking about selling my eggs because my understanding of anatomy was so college-age stupid that I thought I'd be giving away a period. Sure, it didn't really make sense why someone would want to spend $8,000 on a menstruation from an "educated young woman with no hereditary diseases," but I was willing to give them that "miracle."

One afternoon I finally took the bait for a "sales job" that had been running every week. It seemed a little too good to be true, but I was too stupid (again - college) to trust that instinct. The posting read cryptically:

Mountain Subscription Services

$15 per hour. Sales. Flexible hours. Near campus.

Bonus!!! Bonus!!! Bonu$$$$

As luck would have it, a friend of my friend's boyfriend worked as the receptionist for Mountain Subscription Services. *Networking!* I already had an "in"! *Hot damn!* When I went for my interview, I learned that "Mountain Subscription Services" was a fancy title given to a not-so-fancy telemarketing company. I was surprised to see that the manager of the call center looked as if Tom Petty had intercourse with a female snake and she laid a bunch of snake-Petty eggs, and the ugliest hatched and was making his way in the telemarketing sales world in Seattle, of all places. This fact made it *extremely* difficult to take him seriously (and not zone out with a vivid visualization of Tom Petty fucking a snake. *By the way, RIP, Tom Petty.*) From the second I greeted him, all I wanted to say was, "Great to meet you, Petty Snake."

After our preliminary chat went well, he brought me to the back of the office building, which was the location of their large call center. There I was greeted by glares from humans that were my age. These ghouls were not so much humans as they were skinned "Ave Rats." The term "Ave Rat" was a common nickname for punk/hipster/terribly unhappy white people that hung around the main drag just outside of campus known as "The Ave." Even though I detested the Greek system, the Ave Rats didn't care—they could smell sorority on me. The fact that I lightened my hair and they darkened theirs, the fact that I dabbled in pastels and only used eyeliner sparingly—it was enough for them to hiss pagan spells at me whenever I was near. Indeed, the feud between the Ave Rats and the Greeks was an ancient one. It was a grudge so bitter that it could be likened to the *Twilight* series and the bad blood between the vampires and the gay wolves.

Knowing that Ave Rats were definitely day-walkers, I figured my best approach was to kill their undead souls with kindness.

"Hey, guys," I whined like a cheesy 10th-grade JV cheerleader.

My approach did not work. They only furrowed their shaved eyebrows and flared their pierced nostrils. This only made me want to smile even more, pretending I was a pageant contestant about to answer a question with prepackaged saccharine. Somehow their hisses and hushed cackles behind my back made me want the job even more.

To secure the job, I focused all of my attention on Snake, who was wearing (and I'll *never* forget this) acid-washed jeans and a button-up short-sleeved shirt with floating Mai Tais on it. He liked me, which he expressed by staring at my ass and chest. *Fun!* He brought me into his office and playfully demanded, "Tell me a little bit about yourself." I explained that I was a college student looking for a rewarding career opportunity "helping people." When I was younger, I had less of a soul than I do now, and I could land literally any job interview by copying Oprah's technique, which was to "pensively nod and lie."

Petty Snake explained that I'd be calling magazine subscribers with scripted pitches.

"You can act good, I'm sure." He smiled and licked his thin lips.

Petty Snake explained that he'd get a cut of whatever sales I made, and if I made a lot, as he was sure I would, I'd also get a bonus. The thought of fifteen dollars per hour was a very good thought for me—I had made half that at my last job selling shoes at Gart Sports.

"Basically," Petty Snake continued, "if you read everything on this sheet and don't try and write it more good, you'll be making big bonuses." He was so fixated on making it clear that he wanted to dry-hump me that it didn't disgust me; it was just kind of amazing.

For fifteen dollars per hour, Petty Snake didn't scare me. I was running down a (God-damned) dream. I accepted the job offer and shook his scaly hand, letting him lead me out of the call center so he could have a "smoky smoke." As he cupped an unlit cigarette in the light Seattle rain, he called out, "Oh yeah, your shift is seven a.m. to ten a.m. every weekday."

"Great!" I told him, still riding high on the promise of money and forgetting the quality of my morning voice (and morning breath).

My alarm went off at six a.m. on Monday morning, and my first thought was a cool "why am I even alive?" I asked the question five more times and an answer emerged: a vision of wads of telemarketing cash. I kicked off three down comforters that covered my lower bunk bed that was part of a forty-person basement "sleeping porch" (which was the cute name given to the bunker where lowly underclassmen slept in sororities and fraternities).

There are three things that you should know about me: (1) I am not a morning person. (2) If I'm asked to do something by someone I don't respect, I have a compulsion to do the exact opposite. (3) I have a cursing problem. These three facts make me a less-than-ideal candidate for a telemarketing job that sticks to a strict (and poorly written) script and targets the "Greatest Generation" (not fans of foul language) living on the East Coast (three hours ahead and thus requiring early morning shifts).

Despite these three truths, I trudged through a rainstorm at six thirty a.m. to make it to my very first shift. The rats were out having their cigarettes and seemed confused when I greeted them with an enthusiastic "Hey, y'all!" I blasted through the doors of the sleepy call center and went straight to Petty Snake's pit. He set me up on my workstation—a dated computer, a phone with maybe fifty buttons, and a headset attached to a separate device.

"Now, since you're new, we have you on the office speaker to"—he slurped some coffee, adjusted his balls tucked up deep inside his acid-washed jeans, and snorted— "keep you on *quality control.*" He checked out my 'tits,' as I'm sure he called them, and smiled real big-like. *Gross.*

"My calls are going to be on the loudspeaker?" I asked, suddenly uncomfortable with an entire cage of rats judging my sales tactics.

"Yep, *everyone* can hear you . . . so don't screw up," added a woman with bright purple hair who had been listening in from the call center floor.

"We do this for all the new employees so we can give you"—he looked at my tits again—"some tips . . . *nice* tips."

Demon Rat Woman (DRW, as I renamed the purple-haired young woman) did the unthinkable and smiled at me. This rat could smell me sweat, and she took in the scent just like she'd take in a hunk of Swiss cheese. I couldn't let her win, so I straightened up my human spine, firmly planted my two human feet, and brought back my pensive Oprah (the ultimate human) nod. Petty Snake told me during my interview that my bonuses were in direct competition with the sales rats. A competition? *Yes, please.*

"All right . . . let's get selling!" I cheered.

It was unlike me to be so enthusiastic at such an early hour, but I wanted to watch DRW crawl back into her rat hole. I'm not a betting woman, but it's a no-brainer that a jolly (and competitive AF) sorority gal can sell more than an angry rat.

Petty Snake distributed our scripts and the order log and walked me through the database they used to track and harass customers. I'd be calling customers on the East Coast, meaning these were retired folks who were home watching *The Price Is Right* and clipping Pillsbury coupons at 10 a.m. Old people were totally in my charm wheelhouse. I visualized the cash...the power...I was ready to sell out.

"Hi, is this Mr. Robert Gordon?" *Great start,* I thought to myself.

"Yes . . ."

"This is Christie calling from Mountain Subscription Services. How are you doing today? I'm just calling to check the status of your *Golf Digest* magazine. Is that still showing up in good form for you? Pause. Okay, great, because I'm calling about a special offer for a two-year renewal at thirty percent off the retail price. If you just get your credit card information, I can get you well on your way to enjoying more *Golf Digest* for an incredible price!"

"What in the . . . hold on a second there. . . ." Robert yelled out to someone who was likely in another room, though he screamed as if that person were in fact trapped in the phone's receiver. "Barbara, BAR-BRAHHHH! Did you get something called the *Golf Digest* magazine? *WHAT?*" As if it were even possible, Robert yelled louder, "Why in the *hell* are they telling me to renew! It's . . . ahh . . . okay . . . oh, I see."

He exhaled loudly, adding a chill to the already chilly call center.

"I don't know who you think you are telling me I have *Golf Digest* when I have never touched a dang golf stick in my life . . . but . . ."

Mayday! Mayday! I was losing control of the ship and could feel Snake's eyes upon me. The whole room was listening to the call, watching me attempt to hit the golf ball out of the sand trap. I jumped to the "no" section of the script.

"I'm sorry to hear that, Robert, and I sincerely apologize for the mix-up. Luckily we have many great magazines at rates you won't find anywhere else."

"My name is Bob and I want you to *never ever, ever, ever* call me again. You hear me?"

"Yes, I'm so sorry to hear that—"

"*Never!*" he screamed, in a voice that was so bitter-sweetly similar to Jerry Stiller.

Click.

It's a strange feeling that courses through your veins when you show up to do a service-oriented job and end up doing it so poorly that a complete stranger declares that they don't want to hear your voice *ever, ever, ever* again. Petty Snake rolled up in an office chair before I could move on to the next call. I was hoping we could all just pretend it never happened, that I didn't lose my telemarketing virginity in such a sloppy and fruitless manner. Demon Rat Woman leaned in as Petty

Snake approached; her eyeliner was so thick I wanted to dip a quill pen in it and sign the Declaration of Independence.

"That was *hella* brutal. Probably should wait for him to respond to your question before you move on to another one," she advised, as if she were some villainous high school jock in a teenage coming-of-age comedy. "Oh," she continued in a droll tone, "*and...* you don't actually *say* pause." She turned to look at a white guy with thick blond dread-locks, whom I'd already nicknamed "Rasta Rat". They snickered.

"Yeah, so Jade's tips are good. You gotta just slow down and let *them* talk. We're gonna mark him as a 'do not call,' and just to tell you, I don't like those. A 'do not call' is like an F on your report card. Now, you don't like getting F's, do you?" Petty Snake condescended, in such an uncomfortably sexual tone that it took every ounce of self-control to *not* chuck a stapler at his head.

"Nope," I said sharply, to quickly put an end to his slithering.

"Good girl. Let's try again and this time let's take our time . . . no rush . . . *mmmkay?*"

"Yep," I confirmed.

"Hey, Chrissy," Petty Snake beckoned as he rolled away, "just *real* nice and *real* slow."

The next call went straight to an answering machine of a man who sounded exactly like Bob. I shuddered. The trend continued for a while— "dead leads," as Petty Snake would say. Finally, I got to a woman who sounded as if she had one of those really extravagant low-hanging, fleshy goose-like necks. She gobbled 'hello,' and when she heard where I was calling from she told me, "I'm not interested." The bad news was she hung up immediately after that, but the good news was she didn't warrant another "do not call" on my report card. Goose Lady was a D+. Despite my progress Snake forced me to listen to Demon Rat Woman's calls to see how she handled telemarketing copy.

I folded my arms and rolled my eyes. Petty Snake switched the speaker from my phone to hers, so all the call center could hear her rat-squeak.

"Hi! Yes, Mr. Weimer, yes, it's Jade. . . . *Mmm hmm*, I just wanted to see how your subscription to *Reader's Digest* was going. Still enjoying it, I'm sure?"

Watching Demon Rat Woman transform into a human was an outrageous sight—she was oozing charisma and charm; she had this stranger right in her pocket.

"I was looking through some of my clients and I thought, here is someone who could benefit from this new deal we have going. Now, I'm not calling everyone, and it's not going to be around for much longer . . . but, I think . . . definitely, yes, *you* are the one that needs to get on this gravy train."

Wait — what the fuck? Was DRW closing the sale?

Within minutes, she was recording his credit card information with a pen that she yanked out of her fishnet stockings. She scribbled the numbers, nodding and chuckling like Kathie Lee Gifford on laughing gas. My bonus was in direct competition with *this* freak? I was totally and utterly *boned*.

"So, what did you notice with Jade's style?" Petty Snake asked, placing a thumb to the place where he once had a chin.

"Good . . . it was . . . good." I said "good" as if I were a pageant contestant who had received fourth runner-up. The rats loved my squirming. They swished their textured tails in the air and chattered their teeth together in triumph.

Petty Snake further punished me by sitting next to me for the rest of my shift and breathing cigarette-coffee-asparagus breath onto me. I ended the first day with my highest grade being a C-, which was "please call back at another time." I walked out of the call center with my shoulders slumped, leaving behind a pack of rats who were going on break before their next shift. They weren't in college; why would they be? They were *crushing* it in the sales world.

I made it to my 10:30 philosophy course about ten minutes late, which was found unamusing by the professor (who looked exactly how you'd expect a philosophy professor to look – like he was Santa Claus's twin communist brother). I didn't read Plato and therefore didn't care to discuss it, but I was called on to answer a question. I made up an answer using big words and hand gestures. Perhaps I was borrowing a technique I saw Demon Rat Woman use and that's why, miraculously, it worked.

The next day I was up at 5:57, dressed in a collared shirt and black business pants from Express (which was the Ann Taylor Loft for college-aged business women). My walking commute consisted of slamming some English breakfast tea in a to-go mug and reciting lines from Alec Baldwin's overrated "Always Be Closing" monologue in *Glengarry Glen Ross*. I decided to try a new approach, one that was inspired by my experience successfully BS-ing a response in my philosophy class: go off script. I was still being broadcast throughout the entire call center, but I had a feeling they were gonna like what they heard.

My new leads were based in Long Island, from which I'd moved three years earlier. Technically speaking, the game was on my home turf—how could I possibly lose?

"A. Yeahhh...Hey . . . yo . . . Liz . . ." It was 7:07 a.m. and the entire call center got to listen in as I transformed into some Andrew Dice Clay-Edie Falco hybrid.

"Yes, hello, this is Elizabeth."

"This is Chris. Oh, I'm so glad I caught you. How you doin' today?"

"Not bad," she responded, which is Long Island for *what in the hell do you want?*

"I'm callin' from Mountain Subscription Services, cause I got *the* deal for you." At this point in my dialogue, I had flipped my collar up, really getting into character.

"I'm not interested," Elizabeth responded, flatly.

"Oh, no? Let me ask you one little question before I go," I pleaded.

"Okay . . ." Elizabeth said, humoring me.

"Do you like savin' money?" The question rolled off my tongue like a cactus.

"No, I hate it," Elizabeth quipped—as dry as dry ice.

Shit.

"I got any magazine you want . . . in the world. . . . I can give it to you for thirty percent less than asking price."

"You got *People*?" Elizabeth asked, nibbling the bait.

"I do. . . ." I lied.

Petty Snake ran over to my desk and waved his arms as if he were one of those airport tarmac guys trying to stop a 747 jet from squeezing into a compact parking spot.

"I . . . hold on one second." I struggled to find the hold button, until Petty Snake slammed an ashy finger down on it.

"*What are you doing?*" Petty Snake screeched, angrily.

"I'm selling magazines?" I was genuinely confused by his question.

"You went off script!"

"She's from New York; I can't read her a script."

"You can't sell her *People*—we don't sell *People*! You're selling *Cooking Light*! Once she's on the hook with that, then you up-sell with *Golf Digest*, *Reader's Digest*, or *Digestion Digest*."

"No one cooks light in Syosset!" I knew the second I said it that Petty Snake would curl up into a ready-to-attack coil. He lowered what remained of his chin and narrowed his already narrow eyes.

"Let's have a meeting in my office. Jade, can you come over here and clean up this mess?" He motioned to the phone on my desk. Jade, who was listening to Dice-Falco on the intercom, smiled from ear to ear.

"Gladly," Demon Rat Woman stated, turning toward me to show me her teeth.

What proceeded in Petty Snake's office at all of 7:15 a.m., was his tried and true business "man-o-logue" which was like listening to a Sales 101 TA on meth. I listened as best I could, but my mind kept wandering to the woman on the line who was getting sold to by Demon Rat Woman. What if she really did want *People* magazine? Like, what if she just lost her favorite cat in a tragic accident and she just needs the stupid stories and colorful lies told in *People?*

Once I was back on the call center floor, I stuck to the script, and kept my tail tucked between my legs. My sales grades were poor - I had F after F after F. I was beginning to wonder how anyone sold anything; that was, until I reached a man who wanted to *talk.* After he responded "no" to nearly every script prompt, I tried to end the call (which is a big no-no in sales). However, he wouldn't let me off the horn—he wanted more conversation. I finally struck gold when I offered him *Cooking Light* and he accepted. It took about ten minutes for him to find his effing credit card, but, there it was. *Done.* First sale logged, with all the sales rats condescendingly clapping after I ended the call.

With that call, I had stumbled onto something profoundly prostitutional; I could talk to lonely old men and women like a platonic sex phone operator. When they reached climax in our conversation, I would simply run their credit card and take my cut. It wasn't sleazy; it was business.

Over the following three days after this discovery, I'd talk to clients about the weather, about sporting events I hadn't watched, about soap operas, gas prices, salad dressing, polar bears in captivity, world peace, absolutely anything *except* magazines. While Demon Rat Woman, Rasta Rat, Fat Rat, and their cheesy crew were closing deals and slapping claws, I was getting gripping updates from old farts watching the "Showcase Showdown" on *The Price Is Right.*

At the end of my shift on Thursday, Petty Snake called me into the room to discuss the importance of "believing in the script."

"These pitches work," he began again, like some televangelist-reptile hybrid. "You just have to *want* to sell them."

"Okay," I said with a half-hearted nod.

I walked about halfway to campus before I decided I was too tired to attend my philosophy class. My own philosophy was a little bit screwy—I wasn't capable of making any bonuses that could pay for the classes I wasn't even attending.

On Friday I sat at my desk and went through my calls using the script. It was all very mechanical — I pressed a button, listened for cues, recited the script, awaited rejection, followed with a counter, awaited a second rejection, and hung up the phone. I was a mouse on a wheel.

When I was nearly done with my shift, I got a tiny nibble from an elderly woman who took interest in the script bait.

"That sounds like a great idea. I think I'd like to sign up for the three-year renewal rate. That's the best deal, right?" Her voice was scratchy and exquisitely hopeful.

Petty Snake slid over, smelling a sale on the tip of his forked tongue.

"It's a great deal," I told her, nodding at Petty Snake.

"Let me get my credit card. . ." I heard her fumble around in what I figured was her family room. There was a TV on in the background; my guess is it was one of those boxy giants that sit on the floor, in front of a plaid couch, adorned with a "BLESS THIS HOME" pillow. While I was holding for her credit card information, Petty Snake signaled me with a sly grin and two sleazy thumbs up. She returned to the phone, but not before some plates fell to the ground and made a large clattering. The rest of the call center cringed at the sound - I was still being broadcast on the speaker for 'training purposes.' "I'm . . . sorry about that noise. I was just wondering something. I don't know if this is a good idea for me to buy right now."

"Well, we can't guarantee this offer much longer. Today is our last day." Petty Snake watched the lie leave my mouth. I hated myself for saying something that wasn't true, for the express purpose of getting her credit card number.

"It's just that with my cataracts now, the doctor says I can't read anymore. I don't know. It sure is a good deal." She left the sale up to me, it was clear; it was a Mad Libs sales moment. I could fill in the answer for her with anything I wanted. I could make a cool seventeen dollars off the sale and now have more points toward a bonus I might not get.

Petty Snake was gesturing for me to look at him but I already knew what he wanted. It was more a question of my own philosophy, or my own sense of ethics. Should I sell magazines to someone who cannot read them, if I stand to make money off of the transaction?

"You know what? I think you should take care of your eyes," I said.

"You think so? Well, I bet you're right then. Thanks for thinking to call me and tell me about that great offer. Maybe if my eyes get better I can call you?" She asked, in a tone that was impossibly sweet.

"Okay. Just make sure to take care of yourself," I added.

I knew that the moment our conversation ended so would my short career in telemarketing. Petty Snake rattled, leaned in, and hissed at me to follow him to his pit. I followed, knowing I was about to get squeezed out of a sales job.

"You had it in the bag. She told you she wanted the product and you didn't close." He shook his head, trying to make sense of the situation at hand.

"She had cataracts. She's going blind," I told him with an attitude.

"So what? We had a product that she wanted to buy and you didn't sell it. That is your job."

"She'll be blind before the three-year subscription is up!"

"That's not *your* problem." He took a deep breath in and tried to get through to me: "it's just a sale."

Petty Snake actually had a point, but at the time I just couldn't see it. I repeated the cataract line about five more times, finding it impossible to understand how *I* messed up. Eventually he muttered something like "this isn't working out" and while I knew it was coming, it still stung. Outside the pit, the rats were aware of what was happening, but they didn't snicker like I anticipated.

I grabbed my backpack and walked toward the reception area, turning around one last time to prove to the rats that I left with my head held high. I spoke in a crazed sing-songy voice: "Good-bye everyone and thanks for the memories." I expected them to be scared by what was an outright manic moment, and they responded appropriately by just ignoring me altogether.

Petty Snake watched me exit with an "I pity you" look on his face, which was quickly interrupted by one last once-over of my tits.

I showed up early to my philosophy class for the first time that quarter. The professor (and communist brother of Santa Claus) approached me to tell me I was failing the class. He told me he enjoyed my first paper and would consider working with me if I could explain what happened—a family emergency, an illness, a supernaturally powerful hangover.

It's true that "faking tragedy," as I coined it in college, was my specialty. I could make up anything on the spot and convincingly convey, say, a case of leprosy. Despite this, something about Santa's brother just reminded me of the old people I'd been trying to swindle. I had spent the entire week lying to strangers for a reward of cash to pay for a class I couldn't appreciate. It seemed that there was too much lying going on. Just like my decision to back out of the sale with the cataract woman, this too was an oddly philosophical moment for me.

"No," I told him, "I was just busy with a job."

Santa's brother gave me the option of submitting a few extra-credit papers on comparative philosophy critique. It was a generous offer and one I countered by dropping the class. I just couldn't sit in and listen to some white guy blather on about the drivel of some older dead white guy. The course was especially worthless at that point because it offered no practical explanation for a world where people are rewarded for selling magazines to the blind.

The walk back to my sorority that morning was extra long and extra cold. I passed by a cluster of Ave Rats who gathered near the awning of a secondhand record store. On any other day I'd pass them and look off at some distant thing ahead while they'd growl about "the man" or "the system" and how my friends and I were just stupid North Face fleece-wearing cogs. Not that morning. That morning, I got a good long look at them. On that day, their heavy eyeliner just made their pupils look like some kind of perfect bull's-eye, which no longer looked scary or threatening to me. I should have seen them as "unhinged" and "reckless," but all I saw were magazine sales and dollar signs. It was a horribly depressing thought—even the Ave Rats could be bought.

Once back at the sorority, I took out the trusty college newspaper and flipped to the classifieds section. I made an interesting discovery: the psychology department offered cold hard cash for research subjects. Without any hesitation, I pulled out my clunky Nokia cell phone and called the number to schedule an interview. If telemarketing taught me anything, it was a new philosophy, a realization of sorts—that no matter what we look like or how we dress, we're all just a bunch of rats. Maybe I wasn't a sales rat, but I could certainly be a paid lab rat.

CHAPTER 7
Spag Facked

If you get hired as a waitress without any restaurant experience, in a city as overly service oriented as Seattle, there is most definitely a reason why - the restaurant sucks. In 2003, a friend of mine recommended me for a job at The Old Spaghetti Factory, located just up the hill from the piers on Puget Sound. My interview took place between the lunch and dinner shifts, so it was quiet enough to hear a Muzak version of the delicious theme song from *The Godfather*. The ambience of the Spaghetti Factory, with its kitschy décor and wafts of robust marinara, was enough to inspire me. Like at the start of most new adventures, I was giddily naïve: *If I can get a job as a waitress, I'm pretty sure I can be happy.*

I got the job and began my training in The Old Spaghetti Factory basement, which sat below the industrial microwaves and gas stoves that served as their kitchen. Our trainer rolled in a TV on wheels and inserted a thick VHS cassette to kick off our spaghetti edification. A fuzzy font appeared on the screen all wiggly and warped (as is the standard for tired VHS tapes): "Part One: The Spaghetti Factory Family Values."

Here's the thing. I adore corporate training videos, in the same way I love *Extreme Makeover: Home Edition.* I'm all for savoring the carefully curated "family" ideology that manipulates me into believing that what I'm doing is good for Americans. The video for The Old Spaghetti Factory was perfection, too; it had a dystopic quality, similar to Arnold Schwarzenegger's world in *The Running Man.* The hue of the lens filter was grainy and yellow, the sound was warped and eroded, the faces of the waiters and customers were covered with 1980s charm - like pixilated mustaches. Even the CEO of The Old Spaghetti Factory, who narrated the training video, was a real-life 1980s video version of Homer Simpson's boss, Mr. Burns. He explained his "vision" to the audience (me and four other new hires) as if we might be part of his Spaghetti family, too. Mr. Burns' tone in the video urged all of us servers to see him as a family member, a father figure (who could one day call on us for a kidney or two).

"Who benefits from family-style dining at budget prices? *Everyone.*"

Mr. Burns explained The Old Spaghetti Factory is a uniquely American restaurant because it offers everyone unrivaled value. With the purchase of every entrée, customers would receive:

Choice of: coffee/tea/iced tea/milk

Warm bread served with real butter OR garlic butter

Salad with real croutons OR minestrone soup

Spumoni ice cream OR vanilla ice cream with hot fudge

Thanks to Mr. Spaghetti Factory's generosity, "Joe America" could order a "classic marinara," and he would get a five-course meal for the grand total of $6.95. While I was busy daydreaming about the amount Mr. Burns' offspring spent annually on psychotherapy, I missed the genius of The Old Spaghetti Factory business model. A week later, I would figure out its Americanness:

+ Purchase cheap premade sauces and noodles with zero nutritional value

+ Hire 15 "chefs" to microwave and boil said sauces and noodles

+ Hire waiters clad in Oxford shirts to prepare beverages/ buttered bread/salad or soup/and dessert for minimum wage

---

Profit margin for Mr. Burns = 93%

Profit margin for Mr. Burns' family psychotherapist = 7%

We reached a section in the film called "Turn 'em and Burn 'em Service" where the waitstaff took on the noble "responsibility" of getting customers in and out faster than assembly line workers cranked out a carburetor at the Ford factory. This requirement demanded a quality that I never have nor ever will possess – a reasonably good short-term memory. (Side note: I've done this many times, where I'll walk to the bathroom, sit down, and forget what I'm doing in there. *Oh right! Take down pants and pee.*)

The tour concluded with a complimentary meal of our choosing. I chose Mizithra (a so-called 'cheese' made only at The Old Spaghetti Factory) and mushroom sauce on spaghetti. If I were a food critic, I'd describe it as "noodles that had sat in a bathtub for too long, topped with a sauce made of one part ketchup and one part antibacterial soap." What the pasta lacked in flavor was made up for by the "bottomless" sourdough loaves that were housed in deep heater drawers. Following our meal, we were given a painstakingly boring tour of the kitchen, bar, and supply rooms. It was explained to us that before each shift, we had designated chores to complete. We'd all come to find out that the worst setup job was scooping trays of butter and the best was refilling the salt and pepper shakers. I came to find out that at most every shift, I was scooping butter and, consequently, my Chevy Celebrity's upholstery smelled like I was a full-blown butter dealer.

When our tour was complete and I was waiting in the kitchen to shadow a "pro server," I felt a wad of something cold hit my neck. I grabbed it and saw it was a wet macaroni noodle. Turning to see where it came from, I caught a group of Mexican cooks giggling uncontrollably.

"That's sort of a thing here," our trainer explained to me, nonchalantly. "I've been hit by every noodle. You just sort of get used to it."

"Nice shot, guys." I turned to the cooks and gave them a thumbs-up. This made them giggle louder.

Once I had completed my week of "shadowing," and I had passed all food-handling exams, I was required to take a quiz on the Spaghetti Factory ideology. Surprisingly, I passed the test and was allowed to purchase my uniform—a pale-blue, short-sleeved men's Oxford button-up shirt from J. C. Penney. Completing the look were khaki pants, black orthopedic shoes, and a fanny-pack apron with The Old Spaghetti Factory logo to make it official. This ensemble gave us all the "factory look"—we were wholesome, hardworking noodle assemblers.

After training, exams, and server shadowing, I was officially a Spaghetti Factory "resident"—meaning I still had to be chaperoned for another week. I was paired with Pam. She was probably in her early 40s and she had a look about her that said she'd done whip-its from the ripe age of three, but *hot damn* if she wasn't a damn good waitress. Pam had the short-term memory of Raymond Babbitt (Dustin Hoffman's character in *Rain Man*) but the personality of a school nurse.

We worked well together during my second week because she did all the work and I delighted in playing the part of waitress, presenting our cheesy script with the greatest of enthusiasm.

"Welcome to The Old Spaghetti Factory! My name is Christie and I'll be taking care of you today. Is this your first time at The Old

Spaghetti Factory? Oh, it is? Great! That is so great! First off, on behalf of The Old Spaghetti Factory family, let me say, 'Welcome!' I'll tell you a little bit about how we work here and how our restaurant is a little different from what you might be getting elsewhere. With the purchase of all of our entrees, you receive complimentary . . . "

I rattled off The Old Spaghetti Factory's philosophy of "abundance for all" and stood by and watched as each family member ordered a desired complimentary beverage, with adorable little modifications like "coffee with three ice cubes" or my favorite, "one-third of a glass of orange juice with two-thirds a glass of Sprite." They were charming idiosyncrasies that humans at restaurants tend to have—being unsure of what they want as an entree, but sure that they want extra free stuff. Oh, the humans loved to change their order from soup to salad, and back again to "soup with a side of croutons!" There were refills and re-refills. The dessert orders were often given with the request that they get "a lot of spumoni this time, because last time I got a lousy scoop."

What these humans did not realize is that their idiosyncratic noodle demands held up the assembly line at the factory. Nevertheless, when I had Pam with me, we were unstoppable—like two great pimps, tending to six tables of horny-for-spaghetti clients. Pam gave me commands to make salads and soups, while she would submit orders to the microwaving chefs (the group of Mexican noodle chuckers). Oh, and Pam could punch in orders like she was Ray Charles tickling the ivories. During my second week of training, I developed OCD for scooping perfectly symmetrical helpings of ice cream. This was a challenge because the freezer was always too cold, the ice cream levels too low, and that meant I ended up lowering my entire J. C. Penney Oxford-clad torso deep into the tubs. This dedication to symmetry left smudges of ice cream and spumoni all over my boobs—and all that time bending over also meant that my ass was a prime target for noodles.

When it came time for me to graduate to full-time *'all by my seh-hh-hehh-helf* waitress, I, like all recent graduates, was filled with an unwarranted confidence. It was precisely at this moment that a seasoned server, who had the jawline of Brad Pitt, asked for a volunteer to cover his Fourth of July shift so he could go be handsome near a lake.

"I can cover for you," I offered.

"*You?* Are you sure? Aren't you new?" He didn't really care, but pretended to.

"Yeah, but today is my last day of training."

"Yeah, but my section is in *the trolley*," he said, whispering "the trolley" in a tone that stopped all movement in the kitchen.

Oh. The trolley section. For those unfamiliar, the trolley section is a staple at all The Old Spaghetti Factory chains and is pretty much exactly what it sounds like. It is a real-deal trolley parked inside a massive Italian garage (I mean, Italian "restaurant"). To have a dining experience inside the trolley, however, means something very different altogether. Why? Well, because when you get a table in the trolley, you are guided up three *real* stairs into a cramped train car full of spaghetti people, shoveling what is effectively airplane food into their gullets and releasing appropriate levels of silent-but-potent public farts. To dine in the trolley is to be elevated above your spaghetti peers. It is a privilege so impressive that human families wait for hours just to say, "well, *we* ate in *the trolley*" to their jealous neighbors.

Now, I'm all for recreating childhood by way of overrated gimmicks, but nothing will prepare you for The Old Spaghetti Factory's trolley groupies. They are the Trekkies of the spaghetti-eating world; they are *the* next generation of nerdy restaurant diners.

I agreed to take the hot guy's Fourth of July shift and was joined by two of my friends who were also working as servers. We pre-gamed for our shifts by taking shots of watered-down Dr. Pepper from the soda machine, and waited for our sections to fill up.

"Who's in the trolley section tonight?" some wormy pothead bus-boy asked.

"I am," I bragged.

"*You?* Well, you've got like five four-tops already sitting," he said, while looking in the direction of the trolley.

"Let's do this!" I said, like an idiot. Deservingly, a macaroni noo-dle flew into my ear, settling close enough to my eardrum that I was mildly concerned about permanent damage. I ignored the cluster of dishwashers who giggled uncontrollably at my reaction. I cleaned out the goop and headed to the Troll-ites (elite trolley diners).

It should be noted that The Old Spaghetti Factory in Seattle has a view of a parking lot, but, beyond that, one can see a sliver of Puget Sound, where fireworks would soon be erupting. This meant that the entire west-facing side of the restaurant was teeming with Americans in what I'd call "expressive flag-inspired" ensembles. In the trolley, the flag-wearing diners were packed in tightly and as a result, it looked like the sex scene in *Titanic*—steamy condensation dripped from the windows, resulting from all the hot mouths ready to order. I began the welcome monologue at my first table and by the time I took their elaborate drink orders, two more four-tops filled in. I'll admit it, the sight gave me anxiety, but I told myself my next flaggy guests would have simple drink orders and maybe even be sides-less. I was wrong. They were not simple orders.

Other than being claustrophobic and agoraphobic in public spac-es, I also have (as I've mentioned many times, right? I mentioned this, *didn't I?*) an award-winning shitty short-term memory. These qualities do not serve one well when waitressing in a trolley. I attempted to ap-ply free association techniques like "Guy with bloodshot eyes wants *Diet Coke-aine* refills" or "woman with *chunky* earrings wants *chunky* minestrone." These memorization techniques were always botched in some spectacular way. I'd put down a Coke for a different roughed up guy and say, "here's your cocaine, sir!" This wasn't just any other day in the trolley either – it was our nation's birthday and with that came a 15% increase in spending, which resulted in a 95% increase in order complexity. Some high rollers upgraded to cheesy garlic bread, while others wanted to split a five-dollar cheesecake slice for the table, but they all also wanted 'extra free' spumoni ice cream. It's funny how these classy order add-ons gave the Trollites an entitlement to behave like Kanye. I ran in and out of the trolley, sweating like a hog, and sometimes with a manager tagging behind to apologize for the delay. I'd successfully deliver a chicken parmesan only to get tapped on the shoulder asking for a status update on some *goddamned* mozzarella poppers. Instead of calming down and leveling with the Trollites, I decided I'd show them how hard I was working by huffing, puffing, and not wiping the sweat around my temples and armpits.

I was attracted to working in the trolley section because of the promise of good capitalist tips, but on July 4, 2003, the trolley section became more of an experiment in socialism. Servers who were in other sections jumped in to share in my burden, doing so with the understanding that I would tip them at the end of the night. The reality was, those in the trolley had the highest expectations of service and I was not performing at a level to earn trolley-level tips. I learned to ignore the insults and the overheard conversations between my manager and the patrons, who asked, "Is this some kind of a prank? Why is she *this* bad?"

When the clock struck ten p.m., the crowds began to slow and the trolley lost much of the steam covering its windows.

A couple in their early seventies took a romantic two-top in the front section of my train. They were on a first date, they told me, and they wanted to celebrate with a bottle of "something special." They hadn't seen how bad I'd been that night, and so I saw it as a blank slate to reestablish myself on my first official night as a waitress. I wasn't a wine drinker, but to the new couple, I spoke about the wines as if they *weren't* mulled from the urine of Robert Mondavi himself. I bull-shitted about their full-bodied flavors as if they might be the perfect facilitator to incredible seventy-year-old first-date sex.

"We'd like a bottle of your finest spumante," said the old gentle-man.

"A fine choice, if I may say so myself. I'll be right back." I clasped my hands behind my back and sauntered over to the bartender to place the order in person. I gathered the necessary ice bucket and stand, like we'd been taught in training, and felt like I was finally owning the role of waitress.

"Remember to open it and pour it for them," the bartender advised.

"Of course I'll open it. Duh!" The truth was, I wouldn't have opened it if the bartender hadn't told me. I would have left the bottle in the bucket and blasted out of there.

Back at the trolley, I set up the ice bucket and stand, showed them the spumante sticker (the label), and prepared to uncork the bottle.

Before I continue, let me just say: in my family's tradition of opening bottles of (see: Cook's Brut) champagne, we go for distance. Meaning, we try to make the cork fly as far and high as possible. Should it make it to, say, the neighbors' birdbath, then the collective wish, toast, or cheers will in fact be granted by the champagne gods. This is all fine and good, but the human beings dining in the trolley at The Old Spaghetti Factory have different expectations.

The couple waited with giddy anticipation as I held the bottle in my right hand, resting it onto my hip, while I twisted the cork firm-ly with my left hand. The bottle had been shaken some in transit, so the cork shot out with a blast so loud and powerful, it sounded as if someone had lit off a firework inside the trolley. Adding to the drama, I screamed *bloody murder* as the cork shot out of the bottle and tore through the trolley. The entire restaurant came to a screeching halt to see what all the noise was about. At the opposite end of the trolley, a table of four held up the cork for me to see it had made a crash landing in their pasta primavera.

"I'm so sorry about that," I yelled through a trolley window to the rest of the restaurant diners, "happy Fourth of July." To the couple awaiting their bubbles, I added cheerfully, "powerful bottle - that means it'll be good." The spumante, as I'm sure you've already guessed, continued to erupt from the bottle and onto the tablecloth, and eventually the trolley floor. What remained of the sweet, skunky spumante, I clumsily dumped into their champagne glasses, topping them off with extra foam.

"We'll take the check now," said the woman, as she wiped spumante off her face.

Back in the kitchen, there was no talking my way out of my epic trolley pileup. For starters, my scream was heard by *everyone*. I may as well have yelled out from the top trolley stair "I'M A TERRIBLE WAITRESS." I cashed out after my shift ended and paid off the busboys, the bartender, and the entire waitstaff that took care of the trolley. My friends, who had finished much earlier than me, were trying to be sympathetic but couldn't resist the humor in my ability to single-handedly eviscerate the trolley's golden reputation.

Somehow, I'd ended up owing money on that shift. Here I thought waitressing would make me happy, and it just so happened that I was truly, *truly*, so terrible at it. An ugly epiphany danced around in my head: *I can't be a waitress; therefore, I can't be happy.*

After I dejectedly doled out my cash to those who'd helped me, I noticed something in the corner of my eye. The Mexican fellows washing dishes were winding up to send a soggy tortellini straight to my temple. Like some freaky spaghetti superhero, I anticipated their angle and caught the tortellini with one hand. I brought it in front of my eyes to take a look at it. Its soggy skin barely covered up its light green pesto guts. It was so silly, so pathetic, so slimy, and so small.

What a joke. This is just a job.

I rolled the tortellini around in my fingers, getting the perfect grip, and chucked it, hard as I could, right back at the guys. They attempted to duck but it was too late. Julio caught the pesto tortellini right in the center of his unibrow. His friends jumped up and took a look—it was perfect placement. There was a brief pause, as is to be expected after you nail someone you barely know in the face with a tired tortellini.

"What the *fack!*" Julio cried out.

There was again another pause in the kitchen, not dissimilar from the pause after my spumante explosion in the trolley. Suddenly Julio and his crew erupted in a delirious, life-altering laughing fit. I joined in, laughing so hard at the silliness of it all.

After that night, with Julio's "what the Fack," we renamed The Old Spaghetti Factory the "Spag Fack." With the new name came new definitions:

Spag Fack became a *verb:* "Stop Spag Facking me!"

It became a *noun:* "You know, you're a real Spag Fack."

It became an *adjective:* "I'm feeling pretty Spag Facky tonight."

July 4, 2003, was the first and last time I worked in the trolley at the Spag Fack. Miraculously, I didn't get fired and I even made some decent money at the restaurant that summer. True, I did earn the reputation as *the worst waitress* in all of Spag Fack history, I also earned another reputation that I'm quite proud of — if ever a noodle was thrown at me, I would catch it and throw it right back. And I *never* missed my target.

CHAPTER 8
The Brentwood Buddhists

S even months after I got a PhD from UCLA, I was offered a ten-ure-track position at "Walkin' Puppies" (name changed to protect the innocent) in Santa Monica. My boss, a transplant from North Carolina and disheartened singer turned Walkin' Puppies CEO, told me at my orientation that I should *never* talk to clients; as she explained to me, "I arrange all of your visits and you just perform your duties—just think of me as your pimp."

It's no coincidence that she likened our relationship to that of a pimp and a prostitute because, as a dog walker, I felt like a lady of the night (though technically I only worked days). I had to sneak around the back of nice houses and fancy condos to locate the lockbox key and swiftly enter in special codes reserved just for "staff." I also wore skimpy outfits for work because my walks would often get hot 'n steamy. I topped off my skimpy outfits with a visor that looked like those worn by Burger King employees. I guess you could say I just *felt* cheap, and at fourteen dollars per hour, I *was* cheap.

I've worked for rich families before as a nanny—in fact, it paid for a good chunk of my college education—but being a nanny never made me feel cheap. Even with the cooking, cleaning, and nursing (just kidding!), it just didn't seem as dirty as when I'd prepare a meal of free-range buffalo meat with organic flaxseed and extra-extra-extra-virgin olive oil . . . *for a dog.* Icing on the cake was waiting for the pooch to "go," so I could check it off on their daily *log* sheet (yes, the pun here was so intended that I italicized it).

Though most clients were friendly, there were a few that stuck out as being sincerely terrible human beings. My favorite client to hate was a dentist, who, after our meet'n greet, wrote an e-mail to my pimp expressing concerns that I was "unqualified." This dentist was the same person who later forgot to add the "staff" code to her home security alarm, which triggered an ADT SWAT truck to arrive and hold me in "custody" until it was confirmed by the homeowners that I was not burglarizing. The greatest irony in all of the dentist's ADT drama was that there was absolutely nothing to steal from the home. It was as empty and hollow as a recently divorced dude's bachelor pad. Though I really hated the house, I secretly loved knowing that the homeowners were abundantly boring, and I took a strange comfort in imagining how they might stumble through their weeknight dinner conversations. "How were the teeth today, honey?" I imagined the husband asking his wife. She, the dentist-wife, would respond, without any trace of emotion, "they were dirty, but I cleaned them. Pass the quinoa, please."

The dentist and her inbred Muppet "Ruby" lived near one of my favorite daily clients, a spunky rescue dog that was a French bulldog/pit bull mix. She was plucked from the mean streets of East LA and named after Pippa Middleton (Princess Kate's sister). Pippa (the dog) was adopted by very important and Liberal (with a capital "L") parents, who were thrilled to spoil her rotten and "do their part." Pippa's parents lived in a perfect Craftsman in Brentwood, and they were self-declared Buddhists. They were also cold, smarmy, and apparently full of shit. This last judgement I know is true because they left a pamphlet on their fridge that said, "Which cleanse is right for you?"

Though Pippa's parents worked from home, she got two walks per day, each walk being an hour long. I often picked up extra hours walking dogs on the weekends, and, while walking Pippa one Sunday, I saw her dad out on his own run. He regarded me and Pippa cheerfully. "Feel free to run her, too," he said. "She loves to run!" It took every ounce of self-control for me not to simply hand him the leash and say, "here you go, feel free to run your own dog, dick head!"

I never did run with any of my dog clients. For me, running another person's dog was like kissing on the mouth for Julia Roberts in *Pretty Woman*. I had to draw a firm boundary there. I've never seen an expression of jubilation that comes close to the one on my dog Magnum's face when he's out on a run. To walk another dog for money was fine, but to run another was straight up puppy prostitution.

Working for people that were hiring folks to walk their dogs while they took their own jogs was digestible at the beginning of my tenure-track appointment. However, I started to change. I began listening to BBC podcasts on my walks, all about economic politics, and I started to really think about that catchy rhetoric of the "one percent."

Pippa was the one percent.

Every dog-walking day, I threatened to hunker down and actually read *The Communist Manifesto*. I daydreamed about revolutions, as I picked up steamy bags of dog shit.

Regardless of the inherent problems with Pippa's parents, I liked the Brentwood Buddhists' lifestyle. I liked their house—it was hip in an effortless and worldly way, like the kind of feelings they sell you in a Pottery Barn catalogue. The Brentwood Buddhists often had music playing and piles of things in their kitchen that expressed importance, a fullness even.

Their house always smelled of the incense that was left out for Buddha to sniff. He, Buddha, lived in the entryway. He had a great big smile, a great big belly, and made it clear every time I greeted him, that he liked me. Pippa's mom, on the other hand, made it clear that she did not like me. I wondered why at every visit. It could be that I crossed an invisible line and talked to her (unlike her maids or gardener), or maybe it was just that she hated my visor. In her defense, it was a *really* ugly visor.

I continued to walk Pippa five days a week, which meant an average of about five of her organic free-range buffalo shits to pick up. Still, I loved Pippa, like I love all dogs. In the midst of a personal crisis, I took comfort in the giddy tranquility that dogs possess. Pippa was once roaming the streets of East LA, and she now had a better way of life than 99 percent of Americans, let alone the world. She was there when I found out some important stuff on the phone, too, like when I found out my best friend, who'd been trying to conceive a child for four years, was miraculously pregnant. Or, when another good friend called to tell me when her mother died and we cried together. Probably the most ironic call Pippa was present for was from the UCLA alumni association asking if I'd speak to students about the rewards of a career in the performing arts.

Like most white people living in Los Angeles, I have experienced my share of depression and anxiety. Sometimes, just having that whole hour with another creature was enough, but sometimes it made me feel worse. It made me feel isolated and weird. *What was I doing with my life? And, why the fuck was I wearing a visor?*

But, whenever I'd return after an hour of walking by stunning mansions and statuesque palm trees, there was Buddha, *so fucking happy.* It hit me: I need to get on his drugs. So, I started reading about

Buddhism. A core belief of Buddhism is in suffering and pain. Buddha sat under the Bodhi tree for forty-nine days and realized the cause of, and cure for, all suffering. Therefore, I gave it a shot. Yep, you heard me, just like the desperate white people before me, I pretended to be Buddhist.

Two months into Buddhism, Pippa's parents tested me when a sculpture was stolen from their front yard. It was a hideous, abstract metal dog that was seven feet tall by twelve feet long. Every day it stood in my way as I tried to get to the lockbox, and I never hated a piece of "art" more. Despite this, they asked my pimp, "Had Christie seen it? Moved it? Borrowed it?" I envisioned stuffing the metal dog up their uncleansed colons. Instead, I paused and listened to my inner Buddha, who told me to . . . *Calm the fuck down.*

The accusation hurt my feelings, and I was especially offended that during the next few visits I was watched not just by Buddha, but by Pippa's mom. She watched me like a hawk as soon as I arrived, when I was outside near their matching BMWs, their hideous art, or their thousands of packages (this was long before the expression "just Amazon Prime it" existed). I started to feel anxiety, like my body was a Jenga game about to topple. I coached myself on walks to *medi-fuck-ing-tate*—which made me even more jumpy. After a month of being monitored, I was hanging by a thread.

One particular day, the weather in Los Angeles reflected my state of mind. We had a torrential downpour with thunder, lightning, and hail. I completed all of my walks and finished up my day with Pippa, who was waiting by Buddha at the front entryway. My clothes and shoes were bloated with water from earlier walks, but I had no choice but to continue my work. Pippa's mom was in the kitchen being a TBB (typical Buddhist bitch). She sat at the counter going through magazines, while soothing Hawaiian music played and a richly scented candle gently flickered. She was delightfully cozy, and I had a bizarre moment where I felt very happy for her. Wait a minute… were these new feelings a result of my Buddhist practice? *Hot damn! I'm so enlightened!*

"Hi!" I said in a tone that reflected a newfound sense of inner peace.

"What are you doing?" she said, apparently horrified by the trail of rain I was shedding in her home.

"I'm walking Pippa," I retorted, all perky and shit.

Pause.

"Well, she needs her raincoat." This line was delivered in a valley girl "uh, duh" tone.

"Uh . . . okay." I had no clue dogs wore coats for utilitarian purposes.

"It's in the third drawer down," Pippa's mom directed, pointing to an entire row of kitchen cabinets that were reserved for the princess.

Once I opened the correct drawer, I was met with FOUR different raincoats.

"Which one?" I knew my instinct to choose the Dick Tracy knock-off would be scoffed at.

"I don't know. *I* haven't been outside." The words stung. She had made it very clear that there was a visible difference between us—she was an insider and I was an outsider, soaked by the extreme weather conditions that she didn't need to know about.

I looked down at the coats again, and chose the down-feathered Gore-Tex shell because I figured that'd be the only time I'd get to dress any living thing in goose feathers in Los Angeles.

About five minutes into our hour-long walk, a deafening clap of thunder scared me so much I started sobbing. I began to turn back until I heard another crack of thunder that sounded like Buddha saying, "Remember about suffering and pain, you privileged white bitch!"

My hands and body were red from the cold and the rain, providing a perfect canvas for the hail that started to spray. It's the only time I've seen hail in Los Angeles, and it came down like a hardened snowstorm that violently harassed the perfect palm trees above me. The hail was just stingy enough that I was sure it was Buddha sending me a side of extra suffering.

Pippa and I pushed on. I wanted to make it to Santa Monica's Palisades Park, with its breathtaking views of the ocean and perfectly manicured gardens. I was certain that if I endured a bitter hailstorm, Buddha would provide me with enlightenment at the very edge of the North American continent. We made it to the Palisades lookout, but the ocean was completely erased by the storm clouds.

Ah, yes. All that effort to get there and literally nothing was clear to me. There was plenty of lightning, but I was left unenlightened.

The walk home with Pippa was even longer. The down feathers in her coat got soaked, and she shook it off, leaving me to carry its soggy, cold carcass the whole way home (much like Linus' blanket in *Peanuts*). Once home, I was surprised to see that Pippa's Buddhist parents chose to weather the storm, and had gone out in their BMW. I hung up her down coat, locked up the house, and cried the whole drive home.

Not twenty minutes later, my pimp called. Even through her stupid Southern accent, I could tell she was mad: "I'm a little confused. . . why did you walk Pippa?"

"It was on my schedule." Any remaining pandering-to-boss skills had been beaten out of me by the hailstorm.

"Her parents went out looking for her. They felt you put her in danger by walking her in a hailstorm."

"I'm confused. It's my job to walk her, so I did my job."

"The topic of severe-weather walking was addressed in the Walkin' Puppies Orientation Packet. If the weather is extreme, we make sure the client has done their potty business, and then we play with them inside."

"So, you want me to play with a dog inside for sixty minutes while both her parents are home?"

"Well, yeah. This isn't that difficult to understand and . . . I know you're not *stupid*."

If I knew anything about people from the South, it's that they coat their insults in layers of backhanded frosting. Pimp's "I know you're not stupid" was as close as she could get to "you're a fucking moron—read the puppy packet."

"They also said that you left the front door wide open," Pimp continued. "This is a huge concern."

It was at this point that I officially lost my religion.

"That's *bullshit*. I locked the door," I barked.

"They said it was open. They have no reason to lie," Pimp growled back.

"Neither do I." I spoke as if I had suddenly become Walter White from *Breaking Bad*.

"Well, you know *I* believe you," Pimp lied, "but how do you explain that the door was wide open when they got home?"

"I have no idea; an act of God?" I was truly and utterly perplexed. I locked the door—I remember the click; the sound was burned into me like never before.

Then Pimp said it, a line that spoke directly to my short-lived Buddhist practice.

"I need you to be more mindful."

You know, like everyone else I have hallucinations of standing up for myself in boss/employee scenarios, but it never comes out the way I imagine. It's usually just a fleeting fantasy that temporarily relieves feelings of powerlessness. Usually that fantasy is enough. However, when I told Pimp the Buddha's honest truth, that I locked the door, she never even tried to believe me. She needed me to be "mindful" and so in that instance I was.

"I need to quit walking Pippa." My heart raced as I said it, but once the words were out I felt lighter, as if I'd actually *done* something by saying I was done doing something.

You know that old saying, "When God closes one door, he/she/they open(s) a window"? Sometimes it's the other way around. I think we're supposed to suffer, we're supposed to be selfless, but sometimes we have to be the ones who shut the door on people, jobs, or relationships that make us feel like dog shit. In my case, a new window (a teaching job) did open up shortly after I shut the door on the Brentwood Buddhists.

Now, I don't know if that's Buddha's "enlightenment," but it's certainly mine.

Namas-fucking-te.

PART III
Dearly Departed

CHAPTER 9
Clog Dancing

I look like my dad's dad. This is something I've tried to fight all my life. I didn't want to look like a Nittrouer almost as much as I didn't want to cart around his Nazi-sounding last name. It was a dislike so strong that in fourth grade, when I learned that the Iroquois tribe were a matriarchal society and thus inherited their mother's names, I began feverishly searching for proof that I was part Iroquois. As it turns out, there was a rumor that my mom's dad, who was tan with dark brown eyes, was a tremendous hunter/fisher/outdoorsman, and who had a legit drinking problem, was a descendant of the Abenaki-Hill[3] tribe. My Dad later told me in a fairly humorless email that the rumor was just that; he said, and I quote verbatim "the Abenaki-Hill tribe was completely fabricated."

Unlike my mom's dad, my dad's dad was very German looking. He had blond hair and big blue eyes that looked like some eighth-grader's science project diorama of the planet Neptune. Poppop was smaller in stature, and his sharp bones protruded from under his skin, looking like they might jump out at any moment. His calves, especially, were

---

3   Probably important to note that Hill was my maternal grandfather's mother's maiden name.

thin and could barely hold up the sport socks he tried so desperately to bring to his knees. Physically we were similar in every way; even our skin was the same fair shade that I've likened to a cup of blue-tinted skim milk. I found out at age nine that my double-jointed left thumb was also a hereditary gift from him. Its freakiness matched the freaky personality traits I also inherited—my sometimes volatile, loud, and stubborn nature. Though Poppop liked order and control, he was also mercurial, impulsive, and at times even romantic. He loved nothing more than to pull the rug out from under himself and others.

That rug-pulling-out quality is exactly what he did to my father and his immediate family when he left all five of them in 1969. It was a time when divorce was just starting to happen, but "not to *you*," as my grandmother once explained it. Poppop philandered, and, when Mommom found the evidence, she tried to stifle her own volatility. It never worked—they divorced and with that, so dissolved the American comforts they'd worked hard to afford. It all went away—the small cabin on Lake Wallenpaupack, the waterskiing boat, the myth of a happy suburban family. If it had taken place today, Poppop's midlife confession that he "just wasn't happy" would be understood as unfortunate but genuine. In his day, however, it was considered cruel and plain ol' abandonment.

Following the divorce and for a period of six or so years, my father refused to speak to his father. Luckily for everyone, my mom bandaged them together for a period of twenty years or so, and thanks to her efforts I got the opportunity to study a seventy-year-old male version of myself. I likened my dad and grandfather's relationship to a Band-Aid and a sore, because they needed each other, but it was obvious that eventually the Band-Aid would either rip off painfully or wear down and deteriorate. Their relationship was haunted by history so much that even the "grandchild distraction" was not enough to help it.

The drill was always the same when Poppop visited with his second wife, a persnickety Southern belle whom we addressed as "Mommom Di." Their visits lasted for a weekend, there was always lots of drinking, and a CD of the Temptations' greatest and giddiest hits played continuously on a loop. If Poppop visited during football season, any and all games were left on, and at some point, Dad and Poppop would stand on our trapezoid-shaped front lawn and "toss the pigskin."

Dad and Poppop posing with the pigskin.

It was clear to me at a young age that I didn't possess the right parts to toss the pig, however good my aim was (and still is strangely good). Instead, I'd stay inside and do girl-approved activities like practice the piano, the flute, or the violin. One time, during my short fling with the violin, when my grandfather saw me practicing, he took a calculated pause and said, "So . . . you're a fiddler now." He continued on the subject: "Maybe we should find you a roof to play on." After that he walked off with a drink, whistling the tune from *Fiddler on the Roof,* "If I Were a Rich Man." I didn't really understand his point in doing this, but knew I was supposed to figure it out.

Other remarks he made were more blatant, like when I went into our freezer and grabbed a roll from my personal "frozen carbohydrate stash," microwaved it, and swallowed it in one gulp.

"So, she seems to *really* like bread," Poppop said to my father, observing me as if I were a baboon in captivity.

"Yep, she's always eating bread," my dad replied.

"That's the Jew in her," Poppop asserted.

Now I knew that my Ukrainian-born and -raised great-grandmother was Jewish, but I had no earthly idea what that had to do with me playing the violin or enjoying sourdough. Aside from any "Jewish tendencies" I had, I also got called out by Poppop for having any semblance of a backbone. Any opinion I expressed was met with him yelling "she's as stubborn as a mule!" Sometimes when I entered the room, it was just "Oh, here comes the mule" and that was enough, he figured, to keep me from saying anything contrarian. It's true — there isn't much of a comeback when your grandfather calls you a mule. Sure it bothered me, but at least mules have some chutzpah.

It was no secret that Poppop was a misogynist — he didn't speak to two of his three daughters, and to this day my aunts and cousins only refer to him as "biological." But Beluga? Beluga adored my grandfather, but not as much as my grandfather adored his *grandson.* Poppop took Beluga to Eagles games and men's fishing trips where they never caught anything but bragged about eating their weight in lobster. I only got one afternoon trip with my step-grandmother and it was to see Keanu Reeves' awkward ass in *A Walk in the Clouds.* Mommom Di was very feminine, and though I *wanted* to be feminine, that was never something that came naturally to me. I was always stuck somewhere in between the masculine and feminine poles.

Poppop never had much concern for figuring out what I was about. For him, it was all about Beluga. I still think most of Poppop's toys—his big-screen TV in his basement, his red convertible, his Winnebago van—were all for Beluga. When we'd go down to Philly to visit them, I never once dared to touch the remote control of his big-screen TV. I certainly loved big-screen TVs, but until I up and grew a penis, there was no way I'd get to choose what we watched.

In Poppop's Chrysler convertible on a balmy spring day on Long Island.

Though the relationship between my father and his dad was strained, Mommom Di made things dicier (pun!). She never had children and refused to pretend that she ever wanted to have adult step-children. Regardless of her cool demeanor, I enjoyed the show she put on. Mommom Di was most of the characters from *The Golden Girls* rolled into one. She spoke with an accent identical to that of Blanche; nearly every word that spewed from her lips was filled with eight extra syllables and drippy, dramatic inflections. Mommom Di dressed like Blanche, too. Her wardrobe had enough sequins, color, and fluorescence to power the city of Savannah. She bleached her short pixie hair the same color as Betty White's, and she had the audacity to say *anything*, just like Sophia. The only character Mommom Di was missing was Dorothy Zbornak, but I could always stuff my shirt with some shoulder pads, throw on a wig from our basement collection, and roll my eyes (almost as well as Bea Arthur).

Far and away the most fascinating feature belonging to Mommom Di, and one that *The Golden Girls* did not possess, were her drawn-on eyebrows. For the most part, her eyebrows were consistent in expression, but every now and again she'd paint her brows as if they were a mood barometer. They could be gentle, light, or angled in a cartoonish "back-off-or-I'll-stab-you-arch." At the end of the night, Mommom's brows were erased, like an Etch A Sketch, but in the morning, they would return — a crystal ball of what disposition was to come.

In the fall of 1994, my parents invited my grandfather and Di up for an annual party my dad threw for his research lab. One of Dad's students was from the South and had for a long time raved about "pig pickins." It's pretty much what it sounds like: an entire pig is roasted in a pit and picked apart for its meat. In my dad's selfish rationale, the party was an opportune time to bring his father's Southern wife for a visit where there'd be some amount of distraction from the tense Band-Aid situation. To my dad, it was a gracious offering of Southern *hospitality* to his distant stepmother. In reality, it was a cold, rainy October weekend on Long Island, where a bunch of oceanography graduate students stood around a smoldering swine in the parking lot of my mom's dance studio (but I'll get to that in a minute).

On the eve of the pig pickin', Mommom and Poppop Nittrouer arrived at our house and sipped on their liquid tradition—gin martinis. Years earlier, my mom invested in a big bottle of vermouth that was reserved for Poppop's visits. It became a liquid timeline for tracking his trips up to Long Island, and the lower the level got on the bottle, the more deteriorated the Band-Aid became. There was a standard schedule for visits with Mommom and Poppop: they'd get blasted on Friday night and wake up the next morning polished and ready for their breakfast. My dad would make an omelet and farm out "bloodies" (Bloody Marys) along with some vague plan for the day. If we were running late for some scheduled event (which we always were) and you asked Poppop the time, he would always answer: "*It's martini time!*" Poppop was an unconventional grandfather, but he was a conventional partier.

On the morning of the pig pickin', there were no omelets served, as my parents were anticipating eating a dead pig outside the dance studio (where it had been cooking for 24 hours). This meal neglect was reflected in Mommom Di's angry eyebrows and Poppop's scowl. I had, for the most part, ignored them because my best friend/ surrogate sibling Becky was over and we were cooking up a plan of our own.

Once my parents had set up a makeshift tarp for the rain, they came back to pick up the children and the "old farts." Mommom Di was in her usual full-face of makeup, bundled in layers of "whhhhuuullll" (wool), which she borrowed from "Chuuuuuhhk" (my father). Her eyebrows were extra angled – she was *not* happy. It wasn't just that her electric-hued, shoulder-padded ensemble was hidden under Dad's smelly, but necessary, foul weather gear; it was the looming threat of the rain erasing one of her boldest facial features. I made a mental note to check her brows throughout the day – if they started to disappear, I'd know she was cranky. If they were erased entirely, I'd know she was ready to erase anyone who looked at her funny.

In retrospect, the act of buying a giant dead animal, smoking it outside a family business, kitty-corner to a strip mall, in October, on Long Island, in the rain, and calling it a Southern *cultural* experience . . . it was pretty damn rude. The only possible hope of enjoying the pig pickin' was to indulge in the icy-cold keg that sat in the corner of a ramshackle tarp. Problem was, Mommom Di didn't do beer. She stood with arms folded, her brows clinging desperately to her face, as the rain began to blow sideward.

In a twist of intentional irony, Becky and I told our parents we were walking to the pet shop in the strip mall to have a look at the living pigs (guinea pigs). When we returned from the trip, we found that Mommom was on her second cup of keg beer. She was loosening up, feeling warmer. As she fumbled with the keg tap, a wind picked up and shook the blue tarp free of its fastening. A bucket's worth of cold October rain dumped onto her head. The second the water touched her hair, her entire body cringed and she shrieked for all to hear.

"*CHUUUUUUUUUUUHHHHHHHHHHCCCCKKKKKK!*"
(Translation: Poppop Chuck)

The noise she made was a bit like the Wicked Witch, and, also like the WW, Mommom Di was *melting*. It was maybe forty-five seconds before we were all in the car again, heading home. Once we were home, Mommom Di changed into more fluorescent costumes and cranked our heat up. She sat in front of my mom in the kitchen and strummed her fingers together, obviously waiting. At this point in the day, Mommom Di's eyebrows weren't so much eyebrows as they were an ode to the letter "V" (she was *angry*).

"Can I get you anything, Di?" Mom asked.

"Well," she said, "I'd like . . . *somethin'.*"

She took a pause in between "like" and "somethin'" so as to give the effect that she hadn't eaten in many millennia. (Side note: Mommom Di's line was so brilliantly dramatic that we continue to recycle it over and over at our family get-togethers, especially if someone is being exceptionally demanding). My mom pulled out her usual go-to hosting tradition of presenting a platter of refrigerated apples, mediocre bulk-bought cheddar cheese, and some stale water crackers.

Becky and I, still waiting to enact our plan, surveyed the situation, waiting for Mom to return to the pig pickin' and the grandparents to booze-snooze in front of a football game. Though I didn't realize it at the time, we could have done literally anything in my parents' house and no one would have noticed it. *What was our plan*, you ask? To steal two pairs of my mother's old pointe shoes from her days in the ballet company. *So what!* So what?! Wearing pointe shoes before graduating from ballet slippers was a crime that would surely land us in a maximum-security prison if we were caught. Now, Becky was a brilliant ballet dancer who had taken classes with my mom up until that year, when she chose to study with a former prima ballerina from the Moscow Ballet. Becky was nearing the point in her dance career that she would actually be put on pointe. She was a born dancer; she had a natural turnout and arched feet, and she was as flexible and confident as a stripper. Me, on the other hand, well I was nearly pigeon-toed, had feet that were as flat as Florida, and the only flexibility I possessed was deposited into my double-jointed left thumb.

I wanted very much to be a brilliant ballet dancer, because, according to my logic that meant you were "feminine," and feminine is the gateway to "sexy," and sexy people were powerful people who had horses (a goal of mine). The only style of dance that I was actually good at was tap. As we all know, there ain't nothing sexy about tap. It's loud, it's spastic, and the costumes *always* required me to wear tuxedos. I was sure I could fake being a good ballet dancer: put on a leotard, stuff my feet in wooden pointe shoes, stand on my toes, and look off into the distance as if I were clinically depressed. It seemed like the requirements to be a beautiful ballet dancer were contradictory: you needed to look aloof, apathetic, waif-like, all the while your feet were in a bind that makes dogfighting seem *slightly* more humane. To dance on pointe meant you were willing to withstand pain, while offering others the pleasure of witnessing your beautiful lie. What a *perfect* emblem for the practice of femininity.

Once the static cheers of a televised college football game were loudly enough, Becky and I headed to the basement to collect our pointe shoes. Our basement housed my mom's former dance studio, where she taught for five years (before our neighbor sued us over "noise pollution"). When the studio was vacated, I turned it into my subscription-based theatre company (that was occasionally intruded upon by my father's workouts on his free weights). In the "backstage" area of my theatre, there was a large storage closet where Mom kept all excess tutus and dance props, as well as the mother lode - a picnic basket full of her old pointe shoes.

Becky and I opened the picnic basket and found there were old shoes, new shoes, and the Goldilocks shoes—those that were perfectly arched and broken in. We held them in our hands, knocking the toe on the wall of the closet, our eyes *wide* with delight. Worried that Mommom and Poppop would report us to the police if they saw we were dabbling in *hard shoes*, we stuffed them in our oversized flannels and gingerly made our way up to my room. Once inside my room, I locked the door and put my desk chair behind it.

"What if they come upstairs and knock on the door?" Becky worried.

"We'll tell them to wait a minute," I assured her.

"No, it takes at least twenty minutes to put pointe shoes on and maybe fifteen to take them off." Becky's estimates were always a little high, mostly because Becky was (and still is) the most anal-retentive person I have ever known. Even at age eleven, her closet was painstakingly arranged in the same color spectrum as a rainbow (red, orange, yellow, green, blue, indigo, and violet).

I examined the shoes—the laces in particular were pretty elaborate (long). The truth was, my grandparents didn't give a *flying fuck* what we were doing. Poppop had his football, Mommom had a Fabio romance novel, and they both were very much on "martini time." Still—I wanted the drama. I envisioned a huge showdown where they'd walk upstairs, burst open the door, and become sick with worry about the damage we'd done to our pre-pointe feet.

"We can camouflage the shoes so when they open the door they don't know we're wearing them," I suggested.

"Camouflage them with what?" Becky asked, her eyes growing to the size of fancy dinner plates and magnified by her perfectly circular eyeglass frames. (This signature look of Becky's would later earn her the pet name "Owly" from her wife).

I looked down at my feet, clad in a pair of ill-fitting wool socks that I'd stolen from my father's bureau.

"With whhhhuuulll," I said, borrowing Mommom Di's accent for dramatic effect.

We gingerly tiptoed to Dad's dresser, making sure Mommom Di and Poppop didn't hear a whiff of what we were planning. Once at the dresser I pulled out six pairs of socks—some were athletic, some were whhhhuuulll, but they all were a men's size 12. This was double our foot size at that time.

Back in my room, we prepared for the premiere of our Long Island Ballet Theatre Company, the LIBTC. At that point in time, my feet were about the same size as Becky's, barely a size 6. My mom's shoes were a size 7, and pointe shoes don't really work if they don't stay on your feet. So, we put on two pairs of Dad's wool socks underneath the pointe shoes so they'd stay on our feet without falling off our heels when we went up on our toes. We laced the beautiful pink ribbon in a crisscross pattern over the hideous green wool. We topped it all off with our camouflage, a pair of mildly discolored sports socks. Just to clarify the pointe shoe situation: both Becky and I had two pairs of wool socks on under a pair of oversized pointe shoes, which were themselves covered with a men's size 12 athletic sock. It was important that we remain casually dressed, in case my grandparents came upstairs. So, we stuck to our grungy 90s look - baggy jeans and dark flannels, polished off with pointe shoes.

Standing in front of my closet mirror, we paused a moment to take it all in. There we stood — in our flannels from Costco, our boxy Gap blue jeans, and lumpy pointe shoes hidden under dingy Wilson athletic socks. *This* was eleven-year-old femininity at its finest.

Me in flannel, taking a casual "selfie" and flaunting my bling

"You ready?" I asked.

"Yup," she replied, her Owly eyes as wide as...an owl.

I pressed play on my CD player, which was cued up to Tchaikovsky's "Dance of the Sugar Plum Fairy" from *The Nutcracker*. The song began with the delicate plucking of violin strings, which inspired our movement to tiptoe around like injured swans. We were dainty, secretive, and delightfully balletic. It was perfect and exactly what we'd hoped for. As the melody grew louder, so did our dancing. And as the tempo picked up, I was the first to discover a dangerous equation:

pointe shoes + athletics socks + hardwood floor = falling hazard

In the midst of a "move," I fumbled to catch my balance, reached out to grab the window ledge, lost traction in both feet, and landed loudly on my ass. Becky could barely manage to speak, she was laughing so hard.

"Are you okay?" she wheezed, while wiping away tears.

"Shh, shh. I'm fine," I told Becky as I limped up. Like a dog shaking off a fresh bath, I stretched out my legs and continued to embody a feminine sugar plum fairy.

The more time we spent in the shoes, the more our confidence grew. Much like Natalie Portman in *Black Swan,* we were overtaken by our commitment to the art of ballet dancing. We moved to bolder songs of Tchaikovsky's—taking an upbeat pointe-shoe foxtrot with the song "Russian Dance."

Ah, but it was "Waltz of the Flowers" that truly captured the spirit of our Long Island Ballet Theatre Company (again, the LIBTC). Oh, it was all so grand! The ferocious French horns, the delicate flutes, the vivacious violins—they begged us to *jump, jump, jump!* We twirled and swirled, holding an arabesque, only to sashay into a Tonya Harding-inspired triple axel. I flew into crash landings with an indescribable grace. I blasted off of the floor only to snag a bit of my Wilson athletic sock on the radiator and clatter down again.

We choreographed oh-so elaborate anthropomorphizing moves to "Waltz of the Flowers," but the real miracle came at the song's conclusion. I held my neck just long enough, forced my chin to the sky, and emitted the proper amount of balletic sadness as I raised my heels and stood on my *God-damned toes for four whole fucking seconds.* Our pointe performance was superb — our feet were evidence of God's grand design. That afternoon we officially became ballerinas, which by default made us feminine.

We successfully snuck the shoes down to their magical picnic basket and were on our way to the kitchen when Poppop called out to us from the guest room.

"Yeah, Poppop?" I responded, staying at the door with Becky right behind me.

"We've been trying to nap for about two hours now. What in the hell were you doing upstairs?" My eyes followed the gesture he was making toward the ceiling. That's when it hit me.

Shit. My bedroom was directly *above* the guest room. I couldn't think of anything clever to say.

Poppop continued, "It sounded like . . . like *clog dancing.*"

"I . . . *haaaaaaaahhhh*ve a headache," Mommom Di slurred in a manner that mirrored the slurry state her eyebrows were in.

"Well, Mule? Have you taken up clog dancing now?" Poppop asked.

Clog dancing? *Clog dancing!* I had just danced the entire ballet of *The Nutcracker* on my damn toes! Next week I would do *Swan Lake* and *Coppélia. No, I wasn't clog dancing!* I was a Goddamn prima ballerina who just happened to perform in denim, flannel, and athletic socks. *Time for this mule to set Poppop straight once and for all!*

"Actually," I began, though I caught Becky's eyes as they took on a "terrified owl" shape, "I was . . ." I stuttered as I thought about it. Becky would actually get in trouble from her parents. I mean, she could have damaged her feet, and the truth was, *she* was dancing ballet and . . . an d . . . I . . . I . . . "*I* was clog dancing to *The Nutcracker,* Poppop."

There was a great big pause. The kind that comes before something *really* loud.

" *Whaaaaaaahhhh!* " Mommom Di laughed so hard it sounded as if someone had stabbed her in her already overworked liver. "She's *clog dancing* now!"

The thought alone was enough to send them both into a tailspin of hyperventilating laughter. I stood there nodding along, waiting for them to finish. When it seemed as if my confession might kill them with laughter, I turned back to the kitchen. Once there, I made a Nestea with lukewarm tap water — a reward for all that 'clog dancing.'

My parents returned home an hour or so later. As expected, they had loads of pig meat to share, though due to their tardiness they were also expecting an even thicker letter *V* on Mommom Di's brows. When Poppop and Mommom Di emerged from the guest room, my parents were shocked to see the shape Mommom Di's brows took. They were arched up at the center and slanted down toward her temples, suggesting a sunnier forecast. I didn't realize that Mommom Di's visual of her awkward, runtish, and overwhelmingly unfeminine step-granddaughter clog dancing was enough to change the state of her brows. Mommom and Poppop weren't completely un-pissed at my parents, but they were ready to pass some pig around the table and toss the pigskin on the lawn the next day.

Eventually, about four years later, my grandfather grew fed up with his strained relationship with his son and he removed the Band-Aid quickly. That experience was one that I also vividly remember. Though, in that case, the angry expression on Mommom Di's brows was not drawn on; it was tattooed on her face with indelible ink. It's a memory that competes for space in my brain. It tries to unpack more painful details and rearrange feelings that I have toward my paternal grandfather and his role in my life.

For a while, I had shelved the clog-dancing memory, replacing it with the night Poppop sped out of our lives and yelled, from his car, "Fuck all four of 'em!" It was a line we repeated and laughed about, but even its over-the-top volatility wasn't *really* funny—especially because three of us were related to him (and potentially possessed that same volatility). It's a line that sends me back to that same place in fourth grade—where I went scrounging for proof that I was an Iroquois and *not* related to Poppop.

Nearly fifteen years later, when I was sitting in a graduate-school seminar at UCLA, a guest feminist performance scholar spoke of a book she wrote called *The Ballerina's Phallic Pointe.* The title made me chuckle, as it is a fun way to speak of the book's thesis, which argues that pointe shoes were designed as a surrogate "phallus" (penis) for women. The ballerina must, as this scholar argued, essentially "strap on" a pointe shoe to partake in a gender dichotomy that always has and always will give privilege to dicks.

Huh, I thought, while staring off in a windowless seminar room.

I pictured a snooty French ballerina strapping on two erect "penises" to her battered feet, and this visual made me laugh aloud in the classroom. I appreciated the penis-pointe-shoe theory, mostly because it undermined any remaining desire or nostalgia I bestowed upon pointe shoes as a marker of femininity. For so long, I focused on what I couldn't do (go on pointe) and how that made me unfeminine. As it turns out, the pointe shoe wasn't the slightest bit feminine. I mean, that rigid, miserable, wooden pointe shoe was designed by a *real dick.* Much like I had used the camouflage of an athletic sock to hide the pointe shoe when I was ten, the shoe itself used a soft pink exterior to hide the fact that it was actually an emblem of masculinity.

While this realization took hold, another dance-related memory unpacked its details in my brain, right there in the seminar.

It was four years after the clog-dancing incident and also the night before Poppop would walk out of our lives for the last time. Poppop, Mommom Di (in her happy eyebrows), Beluga and I were driving to a Chinese restaurant when a radio station played Michael Jackson's "Beat It." I was fourteen going on "when the shit am I going to grow some boobs" and I had long since given up on being a pointe ballet dancer. I was fully aware at age fourteen that femininity was a currency and that I was quite broke.

As soon as the song came on, we had just entered the parking lot, and seconds later we found a spot directly in front of the restaurant. I'm not sure who started it, but we began a collective dance-off in the car, moving so enthusiastically (spastically) that the entire vehicle shook violently. There was something about that song, with its weird and futuristic feel; it's the hypnotic chorus, just the whole *attitude* of the song. It could have been an unfortunate foreshadowing that Poppop would soon "beat it" and not come back, or it could have just been that we all trusted each other for a brief moment to cut loose. Either way, it's a visual I can't shake—the car shaking, our limbs making funky shapes and expressions, and all of us forgetting what we were *supposed* to be doing and just *being* . . . a family.

We were right outside the restaurant, steps from the perplexed host, who watched all four of us "beat it" for a solid three minutes before assigning us a booth at the very back of the restaurant.

It was a great memory to recall, and as my mind found its way back to that seminar room, I had another realization. Yes, my grandfather liked to point out what he thought I was—a stubborn, carbohydrate-inhaling, "fiddler on the roof" who had a fancy for clog dancing. However, had he correctly accused me of dancing the *Nutcracker* ballet in pointe shoes—I would have kept on trying to dance that dance.

All this time I focused on what I wasn't, *feminine*, instead of what he wasn't, a *conventional grandfather*.

But, Poppop could only imagine me in clogs. Protective, sturdy, strong, goofy, timeless, and *stubborn* clogs. Poppop's comments were not a criticism of my choices but a delight in them and who I was, a free-spirited weirdo.

Clog dancing was, and still is, *my* femininity. And it's a way better fit.

So, there I was, many years later in that graduate seminar, raising my eyebrows to mark the shock of such realization — that Poppop was the one on point after all.

A typical summer night. Temptations playing on a loop and Poppop saying something supremely funny.

CHAPTER 10
Miss B., the Muse

It took a solid two years of running to the piano in our living room and crying underneath it before my mom cooked up the theory that I must have some hidden talent for music. It was never "Why are you suffering from depression at age six?" It was "Well, I guess I better find you a reasonably priced piano teacher before you cause water damage."

Aside from playing coed soccer, or dancing, I wasn't enrolled in any extracurricular activities because the cost seemed outrageous given that I was living with a dance teacher. Why would I go to Girl Scouts, gymnastics, or horseback riding when I could just walk down the stairs and take a dance class in our basement? I wanted, almost as much as I wanted a dog, to be a gymnast and a Girl Scout. I figured that those activities that started with a letter *G* were guaranteed to make me more girl-like. If I sold some Samoas and could backhand spring on a beam, then I was well on my way to living my best girlie-girl life.

When our neighbor Judy Kaplan recommended a musicology graduate student and master pianist studying at SUNY Stony Brook, my mom invited him over for an interview. He was young, serious, and brilliant at the piano. In all honesty, he was the worst possible match for me. If you put me in a room with a serious person, I'm *programmed* to piss them off; I honest-to-God can't help it. At the end of our meeting with the young pianist, Mom asked him his rate. He responded with a number I didn't hear but understood to be too high, as Mom did a typical Pacific Northwest nod and smile. She followed this gesture with a melodic and high-pitched "*thanks so much.*" His was a rate for professional six-year-old pianists, and Mom and I both knew I was of a rookie grade.

One of my best pals, Dorothy, lived around the corner from me (if I cut through the grumpy neighbor's yard – otherwise it was a roundabout drive) and she had just started her own piano studies. Dorothy's mother had signed her up for classes with a woman, Lois Baranosky, who she described as "a bit unconventional." This "unconventional" piano teacher could have taught classes in full Kabuki makeup and a ball gown, because once Mom found out her rate was ten dollars a class, it was a done deal.

We arranged to meet the piano teacher after we attended the winter boat show in central Long Island (a cultural activity topped *maybe* by the annual Brat Fest in Madison, Wisconsin). At the boat show, we spent a few hours touring used twenty-foot gas-guzzlers. All four of us, Mom, Dad, Beluga and me, sprawled out in every boat's "cuddy cabin," as my dad called them (the den underneath the bow of the boat, where most adults did adult things). Beluga and I would be silly enough to think that we'd be welcome to sleep in the "buddy cabin" (as they renamed it) once they bought a boat. Little did we know, we'd be sleeping on the convertible saltwater-soaked seats, if we were lucky (as was the case for Beluga), or if unlucky (as was the case for me), the boat floor where much bait had been ground into the bright blue rug.

After the boat show, all four of us drove to my interview with Lois Baranosky on Lubber Street. Ah *Lubber Street*, a name I always liked to say because it reminded me of a name you'd give a respectable whale. You know, a formal whale with a British accent who said things like "Good morrow, I'm Sir Seymour Lubber." Lubber Street was wide, also like a whale. It was well covered with trees that remained naked in March but were teeming with green in June. The house was a single-story, blood-red ranch with two large windows framed by shutters. To the left of the house there was a converted garage that housed a tenant (whom I never actually saw).

Standing behind a glass door, which would become her trademark lookout post, stood a very short, old woman, with a row of *very* twisty, dark teeth that seemed to be in the process of French-braiding themselves. She stuck just her head out the door, a head topped with a mass of dark gray cowlicks that looked like a shorter Medusa-do (hairstylists might call it a "Medusa Bob"). This figure then stepped back, revealing a very well-lit (yet still cozy) living room with thick, green carpet. Seconds before fully forming an opinion on the brightness of the carpet and the darkness of her teeth, I saw it—a baby grand piano. At home, we had an upright piano, also beautiful, but I couldn't imagine how much better a baby grand piano would sound when you cried under it.

The woman was sixty-seven years old going on wizard. It was clear she had put some thought into her wardrobe, which would remain the same for the rest of her life: plaid wool pants, a long-sleeved collared shirt in a variety of clashing pastels, covered by a sweatshirt that advertised PETA or WWF. Another staple of her wardrobe was a pair of thick, oversized, 80s-inspired bifocals that were tucked into her sweatshirt.

"Hi, Christie, I'm Lois," she said, watching me light up at the sight of the piano. She presented me with a small wrapped package. "This is a gift for you."

I looked at her with huge eyes—*was it my birthday and I forgot?* No one had just given me a gift like that, not a stranger, and certainly not someone with such interesting teeth. I instantly liked this woman; I mean, she had taken the time to use wrapping paper and write a very tiny little tag that said "TO: Christie," "FROM: Lois." It was only polite to wait and open the gift elsewhere, since I hadn't brought her anything and I'm sure Beluga would bust me in the face for not getting a gift of his own (he was a whale with an entirely *different* temperament than that of Seymour Lubber).

We stepped deeper inside her house and took a seat on a couch covered with a bedsheet straight out of 1967. A brown and yellow cat approached us, strutting like most cats do, like a human slut.

"That's my Shiny Nose," she said.

"Oh," I replied, not sure why she was talking about her nose. Based on her eye contact with the cat, I modified my response: "He's cute."

"It's a she," she corrected me, "but Mozart over there, he's a he, and Icky, and Bach." My eyes darted around the room—she had *a lot* of cats. I counted four, until three more entered, and then another one, who must have been the king. I held out my hand and he curled around it, purring like all cats do—in that low hum that sounds like they're flaunting the size of their deviated septum.

"That's Amadeus," she said, proudly, as if he were made of solid gold.

I didn't think much about the consequence of owning many cats, because I was seven years old and the judgment part of my brain hadn't yet developed, but my dad's face began turning blue and his eyes looked as if they were bulging out of their sockets. *Why was Dad holding his breath?* Again, looking around, I noticed: there wasn't a surface in the entire living or dining room that wasn't covered with a 60s bedsheet, which was itself covered in thickets of cat fur. In fact, there were cats all around us, closing in, like a band of adorable villains. If I had more of a background in classical music, I would have known that Amadeus and Mozart were redundant cat names. Additional duplications were seen in the three different cats named Johann, Sebastian, and Bach. *Shoot,* even Shiny Nose (who did indeed have a shiny nose) was really just scraping at the bottom of the cat-naming barrel. So, I asked it, the question that my parents and Beluga were literally holding their breath to find out.

"How many cats do you have?"

"Eighteen," she said, as if the number were 'two.'

At Miss B.'s House. Note: two cats, curled up on a cartoon cat comforter, next to a cat-themed rug.

Now, I've never had a problem with cats; in fact, I love *all* animals—but there is something about a cat's eyes that scare me. They're like snakes in drag, dressed up all fancy in a nice fur coat, and waiting for you to let down your guard before they fang you. And *eighteen cats?* How was it possible they hadn't kicked her out of *their* house? How would a kid with attention deficits be able to concentrate on the piano when there were eighteen times four paws—that's seventy-two—when there were seventy-two paws that could tap, tickle, or choke me?

"Would you like to open your gift now?" asked this wizard-cat-witch, bringing me back to the present.

"Really?" I asked, looking at my parents for the go-ahead. It just seemed so strange given that I had nothing to give her, or her eighteen roommates. Even to this day, I can't open a gift in front of people without them opening something from me - even if it's unwrapping a gifted cough drop. I get very uncomfortable.

A nod from my mom was enough of a cue for me to tear away the wrapping paper. I can't recall the wrapping paper's color or design (likely cat themed), but I can vividly recall the texture—thick, crisp, made just for my hands. I ripped it open dramatically, and I was met with a yellow hair band. I pulled the wrapping paper back more to reveal that the hairband was adorned with a yellow treble clef full of irregularly placed white polka dots. It was the most perfect object I'd ever seen. To the untrained eye, it was just an elastic circle marked with a treble clef, but if you looked closer, it was in fact an engagement band, a proposal from a music teacher to her pupil.

I was still clutching the dainty, yellow treble clef hair thing, when we stepped outside at the conclusion of my interview. It was a quiet walk to the car. The winter air was cold and sharp, the ground still very much convinced it was and would be winter for a while. All four of us were still in awe of the slice of Long Island culture we'd experienced that day. From the used boat show to the cat brothel, Long Island gave us a lot to dream about. My mother, confirming in person that Miss B.'s rate was a third of what the musicology robot instructor was asking, was thrilled. Dad and Beluga seemed somewhat intrigued—perhaps they imagined the weekly stories I'd bring home after taking classes from a witch.

So, on that March day in 1989, when I accepted that magical little yellow hair thing, what I actually accepted was a proposal to learn not just about music, but how to hear, how to listen, and mostly how to really *play*.

Beginning with Miss B.

On my first day of lessons, I dropped the whole "Lois" bit and decided "Miss B" was easiest to say, even though she was technically "Mrs. B." In any event, someone with eighteen cats doesn't typically care about those kinds of formalities, so my name choice was approved. Miss B. gave me another gift free of charge—a dainty piano-assignment pad that would be the first of many piano organizers I would own and then lose. The other introductory books she bought were added to the bill—but unlike most teachers, Miss B. never added a handling fee. Each "syllabus" Miss B. created was designed from scratch, tailored to each student and their strengths. My strengths just so happened to be jazz, and very old (and unfortunately very racist) ragtime.

One of my assignment pads from 1993, packed with classic Christmas tunes.

It was a strange feeling for me to own books, fresh books that I actually wanted to read. Music was a language I didn't yet understand, but I carried my books with a respect I never lent to texts on phonics or mother fuckin' mathematics (as I'd soon nickname it). The piano books were more like cookbooks—where I'd not just read, but I'd *make* something that would one day be digestible to the human ear. Every week, the little assignment book had the standard assignments—a classical piece, a jazz or ragtime piece, the scales (major and minor), and boring music theory quizzes. Miss B. knew I would never answer the music theory worksheets on my own, and instead of punishing me or ignoring the theory, we went through them together at our lessons. As a graduate of Julliard and a professional pianist, organist, and vocalist, even *she* struggled with the theory. Miss B. vocalized her music theory frustrations by saying very human things like "*damn this*" and furrowing her thick eyebrows. She made jokes, and I did, too, and because of this, I came to see music theory as just a necessary puzzle—not a necessary evil.

All dolled up for my very first piano recital.

During my first year, my lessons lasted for forty-five minutes. However, it wasn't long before they reached the two-hour mark, the three, and finally toward the end of my tenure, I took all of Tuesday from three to seven p.m. If I was sluggish and bored in the seven or so hours of school, I came alive at lessons, which were structured like a three-act play:

Act I: Conversation involving weekly human and cat updates

Act II: Piano Playing

Act III: Flute/Singing/(PLA) Pertinent Life Advice

Act I, "Conversation," was my favorite subject, mostly because Miss B.'s life was endlessly fascinating to me. It was fascinating not just because she was a magnet to miserable circumstances, but because she told me about her life as if I'd lived it, too. After she was diagnosed with a heart condition in the late 80s, she'd become confined to her house, a condition that cut her social life short but tripled her cat intake. She was lonely and would admit to that, and, as a misfit with busy parents, I shared those feelings, that empty space. I saw how piano, music, and singing could somehow fill it. Sitting at the piano, reading and playing a song—it's actually an intimate conversation. There are emotional hints to each note; there are shifts in the key; there are progressions, digressions; but each bar is reliable, dependable, and honest.

Another comfort to Miss B's loneliness was her Christian faith, a devotion that began after her father died in 1933, at the peak of the Great Depression. His death marked a start to *her* great depression as a twelve-year-old who had simply *adored* her father and lost him suddenly. The Heavenly Father became her substitute, and it was a good thing, because she would be abandoned by another man she loved, her husband of ten years, Jim. Jim died of cancer when she was just fifty-one. Miss B. would talk about Jim at lessons and how he once visited her as a ghost. His presence in the home was undeniable; I'd often look for him in her second bedroom. I'd peer around the corner just to make sure he wasn't actually stuck under a cat or two . . . or eighteen. There were other family members and friends that passed away, and she told me about them—again, not shielding me from the pain she felt. My position in her home was one part Larry King and one part sea sponge—I'd ask her anything and absorb all the answers. Initially my curiosity was an attempt to stall because I hadn't practiced my scales, but it grew into a weekly piano side chat.

Beyond loving God and music, Miss B. loved any composer that wrote, sang, or made shout-outs to God. She made a few oddly suggestive remarks about Handel, but "the one who got away" (three hundred years earlier) was Johann Sebastian Bach. Apparently, as my mother tells it, during a meeting for an adult music-appreciation group, Miss B. had some strong "belts" of bourbon and professed her undying love for Bach before the group. It got oddly sexual, and the women attending, who were of an educated, silk-scarf-wearing type, politely asked her to leave the group. *Oh, to be a fly on the wall for that particular gathering of suburban women.*

Miss B.'s devotion to Christ and God no doubt inspired my interest in the church, a calling that I was quite bold in pursing. At age ten, I'd walk down to Stony Brook's Methodist church by myself on Sundays and sit on the right side of the upper balcony (Dorothy would meet me there). I have *no* clue what the pastor/priest/minister was saying; I didn't really listen or know anything biblical other than the Lord's Prayer. I almost always arrived hungry, perhaps emulating Christ that way, and I simply followed the commands to stand, speak, and sing. I counted the minutes until I could get my little tear of Wonder Bread and bitter grape juice that the puritans were serving for communion. I started singing in the church choir—again, having no real relationship with Jesus but loving the performance of it all. I loved the big choir uniform; it made me feel like a more holy cheerleader. No one at my congregation ever questioned why a ten-year-old went to church alone, or why she chose to dress as Joseph in the Christmas manger scene. (Side note: I wanted a leading role but understood I was not exactly "Mary material"). The good people of the Stony Brook Methodist church let me come and go in their community, sipping hot cider while caroling in the winter, painting eggs during Easter with the Sunday school toddlers, or pretending to work at our church fairs.

Like Miss B., I found a quelling in religion, like a figurative hug from beyond our earthly selves. So, from about the age of ten until fifteen or even sixteen, I wore a cross. I wore the cross not because I necessarily believed that Jesus died for our sins, but because I believed in the people that believed in that possibility. I believed in their graciousness, their spirit, and mostly, how it seemed that divine worship brought out a bit of what we might call humanity. And, just as religion can bring forth a fuller sense of humanity, so can our relationship with animals.

Animals

If Miss B. ran for political office, I have no idea what party she'd run for, but I do know what her buttons and bumpers would broadcast: "ANIMALS FIRST." It was oh-so-easy to shop for her because if you bought *anything* with an animal on it (particularly a cartoonish cat on a T-shirt or stationery paper), she'd take a look at it, baffled, and ask, "How did you know?" One of her favorite gifts was a sweatshirt I picked out at Christmastime from Marshalls. The front of the sweatshirt pictured a beagle sandwiched between two cats (all three of whom were wearing Santa hats). The backside of the sweatshirt showed these animals' butts, with their tails proudly wagging in the air. It's the kind of shirt a hipster would wear today, but there was absolutely nothing ironic about Miss B. wearing it. The shirt was, in her mind, a very literal fashion statement.

Miss B.'s entire home was a neurotic testament to the comfort and pleasure of her cats. Every surface was covered with a sheet for them to snuggle on, a carpeted tower to climb on, balls to bat at, bags to burrow in, fake mice to destroy. Any table or dresser had stacks of catalogues for the animal lover, or magazines from PETA, WWF, or more radical animal activists. In the back of her house she spent thousands of dollars to build what she called the "Cat Enclosure." The design was both genius *and* psychotic. The cats would walk down into her unfinished basement, where they'd deposit a large frothy shit, before moving through a storm window that was replaced by a wooden ramp. This ramp would transport them into a wire-enclosed "greenhouse for cats," a space filled with feline entertainments. The cat enclosure was larger than the main living area of her home, a funky feature that I'd kill to watch a real estate agent pitch to would-be home buyers. I picture some plucky lady in stilettos and a taupe Talbots suit bragging, "And here is the outdoor cage—it's great for giving your in-laws a time-out."

Miss B. knew that elephants were *my* God. Just like God, elephants were unfathomably large and while I never really got to see them, I absolutely believed in them. When I arrived at one of my lessons, I was greeted by Miss B.'s outstretched hand passing on a PETA article about a baby circus elephant who had been beaten to death with a shovel. The timing was cruel—a few days before, I had seen the Ringling Brothers circus in Manhattan for the first time. Horrified that my parents' money had paid the salary of a baby-elephant killer, I had *no words*. Seeing my anguish, Miss B. suggested that I present the story for my fifth-grade class during our weekly "Current Events" report. The reports were a task I dreaded and often complained about. The senseless death of a baby elephant was enough motivation for me to bring the whole class to tears talking about the poor creature. "The lost soul who died on the floor of some metal cage, her precious fuzzy trunk reaching out from the prison bars, for one last sniff of a freedom she'd never know. *She'd never know.*"

Feeling inspired by the uproar I'd caused in Current Events, I started an elephant-awareness group called the Ele Club. It was an invite-only club, where my classmates would voluntarily forgo recess to listen to me talk about and draw elephants on a chalkboard. I found a book on elephants and used it to write quizzes, with multiple-choice answers and a "draw in the blank" section, where each student had to demonstrate a mastery of sketching two different kinds of elephants. There was the "side kind" (a two-dimensional elephant facing the side) and the "silly kind" (a cartoonish-looking elephant wearing lederhosen and holding a balloon). I had no idea what I was saying in Ele Club, and I'm fairly certain at times I made facts up, but I enjoyed performing the role of an elephant priestess, spreading a message of peace for the pachyderms.

Animal awareness took over Lubber Street once and sometimes twice a year when Miss B. held a garage sale to benefit the WWF as well as local cat shelters. The idea was simple: her neighbors and friends would donate their crap to the cause, and her students would help push the crap onto suckers who could not say no to children or cats. Miss B.'s biggest year earned her $1,800 in sales, a record I never did top, but strove to break. I did my part in contributing my own funds, like one year when I bought a black beanbag with babysitting money. Sure, it smelled like hot barf, but I thought it was cool that I could outfit my room like a hip catalogue kid, on a not-so-hip kid budget. You heard it here first though; don't go buying a bean bag chair at a yard sale. I had to leave a bottle of Fantastic cleaning spray underneath the bag because the smell was about as bad as you can imagine. If only bean bags could talk...

It became necessary to dull my sense of smell as much as possible when entering Miss B.'s cat-infused house, by blocking nasal airways and breathing through my mouth. (This same trick would come in handy years later when taking shots of garbage vodka in college). It wasn't only that Miss B.'s home reeked of cat piss and shit; it was that every item that entered her home also marinated in the scent. I would come home from a lesson and the smell would linger on my clothes, my backpack; it would settle into my scalp. It wasn't so much that it was *that bad* either; it's just that it was *that weird* of a smell, and almost immediately your brain would remind you of what cat orifice it had originated from. It didn't help that she had plush thirty-year-old carpets, or that all her windows were sealed shut for fear of cat jailbreak. Every knickknack in her house, every artifact, was laced with the smell, too. Even her nonporous household items—like her rotary phone, her dishes, her autographed picture of Regis Philbin—they also smelled like aged cat waste.

When I was in junior high school, I walked to Miss B.'s house every Tuesday, taking Friends Road as my route to Lubber Street. When I arrived at her home, Miss B. would always be standing behind the glass storm door, her hands on her waist, with a big smile that showcased her teeth in their signature French braid. She had a woman who ran errands for her, Diane, a thick woman with a thicker Long Island accent, who got anything on Miss B.'s shopping list. What this effectively meant was that I got to determine the sweets forecast for the week, which was a level of empowerment I've yet to experience again in my life. I can comfortably say that even if I don't make much of a difference in this world, for a few years I put an end to Hershey's Almond Kisses. (What in-the-actual-fuck is an *almond* doing in a perfectly unassuming chocolate pyramid?)

I didn't need to make any milk request for the Sausalito cookies I always requested, because there were always gallons upon gallons for the eighteen cats and their nightly "milk caps." Miss B. kept the cookies in the fridge because no one else would eat them and they would stay fresh that way. Straight out of the fridge, they were extra crumbly and cool. I felt like a Goddamned queen when I'd bite into them. After spending most of my junior high years feeling *ravenous*, at Miss B.'s I would eat a minimum of four professional, full-time cookies, and three pints of cold whole milk.

Before our lessons would start, I would talk about what was happening at school—what classes I hated and what people I liked. Miss B. had a way of listening to my day-to-day recaps, and following them up with the wild train wrecks of her own life. She never discredited any feelings I expressed about my world, but she'd follow up my story of "My friend Jess fell off her horse" with hers: "When I was your age, my friend Mary from the Bronx died at the hands of a drunk bus driver." Miss B. saw oppression and racism in the Bronx toward the "colored people" (as she explained that black people were once called). She saw abuse and intolerance, and she spoke up as much as she could, but as she got older, her weak heart kept her in its own form of "cat enclosure."

After we had our snack and conversation, I'd help her with a few chores that she couldn't manage. My favorite chore was filling the piano humidifier. The humidifier was a gizmo that the piano tuner sold her, and it was effectively a beer funnel with a blinking light that supposedly kept the piano strings properly hydrated. I would fill it up if the red light was blinking, and the piano would gurgle as it guzzled the water, personifying the instrument even more. There were other things that Miss B. couldn't reach, or in one case couldn't manage herself, like when there was an infestation of ants in her kitchen. At my house, we used toxic Raid huts that the ants would crawl into and spread to their people, but Miss B. preferred to leave out globs of grape jelly on paper towels, centralizing the ant population. Once the ants gathered onto their Times Square of grape jelly, we'd transport them outdoors. It *never* worked. The ants walked right back into the kitchen and waited for more Times Squares to appear.

The Golden Notes

At some point in childhood, I believe all kids should partake in their own Academy Awards/Golden Globes/Tony's. Maybe it's some showy pageant that takes place over the holidays, or on their birthday, or at some sports championship—but they should have a platform that allows them to behave like an egomaniacal jackass for one day of the year. Just like the Golden Globes, our piano recitals lasted about four hours, attendees also dressed up, and by the end of the show they were also wearing fur (of the cat variety). Like the Academy Awards, our recitals took place in February or March. The only thing that differentiated our recitals from the Oscars was the simple fact that our recitals had an even ratio of 18 humans to 18 cats.

Thanks to the introduction of new and cheap music-themed merchandise, Miss B. got her hands on some Oscar-like awards that she had engraved. In 1992, I was up for "Most Improved," which was our Academy's version of "Best Actor." Sure, there were other shades of success at the ceremony, like "Most Punctual," "Most Positive," "Most Likely to Move on to a Different After-School Activity," but the final award given at the show was "Most Improved." We all knew what it meant to be the person who received it — they were the Meryl Streep of piano players.

In 1992, I had "Most Improved" in the bag—*shit*, I even brought my own cheap camera that my Aunt Karen bought me for Christmas. This was to make sure my win was well documented. I practiced beaming a jagged full-mouth smile, looking off to the ceiling, and twisting my body to elongate the hand-me-down Gap Kids turtleneck I'd be wearing. I'd clutch that Golden Note with my right fist—strongly, but casually enough that the other kids would covet my aplomb. I'd be the winner that was down to earth, allowing everyone to hold the Golden Note and congratulate me before I ran off to *dominate* the musical-chairs tournament.

After Miss B. distributed the first three awards, I awaited my turn, breathing as best I could, but knowing my life would forever change once I got my Golden Note. *Fine*, there were only eight contenders in total, but that fact was completely irrelevant when you consider that *I* was the fucking best. The setup was all there— "a very dedicated student, a great singer, with a great attitude"—and then the name was called. It was not my name, but that of my darling pal, Dorothy. She bounded up and grabbed the award, grandstanding like a normal nine-year-old winner. I was burned, man. *Burned.* I pulled down on the neck of my turtleneck—why the hell was it suddenly so hot?

"Sure, I'll take your picture with the award," I told Dorothy after she asked.

She sat on an easy chair with the Golden Note placed next to her on a side table. She folded her arms and focused her eyes directly at the camera, without exposing any teeth—just sharing a full-blown "I DID IT" smirk. I was so sure that I would be the one clutching that perfect piece of plastic, but I was just the documenter, the *fucking photographer*!

The following year, I decided I would take matters into my own hands by producing *the entire show*. Whether I won or not, all eighteen humans and eighteen cats would watch an asshole in her element for four hours. I cast myself to star as a co-host who also performed piano solo, piano duet, flute solo, flute duet, singing solo, singing duet, dance, and Bob Dylan poetry reading.

The program went a little something like this:

Welcome to Lois J. Baranosky's
Piano Spectacular

Hosted By:
Christie Nittrouer and Dorothy Costello

Act I: Classical Music
Featuring the Piano Class of '93
*with additional piano, flute, vocal solos and duets by Christie and Dorothy

Intermission

Act II: Jazz/Pop Music
Featuring the Piano Class of '93
*with additional piano, flute, vocal solos and duets by Christie and Dorothy

Intermission

Act III: Bonus Piano, Flute, and Vocal Performances
Featuring Christie and Dorothy

Finale: Our Prayer for the Future
Reading of "Blowin' in the Wind"
Singing of "Blowin' in the Wind"
* All Reading and Singing by Christie and Dorothy

There were certain performance staples that were repeated every year; the highlight was when Miss B. accompanied herself, singing Billy Joel's "Piano Man" in a Julliard-trained operatic voice. Time stood still when she belted gritty details about the thankless life of a Piano Man playing music at a dive bar.

Miss B., warming up the crowd for our sloppy singing-dancing rendition of "Tea for Two."

Dorothy and I played piano duets together, we played flute duets, and we sang duets. We also danced, though the dancing was more like interpretative sign language to accompany hits like "Tea for Two" and "Sweet Georgia Brown." To this day, I daydream about one day asking the parents who sat through the Golden Notes what they'd call the "lowlight" of the four-hour recital. I like to think it was my flute solos - when I'd screech through every note and hit one that was so offensively off that I'd break down into a fit of hysterical laughter.

"Backstage" — preparing to ruin the show with my flute playing.

Certainly, the most dramatic part of our recitals was when we got to the end of the fourth hour, and Dorothy and I would shut all the house lights off, and emerge with two small candles. We'd approach the audience with a grave, somber tone.

DOROTHY AND CHRISTIE. Now we'd like to share some words about our prayers for the future.

(They pause dramatically.)

CHRISTIE, (*turning to* DOROTHY, *inquisitively*). How many roads must a man walk down, before you can call him a man?

DOROTHY, (*turning to* CHRISTIE *responds conversationally*). Yes, and how many times must the cannonballs fly, before they're forever banned?

CHRISTIE and DOROTHY, (*in unison, to the audience*). The answer, my friend, is blowin' in the wind, the answer is blowin' in the wind.

After we read the lyrics of Bob Dylan's "Blowin' in the Wind" in their *entirety*, Miss B. cued up the baby grand and accompanied us as we sang the exact same song, only this time, as if it were even possible, we sang more slowly than we spoke. It was brutal; I mean, even *Bob Dylan* doesn't sound good singing "Blowin' in the Wind" and we were no Bob Dylan.

At the close of our number, it was time for the awards, so I took my seat on a cat to await my fate. Before distributing the first three awards, Miss B. handed out participation ribbons, effectively offering everyone a little taste of the Golden Note that year. Because of this and because the other three awards were not for me, I knew by the close of the show that I was the Academy's favorite in 1993.

It was a good year for me, 1993. My piano-playing skills had improved drastically, and I had produced my first variety/awards show on Long Island. However bad I was at the flute, I made up for it by taking control of the piano—playing with intention, and not backing down from the emotional cues written in the music. Thanks to piano, I was pushing myself even though I was dreadfully insecure. I auditioned for glee club and choir solos. I stole a video camera from my grandparents and made creative solo projects for school assignments. My fashion changed—I was wearing bold elephant T-shirts and chunky cat earrings. Most importantly, I was the founder and *president* of an elephant-awareness nonprofit. Piano had changed my life.

Yet in that moment, perched on a tabby, I knew exactly what was coming, and something about it made me kind of sad. Though I accepted the Golden Note graciously, I realized, as I clutched that golden validation, that losing the award the year before was far more of a win. Had I not, the year before, dressed up in my best culottes and anticipated the win, only to be (in my mind) humiliated, I would not have advanced as I had in 1993.

Receiving the Golden Note in 1993.

Don't get me wrong, I still have the Golden Note, it sits on my desk and it is gorgeous, I adore it, but it serves as more of a reminder that *not* getting what you want is at times a far bigger win. I really, *really* wanted that win in 1992. Had I won, it would have been far easier to have admired the award for a solid three weeks, and have tossed it in a box of crap for Goodwill donations. I'm also certain that had I won in 1992, it would have been easy to forget what winning a "most improved" award meant. Winning the award didn't make me objectively "the best piano player"; rather, it meant that I made myself the best piano player I could become that year, and *that* is a pretty unique lesson for a kid to learn. In this instance, there were no comparisons between myself and other piano students, it was just to push myself to play *my* best, and I delighted in doing just that.

Getting Serious

Toward the end of eighth grade, it became difficult to see how piano would help me make any money in life. The way I ignorantly figured things, money would come after college, which would come after high school, which I was about to start. It was during this time that my notion of how to spend my time drastically changed. The word *play* vanished from my vocabulary altogether. I could run varsity track and possibly get a college scholarship, I could do stupid community-service-oriented clubs and talk about "giving back" as if I meant it, but what did piano lessons matter to a college admissions officer?

Rather than level with Miss B. and tell her that I had to get "serious" about my life, I started cutting back on practice and missing classes. I attempted to dump the piano as if it were a loser boyfriend. At the end of eighth grade, when she asked what my summer and fall piano plans were, I told her I was "not sure yet," as my eyes wandered off to find a fresh pile of cat barf. "Gross," I said, meanly, when just a year before I'd help to clean it up.

At that point in my life, I thought I didn't need to learn anything more about music. My education was done. Music became Jewel, Mariah Carey, or those delightful little "mmm-bopping" Hanson sisters. Music was something I could listen to but have no stake in. It was just a background that, if chosen correctly, could make you seem cool. Conversations about the Bronx or Bach were *not* cool. I needed to focus on boot-cut jeans and Doc Martens. I needed to cut this "baby stuff" out so maybe I'd have a chance of getting my period or growing some goddamned boobs!

When my weekly sessions had finally become monthly meetings, I sent a fax from my dad's office to Miss B.'s home explaining that I couldn't continue because of "scheduling conflicts." It was the most selfish mode of communication I could have chosen, and it was written in an IRS-like tone. A week or so later, I was feeling guilty, so I sent a follow-up fax saying that I wanted to help with the annual WWF garage sale (just a reminder — this is World Wildlife Fund, *not* the World Wrestling Federation). Miss B.'s response was quick, especially for a seventy-four-year-old using such a then cutting-edge technology: "The garage sale is for currently enrolled students, we don't need your help." Pulling her fax out of the machine and reading the words out loud, it finally got to me: I was no longer her student. I was without my teacher, my mentor . . . my friend.

During that summer, time passed unusually, in that I didn't play the piano. In fact, I didn't even look at it. It just sat there, with its perfectly central location, a daily dose of salt in my wounds. Mom suggested I contact Miss B. after Dorothy told me Miss B. felt badly about the fax. "Just call her," my mom said, standing in the kitchen without pants on (as was her go-to wardrobe in those muggy August months). Mom dialed the numbers, holding out our kitchen phone as far as it could stretch because it was bound to the wall by a super curly cord. *"Just talk to her,"* my mom urged again. I moved closer to the phone, and shakily held the receiver to my face.

"Hi . . . Miss B., it's Christie," I said, as if she would have forgotten a voice that she cultivated.

We spoke for about fifteen minutes, which for old people translates to about two hours. I gave her updates on my summer and she gave me updates on hers: the music, the cats, a new arrangement of Andrew Lloyd Webber's musical *Cats*. We were cordial and kind. We were delicate with each other, but we spoke for the first time as if we were both adults.

At the start of ninth grade, Dorothy continued with her lessons, and we were together again when we auditioned for our school's musical, *Little Shop of Horrors*. During the week of auditions, my parents were out of town and my magical grandmother (see chapters 12 & 13) flew in from Seattle with her best friend, Vicky. The weekend after the big audition, we arranged to train into Manhattan to see *Bring in 'da Noise, Bring in 'da Funk* along with Vicky's granddaughter and Beluga's best friend, Kevin. It was warm and fun, despite the weather that was overwhelmingly windy and charged. It was October 20, and it was as if the atmosphere didn't know what it wanted—hot or cold—so it showed its indecision by kicking up things in its path. The wind wrestled with what it wanted to say and made sure we humans heard it.

As we were standing outside Penn Station and saying our good-byes to Vicky's granddaughter, a homeless man fell to the curb near the taxi queue. Normally I would follow my mother's advice on homeless people in NYC and look away, but something about him drew me in—hypnotized me. I watched as his body twitched from what looked like a seizure. A crowd of Manhattanite commuters gathered; they knew him, and I overheard them as they said, "he was a banker, and he lost all his money in the eighties crash." It was like a movie, us standing around the tragic hero and piling pity on top of him, crushing him until he eventually died. He actually did die right there, right in front of Penn Station. It caused a clear divide between people who chose to watch and those who chose to ignore him. Both choices felt equally gross, equally inhumane. We waited until the ambulance pulled up and did their usual business. The corpse was removed and that was it.

My grandmother was genuinely horrified, but Vicky's grand-daughter was unfazed. She stood there with me watching, looking surprisingly serene.

We walked to the LIRR boards, waiting for our assigned track. We got our track number, boarded the train, made it to Huntington for our transfer, and, as we were travelling on the Port Jefferson line, we suddenly stopped. We waited for about half an hour with little direction from the conductor, who finally told us a fallen tree had blocked the tracks. We were stuck, and we'd wait another twenty minutes before it was determined that the tracks were irreparable. Like a miserable pile of Polar Express zombies, we boarded a bus that drove us to all the train stops, and finally we staggered home to Stony Brook, much later than anticipated.

Seconds after we'd made it home, I was standing in the kitchen when the phone rang. Assuming that because of the hour it was my parents, I picked it up. (This was a major no-no in our household—it was common law that all calls in pre-caller ID days were to be screened on our answering machine.) I grabbed the phone off the wall and pulled the permanently tangled curly cord out so I could move into the hallway. I recognized the voice immediately.

"Dorothy?" I said. "What?" I said, even though I had heard her clearly.

My grandmother was also in the kitchen, so she heard both words, "Dorothy" and "what" and she saw me slide down the wall. The phone cord wrapped around my body and constricted my movement, effectively keeping me down on the floor. I couldn't speak. I was so sad, too sad, and no amount of faux teen angst could cover that up. My next word, "how," was enough to bring Mommom closer to me. Hearing how it happened made it impossible to speak. Miss B. had been startled after a gust of wind sent a tree crashing on top of her house. The scare broke her heart once and for all. For a life-long environmental advocate, it was a bitterly ironic way for her to die, at the hands (or limbs) of a tree.

Waking up the next day for school was brutal, but I did so with the knowledge that God would smile on me and I'd be cast in the lead role of *Little Shop of Horrors*. It'd be the final Golden Note, given to me because someone so important to me was taken away. Dorothy and I decided we would view the list together, and maybe even both our names would be listed as Audrey. Outside the theatre we found the list, which had two Audreys and twelve backup singers (they'd expanded the roles to accommodate the overwhelming number of popular girls that took an interest in theatre). We pushed through a group of giddy girls, as our eyes traced the names—*Nope not our name, nope not our name, nope not our name*—until we got to the end of the list and looked at each other. After two years of being goddamn extras in *Camelot* and *The Sound of Music*, we had not been cast at all.

"Do you have to go to the bathroom? 'Cause I do," I said, in my best stage voice.

"Yes," Dorothy replied, and we marched in silence to a remote bathroom, far the fuck away from that list.

We entered the bathroom and I started in on a rant that began slowly, like an interrogation officer, and ended like Joe Pesci's "what in the fuck is so funny about me?" in *Goodfellas*.

"I mean, who does this Mr. Vizzo guy think he is? What kind of a director overlooks the best talent when there are fourteen spots? Is he blind? Is he deaf? *We* are the damn *stars* of *the* Golden Notes! What about the church choir! I mean, how about our realistic portrayal in the manger scene? I mean, *come on*! We sing like songbirds, like beautiful braces-clad songbirds. Sure, some of our earlier dance work to Paula Abdul was a little clunky, but we've evolved as performers! Who else can do a poetic reading of *Bob-fucking-Dylan?*!"

I punched a paper towel dispenser for an added dramatic release. It was a good moment; it was a little bit of a gift—we could blame all of our hurt feelings on a stupid school musical. At that moment, there was no grief; no wondering about what our lives would be like without Miss B. in it; no concern for her cats, the fate of her piano, her knick-knacks, the things that made her home so special. It was all about the director, Mr. fucking Vizzo... *that big, hairy dick!*

Miss B.'s memorial was held in early November at her neighbor Shirley Layburn's home. I didn't know it at the time, but Shirley was a ventriloquist who had won her own Golden Note, an Emmy, in 1949 for "Outstanding TV Personality." After a life in Hollywood, she settled in Stony Brook and befriended Miss B. Shirley wrote and delivered a beautiful eulogy. Afterward, Shirley took us over to Miss B.'s home, where we were given items Miss B. had willed to us. I was given pieces of her Wedgewood Jasperware china, and I took home several of her piano books, still marked by her distinct cursive handwriting.

Muses

Exactly one year after Miss B. died, my grandmother called to tell us that Vicky's granddaughter (who stood next to me while the homeless man died outside Penn Station) had died. I thought back to that night at Penn Station. It was as if Vicky's granddaughter knew what was coming. Somewhere in her soul she knew, and not just about her fate, but also about the perfectly timed phone call I'd receive when I returned home that night. She knew. . . . all the signs were there, just waiting to be heard.

Years later, in 2012, I was teaching a class on American musical theatre history and I heard a student say something about music that hit me in an old place.

"Why do we *need* music?" I asked my students.

"When words can't fully capture the emotion . . . then you *have* to sing," responded a student who was normally quiet.

The kid didn't invent this notion; anyone who has been to a musical knows that the music begins when the emotion is biggest—the most joy, the most sorrow, the most anger. Still, and unfortunately, it seems to me that music has a reputation for merely *accompanying* things. Music is rarely given its proper credit, as a stand-alone communication technique that captures the most heightened, rich, full, and terrifying of our emotions. That's its job; that's its function. Music allows you to express what you can't say and what you are afraid to feel.

After my student's response got me thinking, I looked up the official definition of "music" and its etymology (or, simply put, its *origin*). Music has always been described as the "art of the muses." In this case, *muse* means something far deeper than how we've come to understand a muse as a waif in a Romantic-era novel or a "manic-pixie-dream girl" (e.g., the über wide-eyed Zooey Deschanel in a quirky Sundance film). In ancient Greece, the Muses were not just teachers, but they also possessed *all* knowledge — knowledge being human emotions *and* our collective history. We learned about all things, human and otherwise, from the Muses, who'd express their wisdom through music and song. In other words, back in the day we acquired *all* knowledge through music. It's kind of like that *Schoolhouse Rock!* thing except, you know, actually effective.

Looking back on my time with Miss B., I am certain that I learned as much as I did because I had a teacher with *no* concept of time. I was never rushed or hurried through a difficult piece. I didn't master a song until I felt there was no more I could learn from it. There was no timeline for teaching, no target to hit, no quantifiable skills to achieve—it was just to play like I was in love with *every single note* I touched.

More than learning how to play, Miss B. taught me how to listen and how to hear *all* sound. The truth is, music is much more than composed masterpieces; music is in everything. Music is a beat, a pause, a chill. It's a perfectly timed rustle in the branch of a palm tree. To hear an ocean's indecision, the particular jangle of tags on a beloved dog's collar, a mosquito's whine, the crash of a treasured vase on tile, even the tinny honking of a Toyota in traffic—this is music, and it has a temper, a humor, a disposition.

Homecoming

I never stopped playing the piano. In fact, I played even more after Miss B.'s death; I played through the feelings I couldn't yet express. I played through the anger I felt moving three thousand miles away from New York to Seattle when I was sixteen (two years after Miss B.'s death). I played through the excitement of holidays. I played at the drunken high school parties I'd throw when my parents were out of town, as a way to feel like less of an outsider. When I went to college, I got a keyboard before I got a desk. In all these moments and many following, when I couldn't think of what to say, I found a note to hit, and chords to collect myself.

It would be impossible for me to ever thank Miss B. for what she taught me, and part of me feels selfishly relieved that I never had the chance to try. The moments leading up to her death were riddled with cues for me to hear. The same day she died, I witnessed a stranger die on the street in Manhattan. The sound of the train screeching to a halt, the frantic whipping of the wind - these were all a song that I heard, and in some sense, I understood what they had meant and what would be coming.

Miss B. showed me that music isn't just the harmonies or melodies we make - music is also the break, the beat, the pause, the sudden and painful absence of sound. Music is the way that final chord sounds, at the very end of our song, as we graciously fade out of this world and on to another. Music is the sound of that newfound silence and there is a distinct beauty to that.

Make no mistake about it, our musicians are our muses, our divine teachers, our modern-day wizards. My wizard, Miss B.—she just didn't bother much with wearing a disguise.

My seventh and final piano recital with Miss B. in 1996

CHAPTER 11

Head First

Poppop Kelly, caught in the middle of shouting, "take the damn picture."

I t was Thanksgiving in 1992, in Southampton, PA, when we discovered it - our step-grandfather had *the* perfect first name. Me and my cousins were uncontrollably hyper when we sang the name-game song from Tom Hanks's *Big*, and Poppop Bart was our favorite victim.

"*Bart Bart boh Bart banana fannah foh FART!*"

Gristly, grumpy, and somehow very Rat Pack handsome at age six-ty, Poppop Bart was not amused by our discovery. "Yehhh, yehhh," he grumbled in a Philly accent. Poppop's accent was thickest when he'd describe a "beautiful hoagie" (which came out like bewwww-D-fool hoooowwww-GEE."

Poppop Kelly, as we also called him, married my grandmother when she was forty-nine years old and he was forty-seven. I never really knew what he did for work, other than it involved the transpor-tation of frozen commercial bread and pies. After he visited, we'd end up with a sack of frozen sourdough bread and cheesecakes. That's all I needed to know about his line of work. The cheesecake didn't last long in our fridge. I'd pop out a frozen slice and drool-gnaw my way through it, in the same way a mutt gnaws on rawhide.

Other than his bakery handling, I didn't know much about Poppop in my younger years. He was a self-proclaimed "Black Irish" who liked the Philadelphia Eagles, cars, and—above anything else—his above-ground pool. I had accepted the fact that we would never be besties, mostly because he showed more sensitivity toward his evil black cat, "*Puhd-in*" ('Pudding' – for those unfamiliar with the Philadelphia twang) than he did his grandchildren. His in-home bar was filled with what I'd call "toys" and what he called "collectibles"—bobble head sports dolls, Hess trucks, and an antique windup telephone. Poppop never understood why we had to touch everything, and we kids never understood why he had toys you couldn't touch.

In 1994, Mommom and Poppop retired to Palm Coast, Florida. They built a small three-bedroom house with a kidney-bean-shaped pool in a housing development that appealed to East Coast snowbirds and was therefore named "The Hamptons." In the spring of 1995, my dad took my mom along on a work trip to Jakarta and sent Beluga and me down for a week to stay with our grandparents. I had never spent a whole week with Mommom and Poppop Kelly, and the thought made me nervous. I was nervous enough that my piano teacher Miss B. (see previous chapter) lent me her beloved stuffed animal, Piglet, to offer me some of Piglet's signature (if not a tad annoying) enthusiasm.

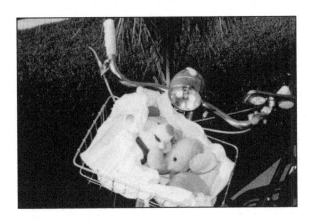

Piglet and Dumbo having the vacation of a lifetime in Palm Coast, Florida.

Being that this was the first time I'd ever spent more than a crowded two days with Poppop Bart, I reviewed everything I knew about him:

1. He liked beer.

2. He liked mean cats that hissed.

3. He did not like me.

Our trip started out fine enough. Beluga and I would get up around eleven a.m., after which we were offered many delicious sandwiches made on the local Publix grocery-brand equivalent of Wonder Bread. We sat by the kidney-shaped pool and listened to soft, easy favorites on Magic 107.7 (which only played The Eagles on a loop), while pretending that we were capable of getting a tan. I also brought a camera and would take various pictures of my stuffed animals in complicated dance moves. I felt some embarrassment about this—I mean . . . I was well aware that kids my age (12-13) were menstruating and smoking, meanwhile I was truly happy to photo document a stuffed moose in a split.

One day, as we were getting ready for the beach, Beluga and I found a beach ball with a painted-on expression that looked *identical* to our cousin Todd. There is no hyperbole here—the resemblance was *uncanny*. We held the ball up to our faces and imitated conversations with our cousin "Todd Ball." Before we found the ball, we had been instructed to help load the car, a request we blatantly ignored. It was one of those instances where siblings get possessed by the giggles, and any adult with a "serious" interference just fuels the flames of goof. We were relentless. I mean, c'mon, our beloved cousin had turned into a beach ball! Seeing our laughter as disrespect, Poppop threw down four cheap and clattery beach chairs.

"For Christ's sake, stop *fucking* around!" he screamed.

It was a jolting moment, to see Poppop so mad that he said "Christ" and "fuck" in the same sentence. We looked down at our feet and were shocked; not so much by his outburst but by the fact that he didn't see the uncanny resemblance to be as hysterical as we did. Our moment of silence didn't last; as soon as we turned back to look at the ball, we fell to the floor laughing.

Once we finally made it to the beach, Poppop calmed down a bit. He took his walk, where he collected souvenirs from the ocean floor that had been washed on shore. For whatever reason, this did it for him. Poppop's shell hunting left him soothed, and it also left his second bathroom *full* of his shells. I especially appreciated the shell collection when I was stuck on the toilet trying to pass one of those Publix white bread sandwiches.

On Easter morning in 1995, my parents called from Jakarta to see how we were doing. Beluga and I were having a conversation about what we would be when we "grew up" and he told me he thought I would grow up to be a diner waitress. I was pretty pissed at him and so I told my parents I wasn't having a good time. My grandmother happened to still be on the line, and upon hearing me say this, she went off.

"Well, I've tried to make it fun for them. I did my best, Chuckie, I did my best. Those two . . . they fight *all* the time. Oh, all that yelling, and the cursing . . . "

She was right. We fought a lot because Beluga was *always* wrong and I was *always* right and to concede would be just plain-old un-American. Still, Mommom deserved better, so Beluga and I decided to suck it up and be "good" for our Easter egg hunt, which took place on the screened-in lanai by the pool. At home, my father always hid the eggs the night before Easter and was reasonably baked when doing so. Given his state of mind, the hiding places were bizarre to say the least, but the eggs were enormously rewarding when found. Adding to our high-stakes Easter egg hunts at home, was the reality that our eggs were of the hard-boiled variety, so we had a potential stink bomb on our hands. But at Poppop's, while Beluga and I were preparing our wet suits for a deep-pool dive to find the eggs, we instead ended the uncomplicated hunt in approximately twenty-two seconds. It wasn't a "hunt" by our standards; it was more like helping someone out who'd dropped a bunch of plastic eggs.

On our last day in Palm Coast, we did the obligatory central-Florida theme-park trip, where we drove about two hours to Universal Studios in Orlando. What we discovered at Universal was that we weren't the only kids on spring break and thus each ride required a two-hour wait. When we were in line for our third and final ride, *Back to the Future*, Poppop started to feel faint. It wasn't hot, but he left the line for a bench under a bit of shade. His prescription sunglasses were covering his eyes, but his expression was all too clear. Something was deeply worrying him. We continued through the heavy switchbacks, moving at an inchworm pace that allowed us to watch him.

The *Back to the Future* ride ended up being my favorite; even though it was a simulation, the ride felt the most realistic. Despite my worry about Poppop, I got lost in the story while strapped into the DeLorean and buying into Doc Brown's manic narration. It wasn't just me either; it seemed like Mommom and Beluga were along for the ride, too. It was the kind of experience you're supposed to have at theme parks, but it lasted all of forty seconds. Despite this, when I was exiting the DeLorean, I felt a level of guilt I haven't since experienced. Two hours after we left him, Poppop was still in the same seat. He was clearly not well.

Poppop was bright-eyed and bushy tailed the following day as he drove us to the Daytona Beach airport. He flew down the freeway and when Mommom nagged him for speeding, he yelled back his classic line of "Ahh, Sonia, relax!" Beluga and I said our good-byes, thinking ahead only as far as our layover in Charlotte, where we'd make a pit stop at the Cinnabon.

Four months and several Cinnabons later, we got the call telling us that Poppop had a stroke and was paralyzed in all four limbs. "Quadriplegic," my mom said, introducing a weird new word to my vocabulary. The label was far too extravagant for what it was, a human who only had control of his head. I pictured Poppop, once fixing cars, swimming in his pool, throwing down beach chairs—all those actions were now gone, now impossible. This sudden loss was a difficult concept for me to process. How could you have your conscious mind and your body but not be able to connect the two? The cause of Poppop's injury was somewhat mysterious because it came nearly a year after Poppop fell off a ladder while painting his home in Southampton. His head (which caught his fall) appeared to be fine, but was secretly biding its time before it broke down. The delay in its breakdown reminded me of the way a star can go supernova but appear intact until its broken light finally reaches us.

Good news came when Poppop gained mobility in his upper body, which brought us to another new word, paraplegic. My grandmother made their home wheelchair-friendly — adding ramps, lifts, and various technologies that gave him some semblance of mobility. She worked tirelessly to give him a sense of autonomy. We knew that Poppop and Mommom's way of life had changed drastically, but my brother and I were the first to go down and see it ourselves, while my parents left for another oceanography trip. If I was nervous to spend a week with my grandparents the year before, when they were "normal" in the eyes of a twelve-year old, for this trip I was scared stiff (forgive the pun).

Just a year later and we were back at the Daytona Beach airport. This time, Mommom stood behind Poppop in his wheelchair. I had anticipated the moment so much that I can still picture it vividly. Poppop had his hair combed over and styled just so, his hands clasped on his lap, and he was wearing a smile that was unlike anything I'd seen before.

Wait a minute. . .

Was it possible that my once-grumpy grandpa was . . . *glad we were there?*

Our conversation on the way to the baggage claim was led by Beluga, who was far more gregarious in that moment then I was. Once we put our bags in the car, we watched as Mommom took out a long, slick piece of wood that looked like a miniature surfboard. She lifted Poppop's wheelchair armrest up, positioned the board under his left side, lifted him onto the board, and then slid him from the wheelchair to the car's front seat. The wheelchair folded up like an accordion and was stuffed on top of our things in the trunk. This same procedure was repeated on our way out of the car, though it was much more difficult to get Poppop back into his wheelchair.

At Mommom and Poppop's house, the changes were abundantly evident. For starters, they had sold one of their cars and used the garage space for a giant wooden podium.

"What is that?" Beluga asked. Thank God, he did, too, because I was dying to know.

"That's my standing box," Poppop said, as if it were a Corvette he had rebuilt.

"What's it for?" Beluga continued.

"It's for standing. I hold myself up and look outside."

"Oh . . . cool." Beluga didn't really sell the 'cool' so well, but he tried.

At my peak of awkwardness, petting Mickey on Mommom and Poppop's swanky living room couch

On the first day of our visit I was abnormally quiet and self-conscious of my apparent awkwardness. I lost control of my own body, ironically enough, knocking into things, saying the wrong words, correcting myself, and bugging my eyes out like a lemur. After our first dinner together, I retired early to my room so I could (again) photograph my stuffed animals. I was hiding but unwilling to admit it.

A selection from my studio portrait session.

"Chris," my grandmother called from outside my bedroom door at around nine p.m. the first night.

"I'm sleeping," I lied.

"Oh, I just wanted to . . ." Mommom opened the door and caught me staging my stuffed animals, and as wide awake as a hamster on Red Bull. "I am gonna get up early with your brother and get the bark mulch at Kmart before the lines get too long. I was hoping you could stay and keep your grandfather company."

Gulp.

"But, I'd *really* like to go pick out bark mulch," I lied again.

"Why would you want to go get bark mulch?" Mommom asked, confused.

"I've just. . . I . . . I just really *like* bark mulch." I wanted to tell her the truth—that I was terrified of having to spend one-on-one time with my paralyzed grandfather.

"If you like bark mulch, you can help us unload it and spread it. We'll be back around eleven a.m."

"Awesome," I lied for the third time.

I handled my responsibility of spending time with my grandfather by sleeping in until 10:45, leaving myself just enough time to get credit from Mommom for being a thoughtful granddaughter. I crept out of my room at around 10:50 and grabbed a roll from the pantry closet. I stuffed it in my gullet, like the teenage animal I was, and peered around the corner to the master bedroom. It was vacant, the bed made professionally, with no sign of human life. Poppop had gone out for mulch, too; so, the coast was clear.

I walked into the master bedroom, which overlooked the small kidney-bean pool. I studied the decorations on their lanai. There were various signs indicating the direction of the beach, or the "pool rules" and a cast of ceramic characters - frogs dressed in bathing suits, a proud seagull, a napping cat—all the things that suggested *life was good.* I studied them for a while, squinting as the sun reflected off the bright white concrete and straight into my eyes. You might say I even felt sorry for the pool decorations. Even they had to plaster jolly smiles on their faces and act like everything was normal when it wasn't.

I was deep in squinty-angsty teenage thought when my grandfather wheeled up behind me, effectively trapping me from a casual escape.

"Good morning, Chris!"

Ah! Who was this guy? Why the heck was he talking so enthusiastically, like he was a Bible Camp counselor?

"I...I...Hi... I thought you . . . went out for the mulch."

"Nope, I was over by the front door." This was said with the same enthusiasm that he used when describing the standing box. I'd later find that one of Poppop's favorite things to do was sit in front of their front door and watch what I could only see to be *absolutely nothing.*

"Oh . . . cool." I was as convincing with my use of "cool" as Beluga had been a day earlier when he saw Poppop's standing podium.

"How are you liking school? Eighth grade, right?" He leaned over in his wheelchair so far in order to grab my line of sight that he nearly fell out of it.

"What? Fine. It's fine." My brain attempted to make sense of the positive inflections he used. I struggled to find the next thing to say. I desperately wanted to be home on Long Island watching *Days of Our Lives*, burning through time like normal kids did on their spring vacations. "I like the pool decorations." It was all I could muster and it was partly true. I appreciated the content feelings they attempted to evoke in humans.

"Really? I think they're pretty stupid. But Sonia loves that shit."

Ah, there he was. There was still some grit and grumble in him after all.

"They're kind of annoying," I said as we both stared outside.

"The smiles are too much. Look at that frog . . . Why the hell is he so damn happy?" Poppop asked.

"That seagull, too . . . what a . . . a . . ." I struggled to say it.

"Asshole," Poppop growled, finishing my thought.

It was a perfectly odd moment to share with my grandfather — bashing a collection of outdoor lawn décor for being *too happy*.

"Do you *really* like school?" He turned his right wheel in just a hair so he could face me. It was similar to the way you'd turn a cheek in toward someone, to show the level of your interest. I had no choice but to be honest.

"No . . . I hate my classes, but I like gym and lunch."

"You have lunch with all your friends?"

"I'm in mod four-five; 'mod,' that means like 'period' four-five, so I only have a group of seven friends in that mod. But, like, most of my friends are in mod six-seven. Last year I was in eight-nine and that was, like, too late for lunch 'cause I'd be so hungry. I guess mod four-five is okay, but I'd rather have three lunch periods. I can't stand math class.

Sometimes I get the hall pass and go down to get some bagels. We actually figured out a way to steal bagels in the morning before lunch. They get them from this place, Strathmore; it's like the best bagel place around. They're still warm when they deliver 'em. They're so good you don't even need butter or cream cheese."

"Oh . . . I know those kind. You always liked sourdough."

"Yep. You just have to heat it up for seventeen seconds in the—"

"Microwave," he interrupted.

"Yeah."

It's funny how an earnest conversation about carbohydrates instills a sense of trust between two people. My conversation with Poppop began with bagels, moved into a discussion of boys and ended with the extracurricular activities I didn't like. I told him about my babysitting work, how I was saving all my money so I could move to Seattle for college and be a 'psychologist-slash-actress.' At that point in my life, I was struggling in school but not willing to admit that it was because I was too scared to even try. Some kids are born trying, others have no interest, and some kids—like me—were terrified of trying and failing.

Poppop and I talked for so long that I eventually plopped on top of my grandparents' bed and ignored rumblings in my stomach for breakfast. I was thirteen and really did have opinions to share. We never stopped to look at the time, or worry about where Mommom and Beluga were. We just talked and talked and talked. We talked like we trusted each other, like family should.

When Mommom and Beluga returned, it was two p.m. Poppop and I had been conversing for over three hours.

"Chris, the bark mulch is here," Mommom squawked from the front door.

I ignored the good news and continued talking with Poppop. A sudden and almost alchemical change came over me, and I wanted to know everything about his day-to-day life. He described his new routine, his standing box, his physical therapy exercises and the latest and greatest addition yet—his hydraulic pool lift.

As the yard was given its mulch manicure, Poppop and I decided to continue talking in the pool. Poppop's pool lift was positioned in the shallow end of the pool, so I could sit on the steps and talk to him. Like most of the other technologies, the draw of the pool lift was that it gave Poppop the control of raising and lowering his seat, a seat that reminded me of the hard-plastic chairs I sat in at school. Poppop's tradition was simple: he got in the chair, cooked in the sun, dunked to cool down, raised himself to cook again, and dunked to cool when he had cooked enough (this sequence continued as needed). When our conversation lulled, we just sat there in the sun, like two lizards on a hot rock, chugging vitamin D through our skin. I'd drift off into thoughts about eighth grade, though this time I thought not about what I was missing, but what others were missing—the sun, the enlightenment, the soft, easy favorites on Magic 107.7.

"Ah, Chris," Poppop grumbled from his pool chair, "you know what would be great right now?"

"What?" I said without moving, deeply committed to dusting my freckles with a bright shade of fuchsia that I'd call 'tan.'

"An ice-cold beer. You wanna go in the garage and grab me one?"

"Sure," I said, knowing damn well that Mommom would be pissed.

I popped out of the pool and dried any trace of water on my body, knowing my grandmother would lose her mind if I was "dripping" on her floors. I tiptoed into the garage. Once my head was in the fridge I heard the garage door open. I was caught fuchsia-handed.

"Christina? What are you doing? What's wrong? What do you need?" It was Mommom doing her usual zero-to-sixty worrying.

"I'm getting Poppop a beer."

"He can't have beer."

Normally I would listen to her, but not that day.

"Oh, okay," I said, pulling a grape soda from the fridge. When she was back to the distraction of mulch arranging, I grabbed a beer and hid it under my towel.

Back at Poppop's perch, I delivered the beer as the Eagles' "Best of My Love" was playing—one of about seven songs played in random order on Magic 107.7. Poppop bobbed his head along, grumbling the lyrics. His movements were subtle and he kept focus on his legs dangling in the water.

"Here, Poppop," I said, proud that I got the beer past Mommom patrol.

"Ah, Chris," he said, grabbing the icy beer and taking a sip, "you're the best thing since sliced bread."

The line made me laugh—not just for being so antiquated but because sliced bread was so low on my list of aspirational carbohydrates. Still, Poppop would say this line again on my next beer run, and the run after that, and after that. He said it until Mommom had to put his catheter in and drain him. For her, sliced bread was *not so great.*

Taking Poppop on a swim. I remember him seeming far more comfortable than he appears to be in this photo.

After just one day hanging out with Poppop, I'd developed an OCD-like need to roll Poppop wherever he wanted to go. As a reward for spreading mulch, Mommom took us to the Kennedy Space Center museum, where I pushed him up and down every ramp. I did not pause to regard crushed tourist toes that got in my path. It was empowering to think that in some way I'd become an extension of him, that I'd become his legs.

I became fiercely protective of Poppop, too. I watched for strangers watching us, and I flipped them off with everything but my middle finger. When Poppop had to use the restroom, Mommom had to bring him into the women's room to use the handicapped stall. It was a reality they were both used to, but I wouldn't stand for any judgment. I stood outside the stall as if I were one of the tough kids at my junior high school. I made sure no one said *shit* about my grandfather. As soon as Mommom and Poppop exited the stall, I watched the bathroom crowd and waited, arms folded, nodding and repeating to myself, "Go on . . . just *try* to say something." Suddenly I was a teenager who *cared*—who wanted her grandfather to have everything he needed to be happy.

Trips out of the house were somewhat stressful for Mommom, who had to pack a trunk full of tools for Poppop, so we spent more time by the pool. With Poppop at his dunking station, me sneaking him beers, and a virtually empty deep end, I decided I'd forgo the teenage malaise and try to learn something new. Up until that point, nothing scared me more than diving. The mere act itself defied logic of any sort. Taking the thing that was most precious and complex, your head, and plunging it before the rest of your body into a substance that isn't always honest about what lay below its surface . . . that was wrong to me on all counts. It also felt wrong given that Poppop's paralysis was the result of a head injury he sustained falling headfirst off a ladder. Despite that, something about the timing seemed just right — maybe it was the inspiration I got from the astronaut museum, or maybe it was the buzz from all the grape sodas. Whatever it was, I decided I had no choice but to throw myself into the water, headfirst.

I began by standing on the edge of the deep end, curled inward like a constipated sea horse. I put my hands above my head and stared into the kidney-bean pool. I waited like this for a while, as the same loop of soft, easy favorites played on the radio. Poppop went in and out of a nap, much like a content cat. Eventually, when I couldn't hold the pose any longer, I had no choice but to fall in. As I fell, I involuntarily flailed my arms to catch myself in the water or protect my head. This only made the splash louder and exceptionally dramatic.

For hours upon hours, I threw myself into the pool, desperately trying to let go of my attachment to my head. I just couldn't seem to get it right, but luckily, I couldn't get enough of my own failure. I splashed Poppop and Mommom, and soaked the audience of the poolside artifacts we made fun of from day one. I got unsolicited tips and pointers from Mommom and Beluga—which only confused my head and made my tumbles more schizophrenic looking. The thing I needed to lead with, my head, was also the thing that was getting in the way of everything.

After three days of silently ignoring the thirteen-year-old who was body-slamming herself repeatedly, Poppop finally spoke up. He kept his head tilted up to the sky, baking in the sun as he offered insight.

"Stop looking at the water. Stop looking down. Think about going up, and for Christ's sake *look up*, too."

Poppop's pointer was a challenging concept to digest — to trick yourself into temporarily forgetting about gravity. I was too busy focusing on my fall that I forgot a crucial element of diving - the lift-off. So, I applied Poppop's approach and straightened out my seahorse shape and forced my eyes to look up. I bent at my knees, sunk back, and sprang into the air with just enough time to tuck my head and pierce through the water like I'd never done before. The height I gained in the air was crucial and exciting, but the exhilaration of piercing through the water headfirst—it's the closest I'd ever felt to flying. I blasted up from the bottom of the pool.

"DID YOU SEE THAT?!" I said, yelling, panting and spitting water everywhere.

"Only took you ten years," Beluga quipped.

"She just had to figure out her takeoff," Poppop said, redeeming my efforts without claiming responsibility for teaching me. He moved his head from sun baking positon to give me a smile of approval. As soon as he'd communicated his feelings on the subject, he went back to sun baking position.

After that first successful dive, I spent my final two days in Palm Coast flying off the side of the kidney bean pool repeatedly. For years, I'd wanted to be able to dive, but I'd focused on the wrong end of the process. The fall, the part where gravity takes over—turns out, that's the easy part.

When we drove to the airport to make our return home, the conversations were 180 degrees different from the year before—they were lively, honest, and for lack of a better word, they were deep.

A few months later, Poppop flew up to New York to visit us during the fall of my first year of high school. It was also the first time he'd gotten on a plane since his injury, and he'd shown no hesitation to make the two-stop flight from Daytona Beach to Islip. He arrived with a smile, and never flinched when he was carried on a dining room chair up and down the stairs of our very handicap-unfriendly house. Poppop was cheerfully doted on by my cousins Todd and Julie, who were also visiting with their mom (AK-47 from chapter 3).

On the Saturday afternoon following his arrival, I found Poppop alone in the den watching college football by a roaring fire. He was seated on the couch instead of in his wheelchair, with his hair neatly combed, and his right arm resting near a side table full of cheesy treats. I clacked into the room, wearing noisy new shoes that had two-inch heels that made me feel especially grown up.

"Hey, Poppop, guess what?"

"Ah, Chris, what's that?"

"I got a B-plus in math." I told him, knowing that at our last conversation I'd sworn off math for good.

"Holy moly, Chris. That's incredible." Poppop said, so sincerely. Then he smiled.

I knew that smile. It was the same smile he had on his face when I'd visit him in the garage, while he was propped up in his standing box. Just a few months earlier, I wracked my brain to figure out what it was about that standing box that made him look like that.

Why was he so happy?

It was a question I couldn't answer when I was in Florida, seeing him standing there with no obvious stimuli. Maybe his happiness came from listening to pleasant sounds — the crinkling made by their entryway palm tree or the grind of a neighbor's power lawn mower, or maybe it was the humming of their spare fridge, perhaps the chirp of a giddy bird . . .

What was that smile?

I looked back at him sitting on our couch. He was back in the Northeast, watching the game by a crackling fire and he was out of his wheelchair. I knew that smile. It was fulfillment. The kind of pure, unadulterated fulfillment that comes from keeping your head up, no matter the circumstance.

CHAPTER 12
Magic and Mommom
Part I

As per my mother's request in 2009, I paired the photo slide show for *her* mother's memorial service with a happy little jingle recorded by the Andrews Sisters in 1940 -something called "Rum and Coca-Cola." It was an unconventional funeral choice to play "Rum and Coca-Cola," mostly because the bulk of the racist lyrics describe how World War II GIs in Trinidad got laid by locals (or, as the Andrews Sisters put it, "made tropic love" to the "native peach"). Nevertheless, "Rum and Coca-Cola" would be the chosen soundtrack to accompany my grandmother's rich life in photographs, however odd it was to hear them paired with the chorus of "both mother and daughter workin' for the Yankee dollar."

My mother's mother, born Cathleen Mary Nicholls in Revelstoke, British Columbia, grew to be five foot nine. She always made a point to talk about the burden of such length. She couldn't sit anywhere too long because it would hurt her "long legs." Sure, she had other attributes, her "almond-shaped eyes," but she'd always come back to her bones—her strong, long, thick bones. Even her home in Seattle was an ode to statues of long women with freakishly stem-like legs. It's no coincidence that with generously limbed spiders she had a no-kill policy, a discovery I made when I was eleven and told her about my hilarious idea to turn a daddy longlegs into a daddy short-legs (by shortening his legs with a pair of scissors). This joke was not met with Mommom's signature laugh, a laugh best described as a subdued version of Phyllis Diller's infamous cackle.

Mommom believed that my hands were her one and only biological contribution to me. This was amusing to me because my paternal grandmother claimed the same body part as her hereditary donation as well. "She has my hands," they'd each declare on separate visits to

Long Island, holding my hands up to theirs to compare the length of my fingers, the span of my palms, and the depth of my cuticles. In truth, if I had to share a feature with anyone, it would be Mommom's hands. They were always well cared for – her nails topped with a rounded acrylic in the same shade as the pastel frosting on animal crackers.

Counter to the uplifting visits with my grandmother, my entire tenure at grade school in New York provided me consistent proof that I was not magical like Mommom; rather, I was "below average." Every year in New York, we took the same standardized tests, the California Achievement Test (CAT) and I scored in a low enough percentile to qualify for Resource Center help. Today we might describe the Resource Center as a place for students who "learn differently," but in Long Island in the 1990s, the Resource Center was known as a place for students who were a "little re-tawd-ed."

Every year was the same: I'd take the CAT test, those test results were sent to my parents, and I'd be notified that the Resource Center trolls would come fetch me from class at some point in the not-too-distant future. The "trolls" were in fact three or so deeply discontented Special Education teachers, born and braised (their faces looked like slabs of meat) on Long Island. All three had mullets in varying shades of taupe and glasses of the most unflattering shape. I never knew when they'd arrive to fetch me, so at various points in my elementary school career, it seemed the trolls would miraculously materialize outside my classroom, announcing their presence each time with the same ominous three-knock combination. After the knock, they'd pop a mulleted head into our room for all the happy Snack-Pack-toting, Gap Kids-clad "normal kids" to see and hear, as they announced in thick Long Island accents:

"We need Chrissy Nuttrider[4] to come with us."

---

4   "Nuttrider" was their delightful bastardization of my legal last name, "Nittrouer"

On these occasions, it seemed I was always dressed stupidly, too—in an oversized elephant T-shirt, or some irregular Marshalls frock or jumper. The trolls started coming for me as soon as standardized testing began, which was second grade, and they continued up until my honors English teacher intervened with a written letter just before tenth grade. Until that intervention, I had no choice; I had to sit through mortifying state-mandated lessons, like my favorite, "sequencing."

The sequencing exercises, which were very popular when I was in ninth grade, involved some lofty brain busters like this: "Sally wants to go for a walk outside. What should Sally do? Should she take her shoes off, or put her shoes on?" My logic then was (and still is) this: *I don't fucking know Sally, and I for one happen to enjoy walking without my shoes on.* These pauses on my part, to wonder about Sally's opinion about shoe wearing, and her personal backstory, did not help me in my advancement from the resource center.

The mathematics tutorials were a little less humiliating because it was expected that I would be bad at math, being, you know, a little girl and all. I had company one year, another student, which was a true delight; finally, I had a partner in retawdation. The trolls would sit us at a computer and we had to answer word problems in order to solve the mystery of Billy's missing ice cream sundae or some low-stakes shit that was as condescending as a Delta Airlines flight attendant explaining how one buckles a seatbelt. The word problems also had incredibly shitty graphics, with pixelated stick figures that were some half-ass attempt to get us 'stupid kids' invested in our assignments. I quickly discovered that I could move the dated 80s avatars very quickly, thus creating a spastic dance I dubbed the "retawd dance." This didn't advance my math skills, but the laughter I experienced, doing *exactly* what I wasn't supposed to do, was what kept me from absorbing a toxic amount of what I'd now call adult bullying. If these Long

Island meat-faced trolls thought I was a "retawd," by golly, I would live up to their expectations. If I learned anything from my time with the Resource Center trolls, it was how to locate a human's Achilles' heel of annoyance and rupture it.

However much the state of New York disagreed, I believed it when Mommom told me that I was a "smart kid." In that vast space between our visits, I wrote Mommom letters and told her all about the ins and outs of my life in Stony Brook. My tone was ten years old going on Charlotte Brontë, but my letters, and their reception, were also an escape to a land where I wasn't a retawded mouse. My hands were my only proof that I had some of Mommom's magic in me, and for that reason they were an exceptionally powerful symbol.

My mom accompanied my dad on a scientific conference or a research trip usually twice per year. If we were lucky, on one of those trips we would have Mommom as our sitter. When Mommom stayed in our home, the entire first floor smelled like Chanel, cigarettes, and rain. Now, I don't know how she transported the crispness of the Pacific Northwest air to Long Island, but it was one of those things that I just likened to one of her magic tricks. If I was on time for school, Mommom would walk me to the bus stop (though this happened maybe twice in my school-going years). Before I left for school, I made sure all Mommom's windows were shut, so as to seal in her smell in the house. This trick of mine must have driven her crazy; as an occasional closeted smoker, she was adamant about no one smelling it, and the opened windows were meant to conceal any evidence.

Mommom in one of her many 80s tracksuits.

We lived high on the hog when Mommom watched us. She'd take us grocery shopping, and we'd pick out the fanciest lunch items of our day: Snack Packs, Dunkaroos, Polly-O string cheese, and real deli counter meat (not chunks of deboned chicken that fell out of our typical sandwiches). Mommom's biggest contribution in our grocery store runs were the Ziploc bags with *real* zippers. All the cool kids had Ziploc bags, not the cheap, thin, fold-over King Kullen bargain brand that we normally purchased and that always betrayed us by catapulting whatever weird and slimy leftovers we were transporting.

When Mommom visited, I told all my classmates stories (at times exaggerated for dramatic effect) about my magical grandmother. Oftentimes I'd lie and say she was still staying with us, when she had gone home weeks before. Even if the stories were somewhat banal in nature, I distinctly remember friends leaning in to hear me share some anecdote about Mommom. People really listened when I spoke about her, and it was this certain magic about Mommom that led me to believe she was a witch. Seeing as she was my grandmother, I decided to try my own hand in magic when I was in fifth grade to see if I, too, was a witch. On the night before she was set to head home, I held a séance so that she would stay longer. Wouldn't you know it? A freak snowstorm hit and she extended her stay by two days. The morning following my successful séance, I took a long hard look at myself in the bathroom mirror and confirmed my new identity. *So, you're a witch, too, Christie . . . so, you're a witch, too.*

Deep Water

Mommom's magic reached beyond the confines of Long Island, too — she traveled with my family, at age five (Korea), age seven and eight (Brazil both times), age nine (Italy), age eleven (Australia), age thirteen (Alaska), and finally, when we got a little older, we met in Aruba, Lake Chelan, or her home in Seattle. All of these locations had one thing in common: they were always near big, beautiful bodies of water. My grandmother was always nearby or in water, and I've theorized that her magic was fueled by water. She'd never complain when she was on a boat; in fact, she seemed to be in a state of bliss. However, when flying on planes, she then drank her weight in rum and Coca-Colas, and when the plane so much as hiccupped, she drank my grandfather's weight. She was even worse in the car; if she were in a passenger seat, she'd recreate the DMV driving test and slam her foot on an imaginary brake. You never wanted Mommom to sit behind you in a car because she'd continually slam that imaginary brake and effectively "foot-fuck you" (as my brother eventually named it).

Mommom had a much deeper connection to water – she often joked that she was part fish, and, for all I know, she might have been a quarter salmon. Her nickname for me and my cousins was "Duck"— probably because we loved water but definitely didn't *need* to be in water to survive, like she did. Personally, I preferred floating on the surface of the water, like a duck, and occasionally diving for something shiny.

Learning to swim is something most of my friends were taught at a community center or a country club pool. When I was seven and spending the first of two summers in Brazil (see chapter 1), my grandmother taught me how to swim. Mommom used a song to guide her lessons, one so dumb it rivaled "If You're Happy and You Know It."

It was awful and catchy, and awfully catchy:

Swimming, swimming in the swimming pool.

When days are hot and days are cold, in the swimming pool we go.

Sidestroke, breaststroke, fancy diving, too!

Oh, don't you wish you never had anything else to do!

Now, these lyrics don't say jack shit about how to float or move your seven-year-old body so you don't drown. Yet, Mommom would sing this, and something about the quality of her voice, and maybe her 80s floral swimsuits, made you want to float to her. She was like some seventy-year-old swimming siren.

Mommom was staying with us at Casa de Bischoff in Belém (see chapter 1), when I decided (after swimming the length of the shallow end 997 times) that I was ready for THE DEEP END. As you may or may not remember, swimming in the deep end is the quinceañera for eight-year-olds. I told my grandmother my resolute intention of swimming in the ever-intimidating zone of the pool known as the "no touch." Our plan was simple: I would jump in the deep end and swim to the floral arrangement (that would be Mommom in her loud swimsuit) in the shallow end. It was a foolproof pool plan.

Standing at the edge of the pool, I made sure my audience was watching (she was) and I leapt without fear. Whatever empowerment I felt in those first nanoseconds was bitch-slapped by the fangs of Ferdinand (the same pooch from Chapter 1), who sunk his teeth into my right ankle. As soon as the pup grabbed hold of me, I screamed and crashed into the pool, gulping a cup or two of unchlorinated

Brazilian pool water. My grandmother swam over to me and caught me as I thrashed around like a prized swordfish hooked on the line.

It didn't take any talkin'-to from my grandmother for me to know I was going back to the deep end - it was just a knowing look that said, "shut up, kid." I gritted my mismatched teeth and marched to the very center above the deep end. Now, up until that point in my life, there were two things that I thought I could marry and grow old with: dogs and pools. On that hot winter day in Brazil, 1989, I became a scorned lover. Like some eyebrowless seven-year-old Don Corleone—with a pouty lip and a pissed-off eye—I made a vow to carry out my revenge.

Ferdinand, looking very panty and very German, stared me right in the eyeballs, then at my feet balls (thanks to nerves, my feet were balled up, much like a fist). Ferdinand couldn't have made it clearer; he was *hungry for foot.* I prepared to jump, and as Ferdinand went to nab my feet, I turned quickly on a heel and I blasted back at him.

"*Nein!*" I yelled.

Ferdinand drew his eyebrows close together and raised them in an expression that only a German Shepherd can truly master, the "*Wait . . .* Huh?"

I chased—no—I threw my runty frame at *his* ankles and as Ferdinand ran away from me, he looked back with another expression of "*Ficken mein Leben!*" As soon as the beast had retreated enough, I turned on my heel and ran back to the platform above the deep end. I launched without interference. Success! I popped up to the surface and borrowed Ferdinand's signature move, the doggy paddle, and swam all the way back to Mommom. She had witnessed the whole thing, and saw me outsmart the big, bad, wolf. For whatever it's worth, in that moment I felt like I was "above grade level."

This breakthrough in Brazil marked the beginning of my sado-masochistic attraction to those "deep end," "no touch" experiences in life, and showed me that water could comfort me, just like it did Mommom.

The Deep End

About three years after our time in Belém, I'd been confidently swimming in the deep end of the Mercer Island Shore Club, which was a stone's throw below my grandparents' house. It was an interesting place, always littered with cliquey blond kids and their nannies or their body-conscious mothers. On summer vacations, my cousin Shelly and I would roll out of bed, and continue our roll down the trail to the pool for public swim (which began at one p.m.). Our activities consisted of twirling and somersaulting in a heated body of water, replicating the most blissful manatees on Earth.

Perched high above the pool, for all the kiddies and their keepers to observe, stood the MISC's high dive, which was a staggering ten feet tall. When swimming below such a magnificent beast, one could really take in its power that much more. Tackling the high dive was on my bucket list, but so were a lot of other things that secretly I hoped I'd actually die before having to cross them off the list. When my older cousins successfully pressured me into taking the plunge, it was at the peak of kid crowds in mid-July. We've all heard of those kids who tiptoe out on that flimsy high dive board, stand there like a mime-in-headlights (far weirder than a deer) waiting for a miracle of motivation to occur, and when that miracle does not occur, they gingerly turn around on the diving board, and exit in the most mortifying ladder descent since Buzz Aldrin was number two to step onto the Moon. Yep. During one summer at Mommom's, *I* was *that asshole* who waits, and waits, and gets to the diving plank, gulps hard and causes an even bigger traffic jam when she has to lumber back down the ladder (à la Buzz).

The following day, when it was just me milling around with my grandmother and grandfather in their small kitchen, I regaled them with a story where I compared myself to a peer who was "better" than me. I was closely shadowing Mommom as I went on and on about my friend.

"I could *never* do what *she* does," I said.

"Yes, you can," Mommom retorted quickly, mid multi-task.

"Yeah, okay," I said in a signature sarcasm I'd picked up from her.

Moments later, I was on my way down the trail to meet my cousin, when Mommom chased after me. I'd made it to the top of their outdoor stairs and was already lost in my head (which at that moment was cooking up a plan to snag a few wild blackberries on my way down the trail) when I felt her grab my arm. Up to that point in life, my interactions with Mommom were so grandparent-grandchild idyllic that the bristle in her demeanor took me by surprise. For the first time in my life, Mommom was not hiding the fact that she was *very* angry with me.

"Hey! You can do whatever you want to do," she asserted with no smile on her face whatsoever.

"Uh...okay." I was genuinely scared and confused. Was my Canadian-polite grandmother bullying me into having better self-esteem? I threw my hand up in a wave so as to say 'okay, thanks, bye' and turned to head down the stairs.

"No. Look at me," Mommom demanded. Utterly terrified, I turned to look at Mommom. Her eyes were narrowed to the point that she looked mean, *so mean* that I distinctly remember looking down to the composite stone walkway at my feet that was such a signature of 1970s Northwest design. "If you want to do something," she continued, "then you will do it." She waited for me to look back at her. "I'm serious."

This was one of those truly remarkable out-of-body experiences, where I watched her as if I were a time traveler coming back to witness this precise instance of inspirational bullying. Part of me still believed that she was bat-shit-crazy for so passionately believing in me, but the other part was struck by the conviction in her voice. My grandmother always spoke with a wispy gentle inflection, but at this moment she spoke as if she were granted only one chance to say this simple line: 'if you want to do something, you will do it.' So, she did it with a sternness that I still can't shake.

Everything that framed the moment was equally vivid; the bright Northwest summer light that bounced off the side of their house, the sharp smell of the air, the hum of the boats and screaming kids carried all the way up to our ears, thanks to the sound-conducting waters of Lake Washington. The way her eyes, which were a sort of golden brown (or hazel as her driver's license promised), caught the precise amount of reflected light and were straight-up phosphorescent. It was like I'd been tapped on the shoulder and told 'hey, no pressure, but - remember this moment for the rest of your life.' Even if I still didn't quite believe what she was saying, *I heard her*, and that was necessary.

When I returned to the pool, I had absolutely no choice but to jump. I felt sick with anxiety on the whole walk to the pool, to the diving board, and on every ladder rung; my stomach doubled its already bustling butterfly population. Standing up on that board with a beautifully full twelve-year-old belly, my teeth (and braces) chattering under purple lips, I took one last gulp of air, and stepped over the edge. Time stopped, my stomach threw itself into my throat, my hands fluttered like an effeminate penguin . . . and then . . . I sliced through the water, and plunged deeper than I'd ever been.

That first high-dive jump was a recommitment ceremony for me and my main squeeze, water. For those formative preteen and early-teen years, my summers were spent marinating in the best bodies of water—without thinking about my own undeveloped body, without pausing to let my fingers and feet de-pucker. Living in water meant I was kept afloat by an element that was so crucial to my grandmother - no matter the distance between us - we were connected through it.

Hearing Things

One of the perks of having big ears, aside from almost never getting swimmer's ear, is that they can sometimes pick up on things—cues, peculiarities, and slight shifts. At age fifteen in Lake Chelan, Washington, my cousin Shelly and I took a tiny fishing boat out on the water so we could exercise our freedom (and pretend to be Christopher Columbus). We took the boat across the lake to our little piece of adult-less paradise—a lone water pipe that was covered by a simple slab of wood. I liked the spot because it was impossible for other humans to get to it, as it was hidden between mounds of jagged rock, which suddenly dropped off right into the icy, blue waters of Lake Chelan.

*Me and cousin Shelly at our favorite picnic spot
in Lake Chelan, Washington.*

Mommom and Poppop knew that Shelly and I were boating across the lake to sit on a water pipe and eat ham sandwiches, drink Diet 7UPs, and possibly even split a Snickers we snagged from Poppop's collection. QUICK SIDE NOTE: Since about 1993, our grandfather developed an obsession with Snickers (facilitated by his Costco membership), and it was his habit to leave them in the freezer so their hardened caramel would effectively make them last longer. To say Poppop was a child of the Depression is to say the pope is familiar with guilt. Poppop found a good thing—Snickers—and bought cases at Costco. Though the resource was abundant, to take a *whole* Snickers for yourself was deemed greedy. Poppop instead handed his grandkids a Snickers bar and a buck knife. Whoever cut it was exempt from choosing, a lesson I learned the hard way when I tried to screw my brother out of about 67 percent of his share. Shelly and I created a little game called "Sneak-a-Snickers," where we'd remove the eight or nine bungee cords holding the lid tight on the ancient freezer. Once inside, we'd sift through about thirty-seven packages of frozen hot dogs, only to find and take just one perfectly frozen Snickers bar. With our loot in hand, we'd run out of the house and into the woods, crying out like banshees.

Now, Mommom knew damn well of our Snickers obsession and that we'd take our loot to the isolated water pipe across the lake. Late one afternoon in July 1997, while we were awaiting word of what Uncle Mike and Aunt Holly were giving birth to (turned out to be a boy, our cousin, Colter), we discovered the beginning of what would be one of the worst diseases to ever touch someone close to us—Alzheimer's.

Shelly and I returned to the dock, tied off the fishing boat as Mommom watched us from a big pine tree that stood by the shore.

"How'd it go?" Mommom asked, arms folded and mouth pressed into her signature smirk.

"Great!" I said, with an enthusiasm reserved only for her.

"You two just love it over there with that woman," she said. "She runs a great little . . . Mexican restaurant."

Shelly and I, being thirteen and fifteen, had no idea what to do except repress a giggle. What in the f-word was our grandmother talking about? Mommom continued to talk about this woman and her excellent Mexican cuisine—an incredibly odd mistake to make because at that point in my life, I had not once dined at a Mexican restaurant in Washington State.

Shelly and I continued to play it early-teen cool, looking out to the water, down at our Teva knock-off sandals, the boat, anything to avoid eye contact with each other and start laughing. Mommom had "lost her mind," and we didn't have the balls to correct her and remind her that for the entire week we had been busy eating ham sandwiches on a water pipe covered with two pieces of plywood.

We followed Mommom up to the house, where she did something she normally didn't do—she made us a snack. Now, one of the best things about spending a chunk of summer with my grandparents was that I could come and go as I pleased. Dinner was never at six or seven—it was usually at eleven and it was always hot dogs. Lunch was sometime around four or five and it was up to us to make it. Breakfast was also up to us and any snacking was usually just binge eating Snickers. Yes, we were a bit like Peter Pan's Lost Boys and thus Mommom's offering of a snack was extremely unusual to us. Shelly and I watched with mouths agape as she pulled out a jar of Prego pasta sauce, poured it into a bowl, and turned to grab a fresh bag of Tostitos. To our combined horror, Mommom took a chip, dipped it in some Prego, and crunched.

"I just love this stuff. It's not too spicy, you know? Here, kids, go on, have some."

Shelly and I eyed each other—it was five o'clock and we had just finished our lunch; it wasn't exactly the best time for marinara chips. Still, I remembered that Mommom was magical (and potentially capable of transforming sauce into salsa just like Jesus did), so I ate a Tostito coated in warm, sweet Prego. It was a flavor I'll never forget; it was the taste of the beginning of something disgusting. It was the first taste of loving someone and losing someone very slowly, and very painfully, to Alzheimer's disease.

CHAPTER 13
Magic and Mommom
Part II

Being observant and outspoken, I took the Prego chip incident to my parents, who took it to my aunts and uncles. Their strategy was to ignore the signs and live in a passive state of denial. *Yea!* When Mommom's odd behaviors and paranoias were public enough that denial was impossible, it was just blamed on her being "drunk." A remedy for this, which was always administered by my grandfather, was to just give her more alcohol to drink. His solutions made her catatonic but non-threatening. To save himself and others from the mean streak that accompanies Alzheimer's, he started feeding alcohol to Mommom earlier and earlier in the day.

In eleventh grade, I moved to Seattle and got a front row seat to witness my grandmother's deterioration. I once adored her home and being in her presence. However, when she was sick, everything smelled different. Much like the Prego chip, it wasn't offensively bad, but it was bland, drained and drowned in secrets. Spending time with someone with Alzheimer's is a bit like going through a fun house mirror. I held my head to the side when I talked to her, looking to see if she was really all there.

Comedy became a universal tool at all of our family gatherings. Instead of seeking professional medical help, my uncles, aunts, and parents sat around the dinner table swapping humiliating stories, laughing so hard that they'd cry. Jokes were our perfectly cruel way of avoiding the feelings that we didn't want to have. Whenever a family dinner got weird, one of us would whistle generic circus music and we'd giggle at how crazy Mommom was. Can you believe it? My hero of just a few years earlier was treated like a circus freak who was the butt of our very callous comedy. Mommom would doze off during family meals and occasionally come to and say the same line that we'd all mockingly quote for years to come: "it's so peaceful here." But those cordial remarks were all Mommom had; the reality was the rest of us were cacophonous and too selfish to consider how disoriented she must have felt.

It wasn't until 2002 that Mommom and Poppop finally had a caretaker come to their home, and by "caretaker" I mean "live-in bartender." Her name was Karen and that's all we knew—that she had a name, and apparently a gift for making stiff drinks and bringing her husband over to talk to my grandparents, who were 98% senile and 100% shit-faced, about "investment opportunities." At one point, Karen proposed that she and her husband move in and live with my grandparents, while serving as their new power of attorney. The proposition was plausible to my grandparents because, at that point in time, Karen was the love of their lives. Karen let my grandparents drink so much that in their drunken stupor they forgot everything, including the fact that they had dementia.

After Karen was fired for being extremely unfit, a new *family* of equally unfit caretakers moved in and took her place. This new caretaking crew would get my grandfather good and schnockered and then they would hit up the bank drive-thru, where Poppop would take out Big Mac-sized cash withdrawals. The cash disappeared, along with my grandmother's nicer pieces of clothing. Many of my family members (myself included) would check on my grandparents and find them both alone in their bedroom, sitting on top of soiled sheets, usually in the dark, with just the glow and buzz from a TV tennis match lighting their faces.

When I was a senior in college, I found a pair of car keys when I was in downtown Seattle and luckily, they were adorned with an Albertsons grocery store "Super Saver" card. On my way to pick up my parents and take them to the airport, I figured I'd better drop the keys off at the Albertsons on Mercer Island. I was surprised to see my grandmother at the front of the check-out line—her hair disheveled, her eyes registering as terrified, as three or four young parents paced impatiently behind her. Once I saw her, I had a genuine, and in retrospect, embarrassing, desire to just walk out and pretend I hadn't seen anything. Whatever ignorant 22-year-old anger I felt toward her for losing her mind was overpowered by the details of her body language. She talked nervously to the cashier, while fidgeting with her pockets and jolting her white bobbed haircut frantically to the right and left. I made my way to her, while frustrated patrons behind her eyed their invisible watches like bad actors in a community-theatre play. When Mommom couldn't tell me where Poppop was, I went through the store hunting for him, literally smelling my way to what I was sure would be a barely locked and fully loaded adult diaper.

It didn't take long before I found him in the cereal aisle, huddled over a grocery cart, crying hysterically. He was trying to make his body move despite severe physical and emotional pain.

"Pops, what's wrong?" I asked, afraid of his answer.

"I fell, I fell," he sobbed.

What he came to explain through sobs was that he fell in the bathroom and managed to crawl to a cart to use it as a makeshift walker. Even with his diaper now clearly visible, his face red, his eyes wet, not one employee stopped to see if he needed help. There he was, making a desperate scene, but treated as if he were invisible—a reality that defines the role assigned to our elderly. Our treasured vet, our beloved war hero, was, as far as he thought, left for dead in a shitty discount grocery store.

We made our way back to my grandmother, who had no idea he had even been gone. The checkout guy, named Sam, gave me a look that said it all: *Who lets their family live like this?* Sam was right. After we purchased the groceries, I walked them to their Oldsmobile and followed them out of the parking lot. It didn't dawn on me at the time to follow them home because my own parents were already late for an international flight. You'd think that we would have hired a different caretaker after that episode, but it would take another year and another stroke for Poppop before the camel's back finally fucking broke.

A year after the Albertsons incident, I was a graduate student living in Wisconsin and after my applications to several summer jobs there were turned down, I decided to go back to Seattle for the abundant (or so I thought) employment opportunities. After nearly two weeks of Seattle job applications out and silence in, my parents and I went to Lake Chelan for the weekend with my grandmother and my aunt and uncle. Poppop was too sick to travel (or ever return) to the cabin, and this fact was reflected in the cabin's master bedroom, which had its carpet stripped and large bed taken to the dump. On my first night there, I sat up in the bedroom that was next to Mommom's room, struggling to sleep – just wondering what she must have been thinking. There she was, sleeping on top of a twin bed, alone, with all the carpet removed, exposing filthy, decaying plywood subflooring. Did she remember the master bedroom's former state? Did she miss the tacky pink carpet? Did she miss Poppop? Did she miss herself, the way she was before she got sick? Did she even *know* she was sick?

The following morning, my parents approached me with a bizarre offer, something they cooked up the night before while I was lying in bed worrying about Mommom. It was a simple question: would I want to be a live-in care taker for Mommom from Monday through Friday? I wondered about the less glamorous aspects of the job. Would she hide my things? Would I have to wash her dentures? Wash her? Change her diaper? Did she wear diapers? I was taking a moment to think this through when I caught Mommom standing outside her room, leaning over the deck railing and looking out over the lake. The water sparkled, it danced, it beckoned her. Mommom hadn't been swimming in years but it was clear that she remembered the water—she still knew its magic.

I took a deep breath, turning away from the sight of her and answered the proposition with a resounding *yes*.

When we returned to Seattle, I stopped by her house to meet with her caretaker to coordinate our new shift schedule. The kitchen door buzzed as soon as I entered; a new sensor had been installed to detect if Mommom had made a run for it. The jarring sound stood out, it signaled that things were different, now that Mommom was under a sort-of house arrest.

I walked down the thickly carpeted hallway that took me to Mommom's room. I knocked on the door and waited.

"Just a minute," she called out with a hoarse voice. She opened the door and greeted me. "Hi, Duck. I'm not feeling so good today."

"What happened?" I asked.

"It's just right here," she said, gesturing to her chest and lungs. "I am having a hard time breathing."

"Mommom, I'm going to start staying here." I stated in a politely pitchy tone.

"With me?" She asked, mildly confused.

"Yes, with you. Is that okay?"

Mommom lit up, the most I'd seen her glow in years.

"That would be wonderful!" she exclaimed.

Mommom's profound enthusiasm brought out the years of suppressed guilt I felt for distancing myself from her and her disease. I sobbed on my way back to my parent's house. I sobbed because, for the first time in a long while, I knew what I was doing was the right thing, I just wished I'd started doing it earlier.

Considering that Mommom had an unpredictable disease, Alzheimer's, I was surprised that we fell into a pretty routine schedule. At nine a.m. I'd make sure she was awake. She was always asleep in her bed, so I'd arrive at her door, knock a few times, repeating in a high-pitched voice, "Mommom, it's Christie." I worried every morning that she'd forget who I was and attack me, which is why I said "Mommom" as many times as I could. When I was granted permission to enter her room, Mommom always said, "I'm just not feeling well, especially right *here*," and she'd point to her lungs just like she did the day I first told her I would be staying with her. I took her complaint as a perfect segue to present her with the four or five morning medications she needed (but often refused) to take. "These will help your lungs, Mommom," I'd lie.

The biggest struggle I faced was getting her out of bed and dressed for the day when she felt "sick." I had a line I used for this daily occasion: "You can stay in bed, but I just thought you'd want to see Poppop." At the sound of "Poppop," she'd perk up and do literally anything to see him—it was the only leverage I had over her, and it always worked. If I was lucky, I could get her to eat breakfast in the kitchen. If not, I'd bring it to her bed. Breakfast was usually scrambled eggs topped with cheese, along with tons of melon, berries, and yogurt. There was also Irish breakfast tea, which she never touched but requested because I was always drinking it. Wherever we were having breakfast, the Lifetime channel was always on. For whatever reason, she loved Lifetime; even the scary movies with abusive, murdering men were soothing to her. My guess is that the corny acting was similar to the way someone with Alzheimer's might deliver her lines, not *really* finding any truth in it. Our favorite Lifetime home movie, which we watched a few times, was the much-anticipated "true story" of murderer Scott Peterson's ex-lover, *Amber Frey: Witness for the Prosecution.*

One morning, my mom stopped over and told me that I was over-feeding Mommom (and myself), and I told mother that she could go "overfeed" herself. Eating was one of the only things Mommom could still understand, talk about, and enjoy, so we dined as frequently and glamorously as Paula Deen. I cooked all the time and picked out the nicest cuts of fish, beef, and pork at the very same Albertsons where I'd found my grandparents just a year earlier.

Grocery shopping with an eighty-year-old with Alzheimer's was much like shopping with an adult-sized toddler. Mommom would grab everything colorful and put it in the cart, and I had to find a way to get it out of the cart without her having a meltdown. Our grocery runs weren't so much runs as they were a slow, sloppy shit show. It took at least an hour to get out of the store—but the wonderful truth was that I had absolutely nowhere else to be and neither did she. My grocery-cart rule was to allow her two wild cards. Her choices ranged from toys to sugary cereal to cookie dough to her favorite: Hanukkah gelt (for the gentiles: chocolate wrapped in shiny gold tinfoil, made to resemble coins).

During one of our trips to Albertsons, Mommom was convinced that it was Christmas. Because I was tired of correcting her, I thought, *Ahh, fuck it, it's Christmas.* To every stranger the two of us passed, it was "Merry Christmas!" The looks alone were worth their weight in gelt.

When we reached Sam, her regular checkout-stand guy, he opened with his usual chirpy greeting.

"Hello, Cathy!"

"Are you excited?" Mommom asked Sam, about to explode with her own glee.

"Excited for what?" Sam asked.

"Santa Claus is coming tonight!" Mommom exclaimed.

Sam, who was Jewish and most likely chose to work at the Albertsons because of its reputation as a go-to kosher market (I mean, they sold gelt in July), looked at her and very bluntly said, "Santa Claus isn't coming to my house."

My grandmother, *horrified* by this statement, held her breath, narrowed her eyes, and snapped, "Well, that's because you're a *bad* boy."

And with that, we waited in long, awkward silence before paying and rolling out with a hundred dollars' worth of ingredients for Christmas dinner.

Back home, as I shuttled the grocery bags inside the house to start cooking our Christmas feast, I noticed something funny. The Christmas lights my grandfather had strung up before his stroke were gleaming brightly. The automatic timer was set so that they'd come on around six p.m. every night. It was then that it dawned on me that my grandmother wasn't bat-shit crazy; she just believed it was Christmas because she trusted the lights.

Our dinners at home (assuming we weren't out tearing it up at the many Chinese restaurants we frequented) were always oddly elaborate and formal. I'd set out the fine china on the dining room table, and we'd dine like it was our last supper. Initially the conversations were clumsy, at least from my end. As I got used to my new gig, I enjoyed the "just go with it" approach. I never got to be Catholic in my lifetime, so I'd treat it like a confessional, knowing any embarrassing personal information would not be remembered by Mommom. Sometimes

Mommom's responses were great, and sometimes they were *the greatest*, like the time I told her about a guy who was just not as into me as I was into him.

"Well, you just have to know that you're very special and so you need someone as *truly* special as you are. Forget about him!" She paused and we shared our own special moment. It would have been a perfect cheesy Lifetime movie scene, except that Mommom continued. "Have I ever told you about my dad? I think you and Daddy would *really* hit it off."

After this statement, she raised her eyebrows up and down in a very Austin Powers-suggestive manner. That was the bizarre beauty of living with someone who had Alzheimer's – moments of "normal" were immediately interrupted by my grandmother suggesting I date my dead great-grandfather, as if he were alive and well, ready to pop over and invite me to the fucking sock hop.

Aside from our trips to Albertsons, we also found drugstores and cheap department stores appropriate for whatever Christmas planning we might do in July. The brightness of a Walgreens or Rite Aid functioned like the perfect museum where we might study the promises on cereal boxes, elaborate cosmetics displays, or our favorite: the "As Seen on TV" aisle. The setting was oddly comforting—the corny music interrupted by "a special on aisle seven," or the stock boy crafting a perfect pyramid for the Tide box army, and all the customers going in and out at varying paces and energies. In a way, it was like taking a walk through a human aquarium; again, there was that same fluidity that I associated with Mommom.

Discount department stores were also great for us, and we shopped like giddy sorority sisters. Anything like TJ Maxx, Marshalls, Ross Dress for Less, where you'd get the same customer service you'd expect in say, Transylvania; these were perfect places for us to be left alone to wander and whistle Christmas carols. Once while we were at a Ross in

Redmond, Mommom took an interest in the lingerie section, and, not wanting to intervene, I let her pick out her items and nodded my head when she asked my opinion. When I wandered near a shirt I liked, she called out to me "Hey, hey . . ." and I waited to see if she knew my name. After a long pause, she called out, "Chris . . . Christie." I came running over and we chatted about the "cute" lace nighty she'd found. Sure, it was *really* weird to weigh in on my grandmother's negligee, but I like to think our shared excitement was not just for "Lamda Phi winter formal with their Glenn Miller cover band," but because she remembered my name.

We took full advantage of the relative vacancy at the discount stores, both of us changing in our respective fitting rooms and calling out when we were ready to present our costumes, just like we used to do years earlier at the classy Tanger Outlets on Long Island. There were a few times when Mommom would forget what she had or had not tried on. I'd look at the same outfit four or five times, and be forced to replicate those *oohs* and *aahs* as if it were the first time. And you know what? I did buy her the nighty she wanted, and though she (thankfully) never wore it, I'll be damned if she didn't feel sexy carrying it out of the store in a Ross Dress for Less plastic bag.

Mommom's feet were always a size 10, but with time they'd flattened out to a size 11, making Mervyn's in Factoria the only store that carried her size. We felt dignified about having five or six pairs to choose from, as if we were solving a tough riddle together. We bought her two pairs of flip-flops, one in a pastel purple and the other in a warm ivory. Both pairs were coated with sequins. Mommom loved these shoes in the store, and even more at home because they were easy for her to put on by herself. Anything more than a flip-flop or a ballet flat, and she couldn't get into it. The trick for anyone with Alzheimer's is giving them back some sense of autonomy as discreetly as possible.

The purple sandals proved to have a magical effect on Mommom's wardrobe, which was fortunate because, up until that point, she was uninterested in changing her clothing aside from two or three shirts (which meant laundry timing was crucial). My Aunt Julie had purchased a beautiful Kaelin tracksuit in a dusty purple color that Mommom loved but for some reason would not wear. It hung in her closet, sadly, waiting for its moment to be showcased. The purple shoes became a color swatch that I would hold up to other pastel tops, cardigans, and capris at Mervyn's. Though she wouldn't wear the beautiful suit, she was thrilled with the other ensembles we found that would match those magical sequined sandals.

Another challenge we faced was getting Mommom to shampoo her hair. My mom arranged for Mommom to see a hairdresser in the Central District of Seattle that specialized in African American hair. There certainly wasn't much of her thin, white hair to cut, but a deal was worked out where, for ten dollars, she got a shampoo and style. The hairdressers were by far the most compassionate to Mommom – they knew she was sick, but they never acknowledged it with more than a knowing glance to me. There was a safety and a warmness I always felt as I sat in the waiting area flipping through *Ebony*. Mommom would find me when she was finished, glowing, feeling feminine, and she'd hold a hand under her bob and ask, "how do you like my new do?" The whole salon would praise the "new look" and how it brought out her best features – her cheekbones, her jawline, her sweet smile.

Eventually, I set up my own "salon" for Mommom in her kitchen. I carefully laid out all the combs, dryers, and styling sprays, and I gingerly tilted her head in the sink, using the extendable sprayer to wash her hair. Sure, it wasn't as glamorous as the styles done by Tyesha, but it was a chance for me to play the part of hair stylist. I'd ham it up, chitchatting like a pro. "So, Cathy, how's your husband doing? Al is his name, right?"

Beyond salons and shopping, we went to daytime movies because they offered a great senior discount, and mostly because it was the summer of food. *POPCORN!* I still have her stub from our screening of *Madagascar*, and I can't look at it without laughing—remembering the manic animation and its impact on Mommom. David Schwimmer, taken on his own, doesn't make much sense to the Greatest Generation, but turn him into an ADHD giraffe and Mommom might as well have taken a gravity-bong rip.

On one trip home from "the pictures" (the movies), I received a frustrating text message from my brother, whom I'd been on tenuous terms with for, well . . . most of my life. Instead of relaying the scenario to her, I simply exhaled loudly and said, "Why is Beluga such a jackass?!" Considering that the previous week Mommom was still trying to get me to date my dead great-grandfather, I was surprised when she said, "All brothers are assholes." Not only did she remember who Beluga was; she also remembered that he was an asshole.

On our daily walks, I had to learn how to be patient when Mommom would take three steps and then stop to show me the same patch of blackberries. It was difficult to keep her walking, but I found that promises of seeing Poppop always sped up her gait. We had a tradition of stopping by the fruit stands on our way home from our daily visits to see Poppop. One rainy day, we plowed through an entire pound of plump, Pacific Northwest Bing cherries while stuck in bad traffic. Let's just say, it was a Christmas miracle that we made it home in time to get to the bathroom.

Although we had a lot of fun together, Mommom still had moody moments, and they were more pronounced in the evenings or around my mother. One evening, I drove the three of us downtown to see a modern dance company perform and this was when I felt officially fed up with Mommom. During the entire rush hour trip downtown, Mommom complained about my driving and slammed the imaginary brake one too many times (which, with her sitting behind me, meant "the brake" was positioned directly under my ass). Once we were at the theatre, she unwrapped a seemingly endless supply of cough drops with the precise crinkle decibel to drive me certifiably insane.

After we had returned from the show and Mommom had gone to bed, I noticed her small sequined black clutch that she had brought to the theatre. It sat on the countertop and was hit by flickering fluorescent light sent down from their 80s kitchen fixtures. I was still angry with Mommom but I had to know what was in the purse. *What could she have possibly needed?* I opened it up. Inside there were cough drops, a picture of my mom on her wedding day, and a small spoon. I pictured Mommom, hours before, clutching this black purse as if it held something truly important. Suddenly I felt a wave of pity for the purse; just like her, it appeared isolated and misplaced on the stark-white kitchen counter. I decided I needed to go in and check on her. Once in her room, I saw Mommom was sleeping peacefully with her arm bent at the elbow just above her head. The Lifetime channel was on. All was okay. I placed her purse on her vanity and patted it gently, like it was a good pet.

The experience of taking care of Mommom also brought me closer to my mom, who is one of those people who always thrives in challenging environments and social contexts. We both had a way of interacting with Mommom that was built into our blood; we could understand her, and still manage to improvise around anything that was too difficult or painful.

My cousin Shelly captured this moment of Mommom,
Mom, and me joking around after dinner.

Another unforeseen perk of my time with Mommom was the time I got to spend with my maternal cousins. There was a magic to our time together, we were close in the same way we had been as kids – just utterly smitten with each other, the way only cousins (and not siblings) can. One afternoon, my cousin Nikki stopped by and we snuggled up with Mommom to watch the be-all end-all marathon of *The Golden Girls.* This was followed by a trip to the Crab Shack, where we ate our faces off during a three-hour meal and then brought our left-over bundt cake (yes, we ordered an entire bundt cake) to my grandfather.

When I was about three weeks into working with Mommom, my cousin Shelly announced that she would like to join the fun, and together we traded off shifts. Our time together was so magical that I would often end up staying for Shelly's shifts and my own, so I was living nearly full-time with my grandmother. I'd cook the dinners and Shelly would make the salad. We'd talk around the table until Mommom got tired. One night, I promised Mommom homemade cookies, which I baked and set out to cool. Shelly and I left the kitchen to watch TV in the basement. When we returned for sodas, we found Mommom leaning over the cookie tray stuffing her face. When she

heard us, she turned around suddenly and said with perfect noncha-
lance "oh hey" with every inch of her face *covered* in melted chocolate.

As I was nearing the end of my time with Mommom, Shelly and
I took her out to lunch for some mediocre Seattle pizza. In a way, the
taste of the pizza and the feelings I had were similar to that Prego
'salsa' we had eaten years before. I was nervous to leave Seattle. I knew
that when I returned, Mommom wouldn't be as well. In this case, time
would *not* heal her Alzheimer's wounds; it would only deepen them.
After our lunch, we drove to the park below Mommom's house on
Lake Washington and the three of us sat there quietly. Years earlier,
the three of us had swam together — Shelly and I climbing up on the
docks to showcase our synchronized jumps that would land right next
to Mommom's unflinching head. That day, however, we couldn't go in
the water; we just watched it from a picnic bench. In the distance, we
saw young kids as they terrorized their grandmothers, while uncles
barbecued, and parents relaxed on camping chairs. I wondered... *Did
Mommom know?* Was she watching these people longingly and remembering younger times? Was she jealous? Was she lonely? Did she *even*
know I was leaving? Did she even care?

I'm not sure how it happened, but Shelly and I started up a
knee-slapping game we learned in 1993. It was a trick we had once
practiced in the backseat of Poppop's Chevy Lumina during the
entire 670-mile journey from Seattle to Bozeman, Montana, for our
Uncle Mike's wedding. Remembering how much the song had annoyed her husband (we sang it for like 11+ hours), Mommom was sent
into a delightful fit of hysterical laughter. Somewhere, somehow,
deep in Mommom's memory, this little nugget was preserved. It was
something we could cling to —all three of us—even if the song itself
was a terrible Raffi-like jingle. It was (and always will be) a perfect moment. The three of us, in soft evening light, bound to a lakeside bench

and revisiting a trick that *annoyed the living shit* out of Poppop. No, we weren't swimming in the water, but we were close enough.

I had hoped that my last night with Mommom would end with her falling asleep early and me shedding all my grief by sobbing in the shower. Or, maybe she'd criticize my driving, or cooking, and maybe we'd have a fight and I'd say something like "Thank God I can leave this hellhole." As I was unloading the dishwasher, I heard Mommom call out to me. I responded with a halfhearted "yeah?" but continued unloading dishes with the hope that she'd forget that she needed my attention.

"Chris," she continued, "I wanna know what you think..."

Her tone suggested "what you think" to be something lighthearted and jovial, nothing deeply philosophical, but more like my position on the Brad/Angelina/Aniston triangle that was all the rage at that cultural moment. I finished up with the dishes and decided to check on her.

"Hey Mommom, here I am." I announced prematurely.

I rounded the corner of the kitchen and found Mommom standing at the start of the hallway, modeling the purple Kaelin track suit, which she'd paired with the purple sequined flip-flops we purchased together at Mervyn's. The two shades of purple were off in a way that made me want to cry—her intention to match her ensemble was right there in front of me, and that, in and of itself, was one of my life's most touching moments. She remembered the outfit and for a moment in time she was herself again, she was Mommom, and it was magic.

Every cell in my body beamed with delight. I told her:

"You look *wonderful*"

"Why thank you! Should we have a drink and sit?" she asked while twirling and posing in her ensemble.

This 'sitting and drinking' was what Mommom and Poppop did — they gathered guests in the living room and paired mixed drinks with Costco-brand cashews that Poppop would heat in the microwave.

"Yes, I'll make us a drink and let's sit," I agreed.

I loaded two glass tumblers with ice cubes, and topped them with a mixture of chai tea mix and milk. We sat and toasted as if there were alcohol in our drinks, and we spoke slowly and confidently, as if we were eased by the liquid we consumed. Across the lake, houses built into the hill twinkled; the red and white light from cars making their way on I-405 made gentle statements. We watched them, admiring the show. Mommom crossed her long legs and smoothed the material of her purple tracksuit, bobbing her sequined flip-flopped foot up and down, clattering the ice cubes in her drink just so.

This would be the last time we'd be in her home together—the very last moment. I knew this and I believe she knew this as well. And it was, to borrow the phrase she used all too often, *so peaceful.*

To give you an idea of what "having a sit" looked like – here we are having a sit in January of 1997 (eight years before our final sit together in 2005).

So Peaceful Here

I was up extra early on May 6, 2009, and was waiting at the Loews hotel in Santa Monica for a producer friend who was filming the Digital Hollywood conference. The hotel sat right on the Pacific oceanfront and on that morning, there was a thick fog sitting on top of the water. The relentless and annoying California sun was pacing somewhere behind the clouds, ready to eviscerate the gray. I was waiting to see where the sun might break through when my phone rang.

"Chris, ahh, Christie?" says my dad in a tone that was one part scattered scientist and one part Russian general.

"Yeah?"

"Mommom died."

Maybe it was the fact that I just so happened to be on the water at that precise moment, but I said with a nonchalant directness:

"Yeah, I know."

I walked to the very edge of the deck that overlooked the ocean as Dad shared the pertinent details. But I wasn't interested in Dad's information, because I was transfixed by the big body of water in front of me. I was comforted by the fact that I knew she was out there...somewhere...back in her element.

There were three years, from 2006 to 2009, where Mommom's disease got greedy. Shortly after I left, it was deemed best to move her into a home with Poppop, a decision that brought them waves of temporary relief. But I don't think of those moments in those three years. I can't. I can't relive the convalescence Christmas party of '07, when Mommom and I locked eyes and it was all too clear that all of her magic was gone.

On the morning of Mommom's memorial in 2009, my Uncle Dave, Aunt Char, Mom, Dad, and brother all went to see my grandfather and show him the photo slide show that I mentioned at the beginning of this story. Just as my mother requested, I played the jolly Andrews Sisters' "Rum and Coca-Cola" song along with the show, but it did nothing to lighten the mood. Beluga, being a dick, sat on one side of Poppop and criticized the slide show the entire time—it was obvious what he was doing, evading his own feelings and attempting to get my sardonic uncle to join in. It was irritating, yet to feel anger toward my brother was better than to wade in what was happening: an old man—again in his diaper, was weaving his attention between a family slide show on a laptop and the infomercials on the outdated boxy TV in front of him. As he watched his wife's beautiful life flash before his eyes, all Poppop could do was sob. We weren't sure if he knew Mommom was gone, even with my mother yelling in an excruciatingly loud stage voice, "DAD, MOM HAS GONE TO SEE UNC, AND YOUR DAD, AND YOUR MOM, AND. . ." But, Mom's attempts to assuage Poppop's pain with a list of dead beloveds just made him cry more. I understood his response and perhaps we both were wondering the same thing...where were these people, *really?*

When the slide show ran its course, my mom and I took one last look through Mommom's room. I knew she had died of a heart attack while in the bathroom and I positioned myself so I wouldn't see that space. It was impossible for me to fathom catching a glimpse of any tile, any linoleum, any surface that she might have gripped or touched on her way out – alone.

As I was turning around to leave the room, something shimmery caught my eye and I paused. In the closet, popping out of a giant black trash bag, there it was . . . one of the purple sequined shoes we had bought together at Mervyn's.

It grinned at me and said "Here I am! Here I am! Thought you could just leave without saying goodbye?" Up until that moment I hadn't broken down, but when I saw that shoe I grabbed my mouth and let out a wail that came from a very old place, a very primal place. Without pause, my mom grabbed me.

"Oh, Chris, what is it?" she asked.

I leaned forward and pointed at the shoe.

"That shoe, that shoe," I shrieked through a bright-red face. Monica, Mommom's very sweet Romanian caretaker, walked by and must have internally rolled her eyes at all my pointing and sobbing about a *shoe.*

Oh, but that shoe . . .

I can still see it—shiny, crisp, functional, and even happy looking. It was perfect - it was her favorite color, the right size, it was comfortable, it was goofy enough with its excessive sequins. The shoe encapsulated my time with Mommom. It held the possibility of healing, of regenerating, of bringing my grandmother back in a time when she had been humiliated and hung out to dry. That shoe - as silly as it sounds, that shoe healed us both. Still, I was unable to articulate to my mother what I was thinking.

My mind flashed back to the fluorescent-lit Mervyn's where I found the shoe. *I was there.* I heard Blink-182 playing on the fuzzy outdated department store radio, I smelled the commercial carpet, the newness of the merchandise. Somehow, I was frozen in time as I revisited the sequence that brought those magical shoes to Mommom. A succession of these perfect little beats unfolded in my mind in a manner similar to the same grade school sequencing exercises I had been mandated to practice by the state of New York (at the Resource Center).

1. Searching every box for a #11 sticker.

2. Finding that box with that perfect #11 sticker gleaming in yellow.

3. Placing the purple shoe on the floor so Mommom could step into it.

4. Watching the back of Mommom's gray bobbed haircut as she stepped into the purple shoe.

5. Holding my breath as she pressed her heel down and seeing the shoe fit perfectly.

6. The moment of anticipation as she pivoted her ankle in front of the awkward, boxy shoe mirror, taking in her new look.

7. The expression on her face when she turned to me – that flash of excitement, the crinkle of her mouth, leading to that smile...

8. Our triumphant walk to the cashier.

9. The perfectly normal chitchat during our transaction.

10. Watching as the Mervyn's bag was handed over to Mommom.

11. And finally, walking out of the store feeling like we'd really found something, together.

How could I possibly explain this all to my mother? I had no way to tell her what I suddenly knew – that Mommom and I had solved our own sequencing exercise. That together we reordered the sequence and, for a short while, an elderly woman with Alzheimer's had reversed the grip of that awful disease. That for one summer, we had done something inconceivable; that we stopped time and took it back for ourselves. I never told my Mom what I was thinking because there is no way to explain what happened during that summer without calling it exactly what it was – magic.

Interrupting this discovery, my mother asked, bluntly: "do you want to take the shoe?"

Do I want to take the shoe?

I ran with this idea for a moment. What kind of home could I give that shoe? I played through the scenarios:

1. I use it as a doorstop.

2. I kill spiders with it.

3. I scare children with it.

4. I slap it on the ground to accompany a big, belly laugh.

5. I place it in a rotating dessert display case and showcase it like a slice of diner pie.

6. I attach it to a sturdy gold chain and wear it.

I took a big breath and got back to the moment. *That shoe, that shoe.* "I can't take *that*," I told her.

And never in my life will I be so correct. Because I can't. That shoe was too precious for me. I can't hold that spirit. Try as I might to cart that giant artifact around, its might is not mine. And as much as I, and we, need to take something with us after death takes someone from us, it's not our place to do so. All we can take is the belief that there will be other sequined shoe sightings, or ducks waddling by, or a faint sparkle in a body of water that's *just right.* We can take *those* winks, *those* nods from above and beyond.

Because *that* wonder is ours to keep. Yes, that's our *magic.*

PART IV
Boys to Man

CHAPTER 14
The Great Pumpkin

B ack in the day, when I was one of 28,000 undergraduate students at the University of Washington, I became an elite member of a very mediocre sorority. The rationale for joining a sorority was so it would make a big campus feel small and make me feel...fat! I didn't really fit into the Greek system, but it provided a tremendous opportunity for me to showcase my unique talent for breaking any and all rules. For that reason, and for a few others (the oddball friends I collected), I adored my two years living in the Zeta house.

My best pranks in the sorority house were made possible by a tape recorder that was required for my riveting "Anthro 101" course. The tape recorder had a function for playback at accelerated speed, also known as "chipmunk mode." Much like Batman's goofy-talkin' antagonist Bane (in *The Dark Knight Rises*), I too terrorized *my* Gotham—the Zeta house. As a freshman, we had mandatory "phone duty," where we had to serve as an operator/dispatch for all five of our sorority's land lines. In addition to this, we had to open the doors like a real-deal Upper Westside doorwoman. Once I discovered that I could use phone duty to broadcast myself as an f-bomb-dropping chipmunk, I delighted in annoying all ninety residents of the house with a play-by-play of sorority life as if I were their chipmunk sister.

In chipmunk voice.

"Sarah H., you have a man on the mezzanine. He looks like he's got a nice set of nuts . . . and you know how I feel about nuts. . . . "

"Julie C., a package just arrived for you from Spokane. If you're not down here in thirty seconds to claim it, I'm pissing on it and bringing it back to my tree."

"This announcement is to inform all Zeta's that tonight's dinner will again be motherfucking *meatloaf.*"[5]

I finally got busted for using the intercom "disrespectfully" when I interrupted an "executive council" meeting held in our formal living room. From our second-floor intercom, I pretended to be our sorority's very serious patron goddess, Themis. To the senior sisters, this was a *major* no-no.

In chipmunk voice.

"Greetings, *earthlings.* It is I, your patron goddess, Themis. Obey my commands and no one will perish under my awesome tits of justice! Deliver one fresh, toasted ham-and-cheese sandwich to room 106. Oh, and bring me two cans of pineapple juice, too. Obey my demands, little girlies, or I'll give you all HPV!"

This behavior and others like it eventually resulted in some well-deserved punishment from the executive council. In one case, I was required to star in our themed fraternity/sorority exchange. Our "social exchanges" were always thrown with a vague theme that ultimately required the women to dress like strippers, and for both groups of young men and women to drink cups and cups and cups of grain alcohol.

In 2001, *The Sopranos* was in its heyday, and so our exchange theme with the Pi Krappa Kri fraternity (name changed to protect the

5   Meatloaf is (and always will be) the most *disgusting* use of meat and loaf. The invention of meatloaf will go down as our species' greatest shame.

innocent) was "Mafia wedding." I would play the role of Mafia trash-ball bride-to-be. It was a role I was born to play. As for the ceremony, I walked down the aisle in front of maybe sixty or more people and exchanged poorly written "humorous" vows with an idiot boy, concluding with our faux priest proclaiming, "You may kiss the whore." I wasn't sure if I should make out with the idiot groom or not, but I identified as an actor and there was an audience, so I decided to go for it. Shortly after the ceremony, during our "wedding reception," I got a divorce. He had, and I say this with a loving heart, the personality of a dead betta fish. Not long after my divorce, a different guy, a tall guy, approached me. Derek. He was thin and he looked a little like 54th Speaker of the House, Paul Ryan (meaning that he looked rich, stupid, and definitely guilty).

"Congrats on your marriage," he yelled over a delicious Nelly song.

"I'm actually divorced. Are you Jewish?" I screeched back, making sure I wasn't wasting my time with a gentile.

"I'm half Jewish. Half German." He laughed.

"Oh . . . so, you must really hate yourself."

"Huh?" he asked, genuinely perplexed.

"The German half hates the . . . you know what, forget it." I didn't feel like explaining it.

"Oh, I get it. Ha-ha. You're funny," he added.

"Thanks for the validation," I said, while kind of smiling.

We continued to scream at each other while rowdy wedding guests bumped into us. Finally, we found a corner near a fire escape that was quieter, and he requested that I continue to do "Mafia voice." He was raised in Seattle so for him a New York accent was considered 'ethnic.' I obliged his request, picturing my beloved school bus driver, Liz, who would scream at us every day: "I'm axing youzzz *one* mowaah time. Youz guys behduhh *sidowwwn.*"

That accent (and its effect on the tall guy) marked the beginning of a very ugly relationship.

Despite the fact that not one of my friends liked Derek, I still did. They thought he was cheap (he'd ask for people to chip in five dollars for Red Bull if we were having the classic cocktail of Red Bull and vodka). They thought he was boring and selfish (he was an engineering major and he was an only child). My friends also nicknamed him "Robot" because of the way he held his arms, which for some freaky reason were not fully extendable at the elbow. They also hated his thick Northwest accent (okay, maybe that was me), a dialect that is best described as sounding like a Southern California accent with a retainer in. He also worked at Costco, which was fine until the day I saw him dressed up in his Costco vest. Sure, I've had some weird work uniforms, but only dogs can pull off vests.

Nevertheless, I was eighteen and like all eighteen-year-olds, I wanted to believe I was in love enough to have sex. Besides, it wasn't like there were better fish in the sea—this was college and most of the fish (like my Mafioso ex-husband, the dead betta fish) were at best farm-raised carp.

About three months into our mediocre relationship, we went to a black-light party at Derek's frat (yep, life was *that* good). I got dolled up in the 2001 sorority uniform (spaghetti-strap top, tight black pants, and frosted lip gloss), and Derek and I made out under a black light after several shots of vodka that had been "infused" with a single Jolly Rancher. It was *incredibly* college-romantic. After we'd sufficiently made out, we went back into his room. He sat down at his computer and told me, "I have something I want you to read."

I walked over to his computer, where a Word document was open on the screen. It was a letter confessing that he was very much in love with me. Now, at this point in life I had never received a love letter, but I had seen (and hated many) romantic movies. What he had presented was a poorly written single paragraph of loosely strung-together Hallmark clichés. Plus, the dickhead hadn't even printed it out! For the love of blue cheese, at least *print* the damn "love document!"

I finished reading it and a thought jumped out of my mouth before I could filter it (thank you, Jolly Rancher vodka): "You cheated on me."

After I spoke I looked around the room to see if it was in fact someone else who had said it.

He denied it, of course, but the way he denied it was all too suspicious. The apparent desperation of presenting an unprinted, unsaved "I love you" doc . . . it was a little too fishy. I repeated the statement "You cheated on me" much like Robin Williams repeated "it's not your fault" to Matt Damon in *Good Will Hunting*. Much like Damon, Derek broke down and began sobbing. He explained that a girl named Marie, a frequent Pi Krappa Kri frat groupie, had offered him a good ol' fashioned BJ (that's "blowjob") in the bathroom. He had accepted her offer and so she performed the job right there in the bathroom.

After hearing this, I balled up my fist (as if to punch him) and slapped him hard across the face. He responded by repeating more clichés. "Please, it didn't mean anything." Despite his attempts to apologize, all the clichés just made me angrier, and so I slunched him again.[6] As I was attempting to leave the room, he grabbed my shoulders to keep me there. This tactic, on his part, brought out my slunchiest slunch yet. I slunched him so hard that he went down, and I stormed out the door.

The following day was especially rough, but for some silly reason I figured the best distraction from my pain was to attend my Psych 101 lecture. As luck would have it, this massive lecture was one that I also shared with Marie. I didn't know her, but apparently, she knew me.

---

6   *Slunch* refers to a slap-punch hybrid, a popular form of drunken aggression most commonly practiced by sorority girls. Also important to note — I've since learned how to punch and quite enjoy boxing.

Amidst all the slunching the previous night, Derek warned me that I shared a class with her. After he shared this information, I demanded a description of Marie. Through tears, Derek said she was "short, with platinum blonde hair, and very, *very* tan skin." *Fine.* I was certain I could go to the massive lecture hall with 500 other students and just ignore her. And surely for most people that could be possible, but with Marie it was not, for you see "very tan skin" was a merely polite way to convey that Marie was *a human pumpkin.*

When I say that Marie looked like a pumpkin, I mean she looked like she was plucked directly from the patch and sprayed with carrot juice. She even had a stem, which was a thin ponytail of crispy white hair. Her hair was thin, limp, and much like the obnoxious fuzz you encounter when shucking corn on the cob. Like all pumpkins, she had no chin. Oh, and let's not forget her eyes — her eyes were pinched tight and were the color of lukewarm black tea. If you haven't gone there already, I'll save you the trouble and just say it: Marie looked like a clone of our 45th pumpkin president.

Seeing Marie in psych class was painful, but I decided I would do the hard thing and forgive Derek and stay together (and by forgive, I mean 'remind Derek of his mistake *every fucking day*). For example, whenever we played that popular college game of Never Have I Ever, I'd open with, "Never have I ever cheated on my girlfriend with a pumpkin." Ours was certainly not the most functional of relationships, but it seemed only logical to an impatient person (me) to take the next step. After enough time had gone by for my Ortho Tri-Psycho birth control to kick in and make me a true hormonal masterpiece, Derek and I set a date to have sex for the first time. Yes, I set a date several weeks in advance. My friends still love to tease me about this, but, what can I say—I find structure and organization to be incredibly hot (also, I'm a *weeeeeeeeeeee* bit of a control freak). I'll spare you the details, aside from this: Derek lived up to his nickname, "Robot."

The hardest thing about choosing to stay with the person who cheated on me was the fact that the pumpkin haunted me – she was miraculously everywhere all the time, like some kind of *terrible* Pumpkin Jesus. "Pumpy," as I started calling her, attended all the same social functions: the fraternity dances, concerts, and, just a week after Derek and I first had sex, she showed up on our camping trip. It was a shock to see her there, mostly because it seemed like dangerous territory for a loose pumpkin (if we ran out of food, we'd eat her first, no question). To survive that run-in with her, I repeatedly visualized a crazed farmer scooping out her brains to make an award-winning pumpkin pie. *Again, definitely not living my best life at this point in time.*

Much like Marie's flat hair, Derek and my relationship limped along, but about a month after our "sex appointment," as my friends called it, Derek and I were fighting like we were on a reality TV show. Though our troubles continued, I tried to keep us together. As my sophomore year of college began, so did his interviews of new blow-job applicants.

This time it was an equally freaky character, not the headless horseman, but "Horse-Face" (a nickname given by my bestie Lindsey). Horse-Face was probably an inch taller than me, as narrow as a book, with a posture most similar to Ichabod Crane, and a face *only* a horse mother could love. Her best feature was her long, horsey hair and her adorable horse-like stupidity. Horse-Face had the kind of look on her that suggested you could stick anything in her (in any hole) and she would keep smiling. Still, I was assured by Derek that he and Horse-Face were "just friends" and I accepted that, until I got the call. . . .

Derek dumped me on the same phone where I'd done so many of my phone duties (*hahaha*) as a freshman. I screamed at him as loudly as I could, shared as many insults as I could muster (heaps of 'em; thank you Ortho-Tri-Psycho!), and hoped that most of my sorority had heard—and *they had.* When I ran to my room sobbing, I fell down and had to be picked up by my bestie Krisa. It was all very Jane Austen. *I gave my virginity to Mr. Darcy who had previously cheated on me with a pumpkin, and wouldn't you know it? Tis a pity he left me for Horse-Face!*

The period that followed, what I now refer to as "the Drunk Years," was as important as it was terrifying to those who were closest to me. Much like Van Gogh's final years at the hospital in Saint-Paul-de-Mausole, it was a productive, if not extremely dark time for me. I purposely hurt people, I didn't want to share, and I wrote terrible poetry.

A year later, after I had dated a few decent dudes, the robot had gotten all the horse out of his system, and he contacted me. He had just returned from an international trip where he got some clarity and he told me the mother of all clichés: "breaking up with you was the biggest mistake of my life." Two weeks later, we were talking on the phone when he defended a mutual friend who had cheated on his girlfriend. "It was just a mistake; people make mistakes," he said.

Right then and right there, I had a thought: forgiving someone for repeatedly making the same mistake can *also* be a mistake! I lit into the robot:

"TWO MISTAKES DON'T MAKE AN ERASER, FUCK-WAD!"

I stayed true to the mantra for three years, and did not see Robot. However, when I was back in Seattle taking care of my grandmother, and feeling mildly nostalgic for shitty college sex, I reunited with Robot. We hung out a few times and had exactly the same shitty robot sex as four years earlier.

During our post-college reunions and following one of our boring romps at his apartment, I laid in bed, deep in thought. It was all very bittersweet, to be with someone who knew me for four years, even if he was a dipshit. He was a decent person, right? I mean, who knows? My grandmother had Alzheimer's; maybe one day I'd get it, too, and just forget he was a flaming douchebag! I looked over at him while he was powered down and in his robot "sleep mode." Still contemplating,

I stared up at the ceiling, where, like the king of all tools, he'd hung a surfboard. *Ugh.* Maybe surfing is cool? *Am I being too critical again?*

BUZZ. BUZZ. BUZZ.

It was his cell phone displaying a text message from "Jessica." I leaned over the nightstand and read the screen.

"Hey, baby, I miss U. Can't wait 2 C U tomorrow. Luv U."

Shit.

Oh no.

I swallowed hard. I've heard this story before.

Just like Charlie Brown's buddy Linus (from *Peanuts*) waited for the Great Pumpkin to show on Halloween, I too was waiting and wasting my life, blindly investing in a relationship that never existed. Indeed, some relationships are certainly worthy of full-fledged forgiveness, but this one was just a trick, an illusion that I kept alive through my own delusions (just like Linus did when he waited for that imaginary pumpkin to show up).

To this day, I find it difficult to pick up a pumpkin and *not* think of Marie, but I don't regret my great pumpkin experience, or my "pumpkin passage" as I like to call it. An old family friend once shared a quote that always made sense to me: "If I could do it all again, I'd make the same mistakes, only I'd make them sooner." So, I'll say this — sometimes you have to figure out who *isn't* worthy of your forgiveness before you figure out who *is.*

PS: if you ever see anyone with a surfboard displayed in their home (especially their bedroom) ...*RUN.* Run far and fast and don't look back.

PPS: pumpkin spice lattes. Boo. They suck.

CHAPTER 15
The 30-Second Fart

I'm not a fan of watching televised sports. I don't like the monotone and post-apocalyptic-sounding announcers, and I can't stand the synchronized oohs and ahs that fans make—it's just further proof that we're all a bunch of sheep. And yes, I know what you're thinking "but you'd like it if you watched the game at my place because we'll have beer and chili, and I make *the best* jalapeño poppers." *OH! OH! OH! Stop the presses! Did you say chili and beer?!* Listen sweetheart, I don't need a sporting event to grant me permission to drink beer at 10 am on Sunday.

With that said, if someone is watching an NBA game, I'll sit down for a hot minute to watch the arms. When I see NBA arms, I feel things. I wouldn't call myself a man-izer by any stretch, but, if I were of the *Mad Men* era, I'd purposely surround myself with long, strong, male arms. I'd only hire "arms" to be my secretaries, and I'd sexually harass them in a non-threatening (non-power dynamic abusing, non-Spacey, non-Cosby, non-Weinstein-y, non-Lauer-y, non-Louis C.K., non...okay you get the point...) way. What I'm trying to say here is: I'm an Arm-y.

And, as it so happens, I have exquisitely sculpted basketball player arms to thank for the most supernatural experience of my life.

Picture it. A late night in Madison, Wisconsin, in the fall of 2004.

He wasn't that smart but I wasn't that sober, *and* he was six-foot-seven.

He looked like Screech from *Saved by the Bell*, only his hair was of a looser curl and he was built like a Goddammed rocket ship. I walked into his house party on a whim with a friend during my first week as a grad student at the University of Wisconsin. I struck up a conversation with him the same way I did with most men I took interest in—as if I worked for the CIA (cool, logical, and always with my shirt tucked in). He was looking nervously at a bleach blond who was eyeing both of us. In an act of desperation, Bleachy had taken off her pants for all the party to see. It was all very *Girls Gone Wisconsin.* Bleachy gave me a look, a big one. I turned to Screech-ship and gave him my official CIA report.

"What's the deal there? She blew you, eh? Now she's feeling regretful and wanting control back. So naturally, the pants had to go."

He was stunned that I had been able to decode her disrobing. I was stunned he was stupid enough to admit to it. It became clear to me in that moment that he was *very* stupid. Ah, yes, but he was also *very* tall. As our conversation continued, I decided to rename him "Arms," only because his real name was the same as another dumb jock I had dated in high school. I refused to date two dumb guys with the same dumb name; now *that* would be very dumb.

We started to . . . I guess you could call it "date," though they were mostly group bar outings or movie rentals. Our hookups were only possible if alcohol joined in, and even then, they were terrible. On a good day, I'm five foot seven—a full foot shorter than Arms—and let's just say that NBA players aren't exactly known for their flexibility.

The only thing I found interesting about Arms was his height and the way he rounded vowels when he spoke in his traditional Midwestern accent. His favorite bar, as luck would have it, was called Johnny O's. If one says, "Johnny O's" in a Midwestern accent, it comes out like "Jaahhhh-KNEE-Ohhhhwwwws." Oftentimes, I'd lie and tell Arms I had a "bad cell signal" and thus needed him to repeat himself, holding the receiver away from my mouth as I giggled at his accent like an asshole. Also, *mildly* interesting and *mostly* uncool was Arms' temper. One time, I playfully pinched his nose and he flew off the handle, yelling at me in his thick Midwestern accent, which just sounded like he was that angry Aflac duck (see commercials on YouTube). I thought his severe reaction was a joke, but it wasn't. Not fifteen minutes after his outburst, he slapped my ass so hard I burped. No, this was not what I'd call a 'healthy' relationship.

Arms and I even encountered a little drama in our fake dating—I didn't like the fact that he was gifted a female stripper for his birthday. Oddly enough, I asked an ex-boyfriend for his input (the same dipshit you just read about in Chapter 15).

"Hey, do guys *actually* like strippers?" I asked, desperately.

"No," said the ex. "They smell terrible—over perfumed and cheap."

His response didn't help—for one, my ex wasn't so much a human as he was a piece of shit, and two, I ended up just feeling sorry for the stripper. I pictured her applying a perfume that her beloved grandmother had given her for Passover/Easter (in my imagining of things, she grew up happily celebrating both).

Though Arms and I made tentative plans to meet up after he watched the stripper, he never did call. In what I think was an attempt to apologize for his behavior, Arms invited me to dinner. I picked him up, because Arms didn't drive anything other than his f-ing scooter (I know what you're thinking, but he was 6' 7"!). We went to a local Wisconsin take-out noodle joint, brilliantly named Noodles. I placed my order of "garlic, chicken, butter, cheese, butter cheese, and extra cheese" and he ordered his, "macaroni noodles with light olive oil." You see, as a basketball player, he was training for the Big Ten; meanwhile, I was training for a big shit.

Back at my house we ate our meals, watching *The Ladykillers* (FML), just killing time to prove that we could. He went into the freezer to mix himself a glass of ice water (again, he's in training) and found a ginger root that I stored in the freezer. He yelled dramatically in a thick Wisconsin accent.

"Oh my Gahhhd. You have a tree root growing in your freezer!" Arms exclaimed.

"Yes, I do," I responded, just to see what I could get him to believe.

"But *why?*" he asked.

"I'm participating in a study to develop a new species of frozen tree, to be grown in a remote colony in Antarctica."

"Ohhhhh. *Wow.*"

Arms' inability to process sarcasm inspired a strong desire in me to binge eat any and all foods my body had difficulty digesting. I busted out Breyers coffee ice cream, and we each had a mug's worth, and then I went back for more. It was simple: I would eat my boredom until I ate his arms.

Shortly after my third mug of ice cream, I noticed some rumbling in my tummy. I ignored it, because that's what we do with gas in public; we tell it to go away, and it (usually) obeys. To coat my internal stew of garlic cheese noodles and coffee ice cream, I made some chai tea. Just as the caffeinated concoction inside me was beginning to talk (and possibly walk), Arms started to tell me about something serious.

"I have to tell you something scary," he started. "My best friend who lives in Colorado—he nearly died last night."

Oh no, I thought. Not the roommate—oh that's scary, yes, of course—but I need to fart. Otherwise I'm going to . . . *fart.* Arms ignored my neurotic arm and leg crossing and continued to vent.

"It was a bad drug trip. They found him lying there on his back and they rushed him to the hospital. . . ."

This continued to the tune of "Blah blah blah, go Paaaahhhckers (Packers), go Baaaahhhhdgers (Badgers), cheese curds, brats . . . Aflac." My mind was on one thing and one thing only: God. Yes, like most disgruntled white people, I'm agnostic, sometimes atheist, but, in this moment, I was Jesus Christ, on the cross, begging for God to prevent the superhuman pressure about to blow. I squirmed, I crossed my legs, I re-crossed them. I turned my body into the tightest pretzel you've ever seen. I tried to scare the excess air away by clearing my throat loudly—all the while nodding and consoling Arms as he blabbed *on and on* about his friend. I prayed to a deceased family friend; I asked her to cause some sudden distraction so I could get to the bathroom and detonate my asshole.

Just as I was about to pass out from holding my breath, I heard a little voice respond to my prayer. The voice came directly from my butt and it said: "*Eeeeeuaaaahhhh. Eeeeeuaaahhhh.*"

At first, I thought it was a fever dream—there was no way I suddenly couldn't control my own body. But, as if an old white man had possessed me, I continued to release what would end up being an uncontrollable, melodic, multisyllabic, THIRTY-SECOND FART. With the first couple of high-pitched squeals, I immediately turned into a bright-red fire truck. I clutched my temples as the supernatural gas played a concerto of Beethoven-inspired high notes. Arms was completely, out-of-his-mind shocked by the duration of my fart and so he just giggled.

Hee hee hee, ho ho ho.

The worst part of the situation was that I couldn't move for fear of what might fall out of me. I was frozen solid — a petrified, red-faced farting deer—caught in headlights that were laughing at me.

The sounds progressed into what you might call a dolphin mating call: *eee, eee, eee, eee.* Then it changed into what I'd call the trombone, a sliding, deep, tonal masterpiece. It was the machine gun expulsion that actually startled Arms, with its violent and seemingly endless rounds of: *furt, furt, furt, furt, furt, furrrrrr, rur, rur, rur, rurt, furt, furt.* My asshole concerto ended on the chipmunk exhale: *hafffffffffffff,* which sounded just like a city bus lowering me to the stop at Humiliation Street.

Somewhere around machine gun, Arms, looking genuinely petrified, asked "Are you okay?"

He was sure I wasn't, because I could not respond. I'd never been more humiliated in my entire life, and I had *zero* strategy for how to recover. My only solution was to act gravely concerned about my own health. Amidst the most amazing fart production of my life, I wasn't even laughing, I was acting *serious!*

To this day, that is one of my biggest life regrets—that I felt ashamed of this supernatural miracle.

I stood up after the thirty seconds and went to the bathroom. I can't fathom the smell I left behind. While in the bathroom I sat on the toilet and felt like . . . shit. I realized that Arms was waiting in the living room, fully certain that I was now taking a *massive* dump.

A few deep breaths later, I emerged from the bathroom saying sadly, "I don't know what's wrong with me." I drove Arms home and along the way we smelled a skunk. The irony was completely lost on him, but, being my witty self, I said of the smell: "It smells like a dog shit his pants."

"Ummmm, dogs don't wear pants," Arms responded, missing the joke (again).

Neither of us laughed. He was right, after all. Indeed, *dogs don't wear pants.*

That was the last time we had a date. He called again, but I played defensive. I didn't like who I was around him. I felt like part of me was lost on him: my sarcasm for one, but mostly my best and brightest farts.

A year later, as luck would have it, I shared a shuttle bus with Arms from Chicago's O'Hare airport to Madison, after visiting my best friend in Phoenix. First of all, NO ONE returns from Phoenix looking good, but if you've spent a long weekend drinking your weight in margaritas, you look *extra not good.* There I was, on the year anniversary of farting uncontrollably for 30 seconds, smelling like stale tequila and taquitos, looking like I'd crawled directly out of Satan's anus, attempting to find an empty seat in the back of the bus without losing too much dignity. I kept my head down *until...*wait a minute. Arms was a fifth-year senior in college a year earlier, and here I was, an accomplished farter (who, fine, okay, *may* have left her wallet at the Prickly Cactus in AZ, and so she smelled like goat bile) but, hey — at least I wasn't in college for a sixth year!

The true tragedy in this story isn't the cruel irony that (of course) I *had* to use the toilet on the bus (which meant I was forced to walk by Arms) — it's that I can't ever re-create the miracle of what happened in those thirty seconds of fart. I know this because I've very earnestly tried to recreate it.

What I did take away from the experience, however, was a nice little litmus test for every guy I met after Arms. I told the "thirty-second fart story" on every first date. My dates' reactions, either disgusted or delighted, said a lot about the fate of our relationship. The experience also forced me to finally own up to the fact that I LOVE FART HUMOR. If anyone, friend or lover, can't appreciate the hilarity of God's great design, that our asses *actually talk,* I can't have them in my life. Farting is one of the most spectacular experiences human beings can share together. Shoot, my "thirty-second fart" story has been used by several of my girlfriends on their dates, and others have retold it to their families around the Thanksgiving table. My thirty-second fart legacy is spreading joy and inspiration for those still stuck in those lame twenty-second fart clubs.

In closing, I'll just say that our bodies often know better than we do, and if we're lucky, they speak up for us. For most of my courtship with Arms, I was sitting on my words, holding in things I felt I needed to say, worrying I might sound vulnerable, uncool, or too smart. I wasted time pretending I could look past things that mattered to me just because he had (*really*) nice arms. But the truth is, and I think this is a great thing about being human, one way or another...shit just comes out.

CHAPTER 16
Mother Nose Best

Mother knows best, that's what they say. Ah, but they don't know *my* mother.

In my case, it's mother *nose* best, because my mother's sense of smell is on par with a grizzly bear in heat. Her olfactory gifts have even earned her the nickname Mama Bear. Aside from her overdeveloped sense of smell, she's physically not very bearlike at all. She's a dancer, an artist, and a connoisseur of cheap chardonnay. Our relationship has thrived because of our ability to go three or four weeks without talking and then to make up for those weeks of "hibernation" by spending four or so hours on the phone. If I'm lucky during one of those four-hour calls, Mama Bear will read off her latest "hisssss-terical" Hallmark card that she has squirreled away in case of a birthday card emergency. Other times, she'll read me the blurb on the back of whatever book-on-tape she's got on loan from the public library. Most of these books will "change my life," she *insists*. Many times, I believe her, but I also put her on speakerphone so those around can chuckle at her conviction.

What sets my mom apart from other mothers is her ability to swiftly and effortlessly extract the truth from her cubs. She's gotten dirt out of my brother, so much dirt that he views her as some kind of a confessional sphinx. I've watched my sister-in-law drop some doozies, not to mention some of the most tight-lipped humans on the planet, who all confide in Mama Bear.

I will say that having a mother who can smell your lies is a great recipe for raising an "inappropriately honest" child. My mother knows every detail about every boyfriend I've ever had, which is why she's disliked most of them. This story, about a Wisconsin boyfriend, is one of my favorites because it involves the utilization of Mama Bear's (long-distance) sense of smell.

Madison, Wisconsin.

After becoming abundantly drunk off Mr. Boston vodka and Diet Cherry Vanilla Dr. Pepper (yes, this was a thing that existed and I consumed), I went out with an old friend (who was in town visiting) to hunt for men. At a hip bar that had a layout like a narrow triangle, I saw two guys sitting down and looking perfectly average. At that very drunken moment, all I could distinguish was that they were dressed brightly, they had eyes and noses, and mouths curled into smiles. With that visual and my drunken state of mind, I could have been talking to a Picasso painting. In any event, the following day I received a call from one of the Picasso subjects.

I told my friend (who also met him the previous night) about the call from the Picasso painting. She didn't respond enthusiastically.

"What's that reaction about?" I asked her.

"It's—it's stupid. It's just . . . his butt was kind of big," she said, apologetically.

"What a weird thing for you to notice," I added.

"It . . . like . . . it wasn't proportional to the rest of him," she said, very seriously.

"Huh . . . well, you know what they say about big butts?"

"Big shits, *I know.*" She replied, predicting my punch line like only a best friend can.

I decided to give ol' big ass a try, and we arranged to have a coffee. When I met "Norm" (we'll call him) I was shocked to see that he looked nothing like a Picasso painting. Norm was very J. Crew, Whole Foods, and the kind of tool that would host a "viewing party" for the Tour de France. He had big eyes, a good WASP-y smile, and . . . wait, holy moly . . . his ass. It was like God ran out of appropriate matches for his top half and his bottom half, so he just stuck two honey-baked hams below his long, boring, white guy back. Norm's hammy ass annoyed me, but he seemed smart, and nice. He was in his last year of law school and I liked that because I've always hated lawyers and imagined we'd have plenty of epic fights.

After we passed the preliminary interview (coffee date), we arranged dinner the following week. In honor of it, I went to Marshalls and got an irregular BCBG very low-cut turquoise sweater that would accentuate my . . . personality. Our dinner conversation was good. Norm didn't have a terribly thick Midwestern accent; it was only a few words that came out nasal-y. Other weird pronunciations: "fire" was pronounced *fuh-eye-errr,* along with "admire" which sounded like *ADD-m-eye-err.* Norm's laugh, however, was intolerable. He clenched his jaw and made a hissing noise on the inhale, like he was hyperventilating in spastic beats. The first time I heard him laugh, I described it in my journal (*yes, really,* I journaled about it) as "a manic-depressive Dust Buster brought to life."

After our dinner date we went back to his apartment, where, upon entering I smelt it. *What on earth is that smell?* Was Norm's entire apartment sprayed down with the musk of a pants-less seventy-five-year-old hippie dude wearing patchouli oil? I tried to ignore the smell because I wanted to like Norm. I mean, he was tall, he was smart, and with him around I'd never feel insecure about the size of my own ass. We got into a heated make-out session on his rug. The smells were especially pungent down there, where two years of his human dander had accumulated.

The next day I called my Mama Bear.

As a dancer and frequent flier, she was (and still is) the queen of public dancing, using any public windowsill as her ballet barre. At every and any given airport, she'd *plié, rond de jambe,* and *grand battement* in black outfits paired with thick eyeglasses—like a nerdy black swan. On this particular call, she was at her ballet barre in the San Francisco International Airport. She was en route to Papua New Guinea to help my dad study ocean mud (which has an oddly similar smell to Norm's apartment - hints of "decomposing sulfuric waste").

"Well, how was it?" she pried, while, I imagine, holding a relevé.

It has always been impossible to not tell my mother what I don't want to tell her. Meaning - I tell my mother everything. This being the norm in our relationship, she can smell when something ain't right, and something wasn't right with Norm.

"We had sushi, soft-shell crab, it was fun, and"—under my breath—"he kind of smelled like shit."

There was a pause so long that I thought she dropped the call.

"Ma? Hello?" I asked.

"He *smelled?*" Mom practically cried as she asked.

"Yeahhhh..." I replied, sheepishly.

"Oh no. *No,* that won't work. I love Dad's smell; he doesn't even have to wear cologne. I love his sweat—it's just *so* good. I could bottle—"

"OKAY. I get it. Well, maybe it's not that bad. I'm probably just exaggerating. Let me double-check." I reached over to my laundry pile and took a whiff of the turquoise BCBG personality sweater I'd worn on our date. "Oh, sweet mother of mercy, that's *bad.. .*"

"What?" Mom asked. "What does it smell like?"

"Like what I imagine Christopher Walken's breath to smell like... dead skin cells, week-old gas-station coffee, and...decomposing whale balls."

"Oh, *Chris.* No. No way. No thank you. Well, at least you know it won't work."

"Maybe you're right."

"I am," she responded with an annoying conviction.

After my conversation with Mama Bear, I called Norm and arranged another date. Even though he smelled like a bad idea, I had to prove Mama Bear wrong. Two days later, Norm and I were deep into our date, and another steamy make-out session, when he pulled away because he had something *important* to tell me.

"Yeah, I am not ready to date right now. I just—I've been thinking a lot about Kate."

"Excuse me...what now? How now? Who now?" This was what I said aloud, but internally, it was *who-in-the-actual-fuck-is-Kate?*

"She broke up with me last summer and I can't stop thinking about her and that's unfair to you. I mean, I miss everything about her. I miss her hair, her skin, her smile, her personality, her body, the way she'd—"

"Yeah . . . yeah . . . I think I got it." I interrupted.

"Do you think we could still be friends?" Norm asked, cheerfully, as if he were suddenly Ronald Mc-fucking-Donald handing out a Happy Meal.

I had a quiet moment where I knew I had a choice—I could walk away and not speak to him again, or I could walk away and concoct a plan to make him rue the day *he* friend zoned *me.* I chose the latter because I was in Wisconsin and I didn't have cable.

"Of course we can be friends!" I said, smiling through a clenched jaw. I gave him a playful slugger punch on the arm and saw myself out.

In the weeks that followed, my "friendship plan" worked brilliantly to get under Norm's stinky skin. Whenever we were together, I poured on the wit and became a *fucking* pun factory. I even went to Target and bought the sexiest set of matching hat and mittens (which is the equivalent of a string bikini for Midwesterners).

One night after studying in the law library, Norm suggested we have a nightcap at his place and discuss a *New Yorker* article he had photocopied for me (yes, he was that much of a douchebag). As I was making a comment, my ol' buddy, ol' pal, ol' chum Norm made a move. Though I was D-FUCKIN-LIGHTED, I stopped him.

"Wait, I'm confused. You can't befriend my cake and eat it, too."

"I'm so sorry," he apologized.

Yes, yes, yes! My plan was working! I left his place and spent four weeks apart from him during the long winter break. When I returned for the next semester, I figured he'd suffered long enough and I could lift our cute little "friendship" clause. We hooked up enough in the weeks that followed to have a tenuous "dating" label. During this period, I completely avoided talking to my mother about it because she couldn't get two seconds into hearing "Norm" and not ask me about his "bad" smell.

Norm and I continued to "date," though he had returned from his holiday break with a revitalized connection to Jesus Christ (of the Catholic variety). He was suddenly talking more and more about his savior and my sins. I met his cousin and his cousin's young family, an experience that straight-up put me off of kids for a solid eleven years (our dinner with the kids was chock full of what I'd call "sticky chaos.").

Still, we continued to pretend that we were a good couple and we even had very (*very, very*) bad sex. It seemed that with Norm's renewed commitment to Catholicism, he took the term *missionary* all too literally. Even worse was the face he made during his "missions." Norm's face looked like a platter at a Friday fish fry; he was pale, lifeless, and creepily wide-eyed. Sex with Norm was what I imagined sex in the early settler times to be like, in like, the worst ways – quick, quiet, and fraught with religious guilt. After we were finished, I was sure he'd do some pioneer shit, like "till the land with the mighty ox" but not before commanding me to churn butter with the other wenches.

When Valentine's Day arrived, a few days after we started having 18th-century sex, Norm completely forgot about the Catholic saint known as Saint *fucking* Valentine. After I told him that his behavior hurt my feelings, he drove over to my place with a "gift." Excited, I watched as he presented his gift—a plastic bag containing a men's razor and shaving cream. "I know you don't like making out with me when I have stubble," he shared. Don't be jealous ladies, but my Valentine gift that year was the late-night company of a clean-shaven idiot. *Winning!*

The truth was, our relationship was on tenuous ground, *but*...we did have fun together, and Wisconsin is one of those places that just might rival Los Angeles in terms of loneliness. I was happy to share his company. It was perfectly satisfactory for us to discuss a *New Yorker* article, or grab a beer together, shaven or not. Knowing I didn't want anyone to weigh in and disturb this mediocrity, I simply never brought Norm up around my mom because she couldn't resist asking detailed questions about his scent. Mama Bear also knew that I *had* to tell her the truth, which would involve describing his scent as if he came with a nutritional label: high-fructose corn-onions, moldy basement, old-man breath, and stale flower water.

One night, Norm came over and we cooked a particularly cozy dinner. After spending some time standing over simmering garlic and olive oil, I thought, *he smells better tonight; this could work.*

As we sat down to eat, we had the usual laughter and sarcastic exchanges. Near the end of our dinner, though, a cool disposition came over Norm. His posture changed and his eyes narrowed – it was as if he'd been given an order from some invisible dictator.

"I've been thinking," he said.

"That's . . . good. . . ." I said, not really listening and quite enjoying the hearty pork chop in front of me.

He got up from the dinner table and very dramatically walked a few steps to my futon and sat down. Something big was coming. I sat down next to him. I put my arm around him, doing my best to ignore the sudden scent of dick-and-balls that coated his clothes.

Just as I wrapped an arm around him, he stood up quickly. He was tall, and from my seated position he looked a little bit like Liesl Von Trapp's Nazi boyfriend in *The Sound of Music*. That's generally *not* a good sign, if the person you're dating suddenly stands up and address- es you like he is an active member of the Nazi party.

"What's the matter?" I asked.

Norm took a long beat while looking at the floor. He raised his head suddenly.

"I will never love you." Norm said, looking at me for the first time like I was a complete stranger.

Norm went on to tell me about Catholicism and purpose and all these holy things, but I couldn't hear it. All I could hear was "I will never love you." This phrase socked me in the gut the hardest because regardless of being a terrible boyfriend, he was, after all my friend. I love my friends; it seems bizarre to me that anyone could call someone a friend and *not* love them. I've always been of the belief that if you love someone you should tell them; why you'd ever deny them of that expression is completely nonsensical to me.

During his monologue, an odd swell of gas came up in me, much like the 30-second masterpiece that I released a few months earlier (see previous chapter). Thankfully, I learned my lesson and saved face in front of Norm by excusing myself to use the bathroom. Once in the bathroom, the horrible smell was, for the first time not his—it was now mine, and it was . . . well, pretty farty. I felt utterly humiliated, hurt, and afraid to face this stink head who told me I was unworthy of his love. *Fuck it.* I gathered myself, fanned the fart smell away with a waving arm, reentered the living room, and put on the show of a lifetime. On his way out and as some sort of conciliatory compliment, Norm told me, in the tooliest tone you can imagine:

"Ughhh . . . but you're *so* hot."

"Yep," I agreed. Following my cool response (it was pretty cool, in all honesty), Norm walked his double-ham ass out my door and that was it.

Mama Bear was out of town when the dumping took place, but I did e-mail her. Her written response was "Good riddance. P-U. That guy did not smell right." Just to be perfectly clear here, my mother never once met Norm, but she *still* insists she could identify his foul scent across continents and oceans.

Before we head into the final chapter, I'd like to go back to the *title* of our story, "Mother Nose Best." When my parents flew in to meet my now husband for the very first time, we arranged to greet each other at the University of Wisconsin's Memorial Student Union on Lake Mendota. It was a beautiful Friday afternoon in April—the place was packed with groups of friends meeting and drinking remarkably delicious Wisconsin beer.

Since my parents had never seen Andrew's face, I decided to have a little fun and with each new guy that walked by, I exclaimed, "That's him!" My dad fell for it a few times but my mom didn't buy it. While I was turned toward Lake Mendota, lost in conversation with my dad, I overheard a quiet sniffling coming from Mama Bear.

"Why are you crying, Mom?" I asked her.

She looked to the very edge of the terrace entrance, where she saw a young man walking toward the lake. This young man didn't know we were watching him; still, he had a distinctive grin on his face, and his poise oozed goodness and warmth. Mama Bear pointed directly at him.

"That's him. That's Andrew. *I know it*," she said, still crying as my dad and I laughed at her melodramatics.

But, she was right. And of course she was; Mama Bear could smell him a mile away.

CHAPTER 17
Going Rental in Reykjavik

One of my favorite pastimes while in grad school was to impersonate Fast Eddie Felson (Paul Newman in *The Hustler*) and hustle unsuspecting suckers at a brewery and pool bar in downtown Madison, WI, known as "The Great Dane." In truth, I'm a terrible pool player, but my hustlees had no idea. So, until I actually played pool, I got to pretend, for a hot second, that I was Paul Newman. Late one night, I approached a group of Midwest guys, introducing myself as Annie Jump Cannon, a skilled pool player who could "destroy any opponent" (AJC is a famous astronomer and was an idol of mine when I thought I might become an astronomy minor). My dear friend Michelle was all-in on the hustle, so while our opponents wrapped up their existing game, we decided a pitcher of beer was a necessary investment.

I didn't notice it at the time but throughout these transactions, Annie Jump Cannon was being tracked by a stranger who was very interested in challenging her to a game. The stranger was dressed casually in a button-up plaid shirt with a brown hat he had spun backwards, making him look like he belonged at a deli somewhere in the Tristate area. He and his friend challenged Annie Jump and Michelle to a game of pool. We accepted. After we "broke balls" (that thing you do when you first start a game, where you explode the happy triangle formation with the one white ball - again, I'm *not* good at pool), I and the backwards hat guy began a discussion of three topics: Scandinavian naturalist female playwrights, big dogs, and European travel. We both had returned from trips to Europe that summer (see chapter "I Love English") and had apparently missed each other by a day in Dublin. "It's too bad," we agreed, that we hadn't met in Ireland. That thought lingered a little longer than either of us expected; maybe because in that moment we were both imagining a stroll down a cobblestone street, with historical sights and smells wafting about, as we ripped each other's clothing off. We were so swept up in that imagining that we forgot entirely about our game of pool. Both of our wing mates waved their hands in front of our faces, trying to break the trance.

To anyone else in the bar that night, it was clear that me and the guy with the backwards hat were either:

Extremely passionate about billiard theory; or

About to suck each other's blood.

The truth was, though we had met just moments earlier, we were, all eight minutes after meeting, very much two little vampires in love. Europe was not just a topic of conversation; it was a romantic metaphor for our could-be relationship. Every European anecdote we shared that night stood as something we *could* experience together . . . one day.

2013

Eight years, two dogs, and one marriage later, that same stranger and I finally made it to Europe. I did eventually get his name, Andrew, though unless he has royally pissed me off, I call him by his nickname, Weasel.

Our trip came after eight years of sad attempts to re-create "European experiences" in Wisconsin and Los Angeles. At the French restaurant down the street from us, we pretended our waiter (an actor from Brazil) was actually speaking with a French accent. On Andrew's thirtieth birthday, I nearly got kicked out of that same French restaurant when I did a "highly offensive" (their words, not mine) imitation of Édith Piaf. My UCLA graduation party took place at a German bar where we happily drank Erdinger and terribly stale "Bavarian-style pretzels" (Los Angeles has no appreciation for the art of making quality carbohydrates). We even spent a few delightful Friday nights parked on the couch after smoking just enough pot so that when we watched *Visions of Austria* on PBS, we were "*totally there, man...*" We took a few trips to Solvang—a Danish town in the Santa Ynez Valley adorned with plastic windmills, mediocre pastry shops, and a handsome bust of Hans Christian Andersen (that I may or may not have assaulted after too many wine tastings).

Planning our trip began less romantically than our initial conversation at *The Great Dane,* as it centered first and foremost on finding the cheapest airfare. As it turns out, flying to Europe by way of the Arctic Circle is the best bang for your króna.

"I know you've always said you wanted to go to Iceland, but do you *actually* want to go to Iceland?" Andrew asked me one night when he was making his signature last-minute dinner called "butter chick" (garlic butter and chicken sautéed together).

"Of course I want to go to Iceland, but don't you hate all things Nordic?" I asked, knowing that as a Leo he'd want to clear his reputation as a Nordic hater.

"Well, it's cheap to fly there and now is the time to go, *if* you want that. We could easily do a connecting flight to Munich." Andrew turned around and lifted an eyebrow to suggest our decision would impact the world somehow.

I feel I should pause here to defend Andrew's position on hating "all things Nordic." Our first conversation at the bar in Wisconsin involved me talking at length about Scandinavian theatre, which was my area of expertise at that point in life. After I'd taught twelve quarters of Scandinavian literature at UCLA, Andrew endured every terrible story about August Strindberg, Nazi sympathizer and novelist Knut Hamsun, or the cultural significance of pickled herring. Probably most challenging for Andrew was when I'd insisted we watch Ingmar Bergman's horribly depressing, divorce-inspiring *Scenes from a Marriage* when we'd been newlyweds for barely three months.

"You like Ireland, right?" I asked Andrew, knowing damn well that he did.

"You know the answer to that," he said, smiling ... onto my plan.

"Well, Iceland is like Ireland on crack," I declared with widened eyes.

"Okay, okay ..." He responded quickly, trying to temper one of my lengthy monologues.

"No, I mean it." I continued, ignoring him. "Iceland is on the Mid-Atlantic Ridge, so it's technically on the European continent *and* the North American continent. It's covered with volcanoes and glaciers, fire and ice, yin and yang. It's geysering and snowing, and it's just the ultimate drama queen."

Andrew continued to listen but rolled his eyes at my descriptions. I am no scientist but I do adore the fact that Iceland is, geologically speaking, "young" and kind of like this hissy teenager stuck in the middle of her parents' divorce (Europe and North America). Andrew always appreciated anthropomorphizing of any kind, so we booked tickets to Iceland for early October when it'd be nice and warm.

Getting There

We flew directly to Reykjavík from Seattle, where we were joined by approximately 7.7 percent of Iceland's population on our flight. Once the initial thrill of Euro-travel wore off, Andrew was hypnotized by the TV screen on the back of the seat in front of him, ripping through Marvel movies while I glued my forehead to the plastic oval window and watched the landscape below. Mount Rainier became the Cascades, which grew leaner, greener, and darker as we traveled northeastward. When we were nearly smack-dab in the middle of the North American continent, a thick, cool fog rolled in. The sun was behind us, backlighting an eerie blanket of smoky fog that coated the evergreens below us. It was as terrifying as it was mystical—two qualities that really do it for a Gemini.

Andrew and I are a great pair of insomniacs on airplanes, though for very different reasons. He loves the inexhaustible movie collections and I love to sit back (without the distraction of the internet) and worry. On the worry menu for that particular flight was the rental-car reservation, which had me set to drive a manual transmission, a.k.a. "the stick shift." I had only driven a stick shift twice in my life and both times for a total of (maybe) twenty-three minutes, wherein I stalled a total of 115 times. Andrew had never driven stick shift, nor did he care to learn—why would he, when his wife *kind-of* could...n't at all? In this particular instance, I insisted we opt for the manual transmission because I wanted to save ten thousand krónur (one hundred bucks).

We arrived in Reykjavík in the same state as two sleep-deprived toddlers ready to meet Santa at the North Pole – we were in no way capable of making rational adult decisions. At the car-rental booth, we were met with a fair-skinned day-walker named Igor. As Igor processed my information, I took a look outside at the tour buses. According to our research, there wasn't much of a cost difference between renting or taking one of the many coach buses that hustled the island. The savings came down to thirty or forty dollars, but for a couple who generally hates strangers and confined spaces, the rental was a much better deal for us.

"You have an economy manual four-door for two days," Igor told me.

"Just say, Igor, that I wanted to upgrade from a stick shift. . . . What would that cost?"

"Stick shift?" *Does not compute, does not compute.* Igor stared back at me blankly.

"The stick thingy, the . . ." I started to act out what most humans call a "manual transmission."

"Ah so, you want to upgrade to an automatic?" Igor offered, without smiling.

"What's the cost?"

"It would be an additional cost of five thousand krónur per day," he said, tapping his index finger along the computer screen.

"*Nope.* Stick shift it is," I quipped, like a frugal sitcom dad.

"Do you want the supplemental insurance?" Igor asked.

I pictured an exploding volcano spewing hot lava on our econo-car, a visual that was interrupted by Andrew.

"*Nope.* We're good," Andrew chirped.

It was 6:37am when we stepped out of the airport and officially began our first-ever European vacation. Our first impressions were identical: "HOLY FUCK, IT'S COLD." The Arctic air blasted through our yuppie Banana Republic fall shells and tipped off the beginning of an extremely f-bomb-heavy vacation.

"Why the fuck are we in Iceland?" Andrew asked, as the wind picked up and caused him to gasp.

"I don't fucking know," I said.

No two people hate cold weather more than me and Andrew. It is a hatred so deep we were willing to move to Los Angeles, the most hollow place on the planet, only for the promise of *not* being fucking cold.

I led the way to our rental car, hoping to remember in those forty-five seconds exactly how one *drives* a manual automobile in the first place. I threw my bags down by the trunk of the car, and immediately made my way to the driver's side door. Normally I approach new environments at a tortoise pace—it's something friends and family have come to tolerate—but on that day, I behaved as if I were a hare on cocaine. As Andrew was fumbling with the bags, I decided I could master driving a manual transmission using the power of intention. I called up a Tony Robbins quote from a book on tape: "The path to success is to take massive, determined action." (Tony, if you're reading this: your quote is tremendously motivational for...say, a serial killer.)

I put my left foot on the clutch, my right foot on the gas and stuck the key in the ignition. Just as I was about to let 'er rip I noticed something different in the manual transmission gear map. This Icelandic beast had the gears all mixed up.

So, instead of seeing what I'd see in an American manual transmission:

```
1-3-5
2-4-R
```

I saw this:

```
R-1-3-5
2-4-6
```

If you missed it, first gear and reverse are in opposite positions on the American and Icelandic cars. *No big deal.* I studied the new map for a millisecond and was so anxious to prove I could drive the manual that I took "massive determined action." I started the car and threw it into reverse, which, as we all know, should move me backwards. Unexpectedly, the second the gear caught, it blasted me forward like the goddamned *Apollo* launch, hurling me directly toward a parked minivan in front of me.

"No, stop, not that way, no! Hit the brakes!" Andrew screamed.

I pumped the brakes, which were apparently not yet thawed out and thus not ready for my "massive action." The car sputtered and stalled, catching a patch of ice that further propelled it toward the vacant rental van in front of us. *Crunch.* My solution was to start the car again, and blast with all my might into reverse. The gear caught and I was launched forward and farther into the bumper of the minivan. Andrew sprinted over.

"Are you okay? Are you okay?" He repeated the question quickly and genuinely.

"I put it in reverse. How come I went forward? How did this just happen?" I was dumbfounded.

"It's okay, it's okay." He meant it when he said it. "Let's just take it one step at a time. Okay?" (Side note: in all my years on Earth, I've never met anyone as patient as Andrew. He never thought to question why I'd put it in reverse when he was loading the bags in the trunk.)

"Okay," I said.

"First step—let's pry the cars apart," Andrew, the eternal project manager, said.

Upon hearing his cool, logical voice list our first order of European-vacation business as "pry these cars apart," I doubled over the miniature steering wheel in a fit of laughter. The econo-car horn responded to my weight with a whining honk that sounded more like a "Huh?" than a "Move it!" This made me laugh even harder.

Andrew, not breaking from his Mr. Fix-it role, got in front of the gnat (our rental car) and prepared to separate it from the minivan. I took my cue. I started the car and put it in "R".

"No! You're pushing it forward, it's gonna crack!" Andrew screamed

"What the hell is going on? I'm putting in 'R'! 'R'-for-fucking 'Reverse'!"

"Well, get out here and help me push it out," Andrew demanded.

I put the car in neutral and joined Andrew in rocking the gnat back and forth to pry it from the minivan. We tried to separate the cars again, and again, and even took running starts to body-slam the gnat free from the minivan. Amidst all of our antics, not one soul stirred; we may as well have been stranded on the moon.

"Why don't *you* know how to drive stick? This is all on me!" I screamed.

"No, it's not! You can fucking do this!" Andrew yelled, knowing I find the 'F-word' to be an effective motivator. "Get back in there and let's try again."

"Andrew, I don't *fucking* know how to *fucking* drive this *fucking* car."

As I was in the midst of a *Jersey Shore*-like meltdown, a miracle occurred, and an American woman, whom I recognized from our flight, walked by us on her way to her rental car.

"Can you help us?" I begged, much to her horror.

She evaluated the situation and lucky for us, she was from Oregon, which meant she was required to be helpful even if we looked like maniacs. She got in our car, started it, put it immediately into first gear, spinning our bumper deeper into the minivan.

"No, no, no —you're going forward!" Andrew screamed at the poor woman, just as a piece of plastic snapped dramatically.

"But I put it into reverse. Hold on, I'll try again." She checked the sticker on the shifter and went to start it again. Yet *again* she blasted forward and further smooshed the cars together.

"NO! NO! NO!" Andrew and I screamed in unison.

Lady Oregon cut the engine and scratched her chin.

"Let me try on my rental," she said, as she exited our car without apology for adding more dent to our bumper.

Andrew continued to rock the rental, as we saw Lady Oregon start her rental car and jolt forward like I had done so many times. We ignored her as she continued a cycle of: start and jolt forward, start and jolt forward, and jolt forward — like she was a kangaroo driving a bumper car. Suddenly we heard her scream.

"I got it!" We watched as Lady Oregon was driving backwards. She rolled up to us and explained, giddily, "there's a lever underneath the knob. If you want to go into reverse you gotta lift it up, otherwise you'll just go into first gear."

"Motherfucker," I said, turning to Andrew, who shared the sentiment.

This hidden trick of lifting the lever, which was not communicated to me or other renters, was the difference between going in two *very* different directions. It was so stupid. It made as much sense as early sea-faring pioneers settling on an island that was in the God-damned *Arctic Circle*.

Despite our rage over the mechanics of our rental car, we thanked Lady Oregon for her tip, and once we applied it, I blasted so far in reverse that I nearly hit the car behind us. Somewhere in our backwards blast off, our extra-long Icelandic license plate clattered to the ground. Andrew, still outside the car, looked over both shoulders to see if anyone had emerged - they hadn't. He reattached it quickly and jogged over to the driver's side of the car.

"Do you want to return this and get an automatic?" he asked, knowing the question was easy to pose but difficult to answer. The car was impossible to drive, but to return it would be *so* irritating. I pictured Igor opening a massive textbook titled "*Nordic Bureaucracy: First-and-only-Edition.*"

"No. Let me have a go around the parking lot and see how she purrs." I started the car again, and like a blender from the 70s it wailed dramatically and shot me into first gear. From there I tore around the rental lot, terrified that losing speed would force me into a stall. Andrew watched me weave around cars, and he grimaced at the litany of liabilities Iceland now presented. The car spit up gravel as it violently screeched up next to Andrew.

"Andrew! Andrew, get in the fucking car before they catch us!"

" *Who* catches us? Why are you screaming and acting like we're Bonnie and Clyde?"

"Get in the fucking car. Now, now, now!" I was WILD with manual power.

Andrew jumped in the car and we flew up to the automated parking gate. Without skipping a beat, he popped out of the moving car, ran around the back, inserted our validated ticket, got back in the car, doing all these tasks without me having to stop the car (and hence stall). From there we sputtered in first gear, barely making it to second, and once out on the wide-open volcanic plains, I got us settled in a wheezy third gear.

"*Holy shit, holy shit, holy shit.*" I repeated my Buddhist mantra with widened eyes fixed decisively on the narrow two-lane road that hovered just above a sea of hardened black lava. The sun hadn't broken yet, but the sky was doing some amount of work to light a landscape that looked to be a vast plain of nothing. We passed a small housing center near the airport in a town called Keflavík, but, after that, it was a lunar void. The car spoke up when the RPM gauge had us at around four. It begged me to change into fourth gear. I ignored it and took a deep breath; I was not ready to take our rocky relationship into fourth gear.

"Where the fuck are we?" I asked as it dawned on me that Iceland was "not the fuck at all how I pictured it." For as far as my eyes could see, it was lava leftovers, covered with bits of brown grass. I was expecting a dramatic and intense landscape, and what I saw was an apathetic hipster at best.

"I don't know," Andrew responded, but not before exploding into a delirious high-pitched giggle, a sound that he reserves for the silliest of occasions.

"Great vacation destination. Truly timeshare-worthy," I added flatly as Andrew continued with his high-pitched little-girl laugh. "You know, I'm feeling pretty jet-lagged. Mind if I take a nap?" I asked him, fluttering my right eye as if I were starting to doze.

"Sure. Go for it," Andrew replied through a giggle.

We were going about a hundred kilometers per hour when three tour buses approached us from behind. The roaring presence of the tour buses sent me into my usual go-to, uplifting, Tony Robbins-inspired self-talk.

"*We're gonna fuckin' die!*" I screamed. Andrew turned to see the line of angry buses gaining on our little shit-car.

"Just keep going, *keep going.* They can wait." Andrew pushed his brows together into a narrow focus point, like he'd reached the hardest level of a video game.

"They're on my ass. Oh, fuck, they're on my *fucking ass!*" I started to slow down, enough to make the engine sputter and cough. "*NOOOOO!*" I howled like a werewolf. "If I slow down, I'm going to stall and they'll just drive over us. They'll flatten us and our heads will pop off like fucking balloons! No one will even know – we're in ICELAND for *fuck's sake!* It'll be years before they find us. *Decades!* We're gonna die, Andrew. It's all over now."

"Just keep your eyes on the road," Andrew said, while dramatically gripping the car's ceiling handle. He turned around to see that the buses had pulled to the left to pass us. "Stay here, stay in third gear, just *stay, stay,*" Andrew coaxed me like I was our (at-times) panicky mutt Magnum.

The busses barreled past us on the left, their draft sucking us even closer to them on the already slender road.

"The road is narrowing! *Fuck!* Why are these roads so small? They're gonna send me off the road. *Fuck!*" Sure enough, after one of the busses passed us and I was no longer sucked into its draft, I veered off, nearing the abyss of black lava rock.

"GET BACK TO THE LEFT. *LEFT, LEFT, LEFT!*" Andrew was no longer calm and collected, he yelled loudly over the roar of busses that had now surrounded us.

As the second bus thundered up to my left, I clenched the wheel hard, and felt the stares of twenty or so geezers peering down to look at the two of us hyperventilating and cursing in our tiny, tiny car.

"I HATE THIS! I hate this so fucking much!" I screeched.

"You're doing so fucking great!" Andrew screamed.

After the third tour bus passed us and we were still alive, we calmed down a bit. We spent our first calm moments bashing early Icelandic settlers and why in the hell they'd chose to *stay* in Iceland. When the tone in the car was starting to lighten up, we reached a bend in the road.

"*Rounda-fucking-bouts?!*" I raged.

"Shit." Even Andrew's positivity couldn't stand up to the challenge of taking a manual transmission through the slow-and-go of a round-about intersection.

As we neared the circles, I decided to gun the engine several times and get some speed.

"What are you doing? Why are you revving the engine?" Andrew asked, afraid of my answer.

"I can't slow down *or I'll FUCKING stall.*"

As I careened toward a large circle adorned with a giant lava boulder in its center (how creative), I alternated between braking and flooring the gas so I wouldn't stall out. The squeal of the wheels around the first turn forced me to brake hard, which shook us into a full-out stop, square in the middle of the intersection.

"Motherfuckers!" I screamed.

"Start the engine and get us out of the intersection," Andrew said calmly.

"No shit, Sherlock! Oh...*oh*. Should I start the engine and drive?" I turned to Andrew, "Is that a *good* idea...to drive the car, Captain *FUCKING* Obvious?"

"Now is *not* the time." Andrew motioned to a car on our left who was politely waiting for us.

I put the car in neutral, started her up, and blasted into first gear. We stalled out just as the polite car decided it was safe to enter. Being worried that they'd slam into us, I slammed our whiny *huhhh* horn as a way to alert them of our presence (of which they were already *well* aware). The horn proved too whiny, so I rolled down the windows (the windows were also fucking manual) and yelled.

"I'm fucking here! I'm fucking here! Don't hit our ass!" I screamed.

I started the car again. The engine exploded forward—it shook and stalled.

And number two, again—the engine stalled.

At time number three, I started to sweat.

And four.

And five.

"You got this, just ease it into first gear," Andrew coaxed.

"*Ease? EASE?!* I want to punch you straight in the cock! If you know how to do it, then by all means . . . go ahead and *drive the fucking car!*" The anger worked to my advantage, and as I put the car in first gear, I burned so much rubber that we were surrounded by a halo of thick smoke. Somehow the gear clicked and we shot forward like a cannon.

"What the *fuck* was that?!" I continued to yell until a gentle downward slope in the road revealed a slalom course of SIX ROUNDABOUTS.

Six roundabouts—all ahead of me, each with an absurd amount of Icelandic Sunday-morning traffic. I looked at Andrew, expecting him to say something annoyingly positive.

"Remember: it's clutch, then gear, then gas." He said, thinking his cute little reminder might help me.

"Gee, thanks a lot, fuck wad!" I quipped sarcastically.

"Fuck you! I'm trying to help!" Andrew shot back.

Andrew grabbed the handgrip above the door and braced himself for the shit show ahead. We barreled onward, headed directly toward the eye of the circle (which was adorned with another *massive* lava rock). As if things couldn't get worse, my steady geyser of piping hot f-bombs had left our windshield "foggy as fuck."

"We're steaming up! We're steaming *the fuck up!*" We frantically rolled down our windows and Andrew hung his whole body out the front of the car, desperately trying to wipe the windshield with his Banana Republic fall shell.

"You wanna stay on Reykjanesbraut even though it veers to the right a little. Then we go straight through two more roundabouts and take our third right onto Hafnarfjar arvegur. After that, you take a left on Vifilssta avegur."

"I swear to buttons, I'm gonna fucking end you! Just tell me *one* Hagar-harf-narf-fjord-fuckity-fuck-fuck street at a fuckin' time, *you dick fuck!*"

As we approached each of the six roundabouts, I alternated between gas and brake, while blasting the whiny horn that sounded off a gurgled "*Huhhhh?*" as a warning. The trick worked, mostly because the Icelanders were wary to enter the roundabout while two Americans were jamming a horn, spitting up heaps of burnt-rubber smoke, and rolling down their windows so the mad woman driving the car (me) could scream, "GET THE FUCK OUT OF OUR FUCKING WAY!"

On the sixth roundabout, we were laughing so hard it was as if we'd been muted. I mean it: we couldn't ingest oxygen fast enough to fuel our laughter. We had tears streaming down our faces, tears that were instantly frozen by the frigid air that was blowing through our opened windows.

Once I finally calmed down, I had an epiphany of sorts.

"Hey, you know what I just realized?" I asked Andrew.

"What?" Andrew replied, knowing I was the queen of non-sequiturs.

"I have no short-term memory."

"You *just* realized that? *Really?*" Andrew asked, visibly perturbed.

"No! I mean I can't fucking remember what gear I'm in." As I confessed it, I noticed a red light ahead, so I shifted into second. The gears grinded and hissed at me, like I'd forced them into a compromising position. "*Tit fuck!* I'm in fourth gear. Andrew, I can't remember what gear I'm in. You have a great short-term memory; why don't you remind me before I shift?

"Okay, okay. That's smart. What gear are you in now?" he asked, ever so calmly.

"*I don't fucking know!*"

"You were in fourth and couldn't go to second so you must be in third."

"Third gear," I said slowly, methodically, as if I was ground control to Major Tom.

"Approaching stop sign in thirty feet," Andrew said, channeling a male Siri voice. "Prepare to slow down."

"Clutch down, shifting into *second gear*. Second gear accepted." I said, like a psychopathic nut.

"We've got a left turn coming up onto Hafnarfjar arvegur and then we're basically downtown."

"This is working—*holy fuckin' Freyfaxi*, this is working!" We hooted and hollered in the gnat, like we had put in the last piece of a complicated puzzle.

Iceland has an interesting little feature on their traffic lights, where a yellow light can mean two things: "light about to go red" *or* "light about to go green." Once we figured this out, we'd approach every red light with the same prayer— "Come on yellow, come on yellow"— because that meant I could keep moving without fear of stalling. We were like two blackjack addicts slowly rolling up to a light that *might* land on yellow. If the light was still stuck on red and we didn't have any runway left, we accepted our fate and stalled out dramatically, like a Civil War reenactor just shot. As a long-time track runner, the yellow light that appeared after the red light (meaning green is coming) also served as a "Runners, take your mark, set . . ." blastoff. We worked out a system where Andrew watched the light and I kept my head down, focused on the "track" like I was Usain Bolt.

We were on the cusp of entering downtown Reykjavík, turning from Kringlum rarbraut, or "Kringy-braut," as Andrew called it, onto Sæbraut, or "sauerkraut," which would take us along the water. I turned my left signal on and waited for a flash of yellow. Upon seeing the yellow light, I restarted my engine, and prepared to go Tony Robbins all the way into Reykjavík. I was feeling confident and proud and stupidly unstoppable.

I got green.

I threw my left foot down on the clutch. I felt the burn in my left calf.

I shoved the stick up and to the left. First gear. Take that!

I transferred power from the clutch to the gas. . . .

"Get ready, Reykjavík!" I yelled.

The car moved a few inches into the crosswalk and sputtered like an insecure lawnmower.

Still in what was a reasonably fresh green light, I restarted the car.

"Here we come, Reykjavík!" I exclaimed.

We rocked forward and for some reason moved back an inch, which is precisely where we stalled.

I pictured Tony Robbins and taking *extreme* measures. I tried again.

Nope.

Again.

Nope.

Andrew started laughing again like a little girl. He let go of the car's handgrip to wipe his tears.

I ignored him and kept trying and stalling, which meant his body was rocking back and forth with each failed attempt, shaking the car on top of its own sputter and stalls.

After *four* light cycles and 30+ attempts to move us forward, the gear caught and I plowed onto Sæbraut. Considering it had taken me seven minutes to get the car to move in any direction, I was not happy when I saw it . . . up ahead in the distance, a roundabout.

"*No, no, no!*" I howled like Neve Campbell in *Scream 2.*

"You can do this. You're doing *so good,*" Andrew said, stifling his own inner 'holy shit' tone.

"*What?* You can't just blatantly fucking lie like that, Andrew."

"You're moving, you're driving. Shit, I can't do that!"

As we entered the black hole (the roundabout) we held our breath. I accelerated and the car cried out "help me" and on its shrillest whine we stalled. Moments after stalling, a Mack truck approached from behind us. I screamed and honked the horn. The truck driver raised his eyebrows trying to figure out if it was me who made the scream, or if it was in fact a native Icelandic bird signaling a mating call. He slowed to a stop and waited.

"Just start the car and get us into first gear," said Captain Obvious.

"Do you think I don't know that? *Really?* There's a fucking Mack truck behind me. Do you think I'm like, *Oh, shit, what was I supposed to do again?*" I checked in the rearview mirror. The trucker was drumming his fingers on the wheel—just waiting it out.

I started the car and we immediately stalled. This happened two more times. Finally, the gears caught on the fourth try, but I only managed to move us forward about a foot.

"Well, we're headed in the right direction!" Andrew said, *so* fucking cheerfully.

I turned to give him a look that only a wife could give, and I repeated the above maneuver, which moved us forward another foot. When the car gears caught, I kept going straight without stopping because as luck would have it — we were lost.

I took us to a grocery store where Andrew went inside to fetch directions from a store clerk who looked, as Andrew later described, like a "half Q-tip, half neo-Nazi." While I waited for Andrew, I turned on the radio and scrolled through my options—there were two stations. I opted for classical music and sat for a moment.

The music flowed out of our open windows and echoed against a brick wall. Behind me, a collection of frosty low-grade mountains rested above calm seawater. It was nearly eight a.m. and it was eerily quiet. Above the grocery store, there stood a four-story apartment building without any lights on. It was Sunday morning and they were still sleeping – *how quaint.*

I got out of the car and inspected the damage to the front of the gnat. Considering our impact, the damage was minor, but . . . wait... something was missing. . . .

"*The fucking license plate.*"

The classical music playing on the car's radio continued to haunt the abandoned parking lot. What does a new license plate even cost in Iceland? Seventeen loaves of *rúgbrau* ? (*rúgbrau* = Icelandic rye bread that produces award-winning farts.)

When Andrew came back, his shoulders were slumped and he looked quite defeated. We got in the car and sat there quietly. Andrew broke the silence.

"Do we want to drive back to the airport? It's only seven forty-five. We can get a new car and be back by ten a.m. We wouldn't lose much time."

His proposition was so blissfully practical. Oh, it was the prudent choice. I thought about it and imagined my Icelandic life in an automatic car—never having to shift, never having to think, perhaps never even dropping an F-bomb.

Then, without responding and without giving him time to clutch the handgrip for support, I released the emergency brake, started the car, and threw it into and out of first gear. We tore around, making smoky donuts in an abandoned parking lot in downtown Reykjavík at 7:45 on a Sunday morning, with loud classical music screaming out our windows. (Quick side note: to the Icelandic woman who stepped out on her balcony in her bathrobe to see why a car was apparently being murdered by a couple laughing like hyenas, I sincerely apologize.)

"I can do this," I told Andrew, in a terrifyingly convinced tone. "It's gonna be weird and ugly, but *we* can do this."

"Okay. Let's do it." Andrew nodded his head and smiled.

We were ready. It was a great moment—full of promise and pride.

I started the car, put it in first, and the entire car sputtered violently before we even made it onto the street. We didn't look at each other because we knew we'd explode with laughter. I pursed my lips so I couldn't smile. Andrew averted his gaze, knowing that watching me try to stifle a laugh would send him into his own giggle fit.

It took *seven* times before we made it out of the grocery store parking lot and to a fancy hotel to ask, yet again, for directions. After we got directions, we stalled *fifteen times* (I AM NOT KIDDING) trying to depart the hotel driveway which was on a slight incline. Our exit was so obnoxious that we got a round of applause from the hotel staff, who watched us while they were on their smoke break. We laughed about this all the way to the street sweeper who cut in front of our car and forced me to stall in another roundabout. The street cleaner made three laps around us before we were able to move forward. We were stuck there giddily lost between inconsolable laughter and fits of rage (an entertaining mix for the sweeper, I'm sure).

Learning Curve

The rest of our two-day stay in Iceland involved a fair sampling of manual highs and manual lows, but mostly there was a steady supply of gut-busting laughter. Oh, it was such good stuff—laughter so deep and awkward that we lost control of our bodies, and our faces ached from smiling with facial muscles we didn't know we had.

After several failed attempts to get out of the parking lot at Thingvellir National Park, I reluctantly stood for this picture with "the gnat."

The highlights: The time a bright-eyed young mother pushing a stroller looked on in horror as I burned a halo of rubber through a busy shopping intersection, while she was waiting to cross. There were the old folks out on a walk who giggled when I again missed three light cycles because I couldn't get into first fucking gear. At one point, I accidentally parked in a reserved spot, which meant I had to do a three-point turn up a hill. The woman waiting for her spot dropped her jaw when, after several failed attempts, I put the car in neutral and Andrew He-man pushed it out of the way. Eventually, she laughed with us, too. Andrew's personal favorite moment was when we were departing the sacred old parliament site, the Althing, and our entire car shrieked so loudly getting into gear that every single human on the tour bus held their ears.

Weasel, though freezing his balls off, is smiling under his scarf.

We were lying in our hotel bed on our last night watching *Beverly Hills, 90210* with Icelandic subtitles when I figured it out.

"I think I've been stalling so much because I've been trying to go straight into third gear."

"Really? How is that possible?" Andrew asked.

"I think the first and third gears are just so close that I have been throwing it into what I think is first gear but what is actually third gear."

"Well, that would explain why we've been burning up the clutch."

"Not that it matters—I mean, we're leaving tomorrow."

It ended up being a very good thing that I paused to reflect on my manual driving technique that evening because the following morning at four a.m., Andrew pulled back our thick bedroom curtains to reveal:

"A snowstorm. A *motherfucking* snowstorm."

We hadn't driven in snow since we were in Wisconsin, six years earlier, but I sure as shit hadn't driven a manual car in a blizzard in Iceland. We had no choice but to weather the fucking storm. We gathered our suitcases and rolled them out onto the snow as we slid on the sidewalk in our thin-soled fall footwear. Andrew scraped the snow off the gnat with a courtesy map of Reykjavík, and he used his suitcase to clear a reverse runway behind the car.

I started the gnat. I got us into reverse and made the transition into first gear. We were both dumbfounded that the car was moving on the first try. We held onto that enthusiasm until we fishtailed into oncoming traffic. Luckily there were no collisions. It was at this point that I left atheism behind and became a full-blown born-again Christian.

For one hour and thirty-two minutes, we drove in a pitch-black blizzard, navigated around roundabouts, on narrow one-lane highways, bordered to the right by volcanic boulders and haunted by the whine of the over-worked windshield wipers and the clunk of chainless tires, picking up and spitting out heavy pancakes of snow. We were repeatedly passed by four-wheeler beasts which kicked up sludge that blanketed our windshield and temporarily blinded us. Without saying anything, Andrew extended a rolled-up map out the window to clear the sludge away, as I continued to curse and pray. We handled our fishtails and the faulty defrost system, keeping our eyes glued to the faint trail of tire tracks in front of us. The snow thickened when we were on the highway and it came at us from a pitch-black void (much like it does on the Magic Mountain ride at Disneyland). Though we were certain our flight to Munich would be cancelled, we were determined to get to the airport for the sole purpose of *never* having to drive stick shift again.

When we were ten minutes outside Keflavík, we drove through some kind of magical wormhole and the blizzard turned into a gentle flurry. We were convinced it was some kind of prank, until we figured out there was probably a good reason for building an airport in the balmy Gulf Stream breeze. We pulled into our rental-car return lot without one single stall or shutter. As our attendant checked our snow-covered car for damages, we eyed each other, knowing that our license plate was still floating around on the volcanic plains.

Feeling quite giddy that we made it through the storm.

"Okay, you can go," said the rental car agent, Thor Thorlorson, without smiling.

Without any time to spare, we sprinted through a wintry mix, getting to the airport just in time for our flight. We made it through security, looking over our shoulders, wondering if we'd be called out and hauled away for the state of our gnat. After we first took off, I looked out the window and watched as the magical Iceland grew smaller and more distant. Then, when all I could see were heaps of ocean, I decided to stop worrying and watch a movie with Andrew. We synced our screens and got lost in someone else's adventure, until we made it to Munich and started our next one.

Changing Gears

Two weeks later, when I was back in the typical Los Angeles commuter grind of stopping, going, cursing, spitting, and crying, a familiar sound caught my ear. It was the whine of the RPM gauge, as it jerked up and down with each time I blasted the gas and slammed the brakes. However, unlike Iceland, my car in Los Angeles was an automatic and so it didn't stall when the RPM was thrown out of whack.

Huh, I thought. It's incredible how human beings have perfected the art of taking things for granted. Here I was, my first time driving since Iceland and I had already taken my automatic car for granted.

I took a moment to remember Iceland — how easy it was to start the engine of the manual transmission, but, how impossible it was to move forward, just one inch. Beyond the challenge of getting into first gear, actually shifting into second, third, fourth, and fifth was virtually impossible. The fear I continually faced once *finally* getting the car to move in Iceland was - what if something unexpected popped up and I was forced to slow down? I'd break down and have to start all over again from scratch.

Opting for the manual transmission in Reykjavík was a totally illogical choice. It made absolutely no sense as to why someone would *choose* to operate a vehicle they didn't actually *know* how to operate, all in a foreign environment. Nevertheless, Andrew and I agreed to it, even if it was scary and for all intents and purposes, kind of outdated. Thankfully, it's an experience, a memory, that I can't shake - stuck with my very best friend, utterly clueless, and totally lost, but figuring it out together amidst fits of f-bombs and gut-busting, doubled-over, pants-pissing laughter. Oh yes — I'd choose that illogical, pain in the ass, piece-of-shit manual again in a heartbeat.

As it so happens, our ride in Reykjavík turned out to be the perfect metaphor for us, when, a few years after the trip we were faced with an exceptionally painful struggle with infertility. Before we were given an official diagnosis, we tried everything and anything to get into first gear, but, just like our first two days in Iceland, we sputtered through many light cycles. Unlike Iceland, however, in our instance of infertility we were particularly humorless. Just like our manual rental, Andrew couldn't drive, and so the burden and humiliation of stalling fell on me. Those feelings - the lack of control, the fear we might never ever move forward all the while watching others effortlessly pass us

- it was a painfully spot-on parallel to our rental in Reykjavík. There were even those moments during our struggle to get pregnant where I wanted to get out of the car and leave it on the roundabout for good. But, somehow, Andrew inspired me to start the car and try, yet again, to move forward.

In our case, getting pregnant with our daughter, Vickie (Victoria), was bizarrely similar to the experience of driving a manual transmission. It was a lot of work, a huge pain in the ass, *ah* –but when we got into first gear, and we saw a little flicker of light flashing on a screen that was our daughter's heartbeat, there was no fuller feeling - until - all the stuff that came after first gear. All the other shifts that built on top of each other until we made it, *finally*, into fifth gear. And, being with her perfect little spirit, watching her bright character unfold, hearing her laugh at the inherent silliness of it all; that was the same moment you get in fifth gear, when you're blasting down an open road and you realize that all your patience with shifting and changing gears have finally paid off. It's a feeling you just can't get with automatic.

So, yeah, I'd choose the manual every time.

And I'll repeat it to you for posterity:

I'd take that journey again,

And again,

And...

Again.

Stuck on the side of the road in Iceland, laughing our
asses off, and taking a picture of our intended destination ahead
(the Blue Lagoon), just in case we didn't make it.

BIO

Christie Nicholls is a Los Angeles based SAW (stand-up comedian, actor, and writer). After earning a PhD in Performance Studies at UCLA, Christie finally admitted that she wanted to perform herself. Whether in front of a camera, or a live audience, Christie will embody any role, from traditional leading lady, to Jane Fonda, to Richard Nixon, to her original characters, to your Mom (no really, she's excellent at impersonations). When Christie isn't writing, or performing, or prank calling, she's playing with her daughter Vickie, her husband Weasel, and their two rescue mutts Maverick and George Carlin. Or... she's probably in the hot tub. Yep, check the hot tub.

Christie is a splendid conversationalist.
Start one with her at www.christienicholls.com

Made in the USA
Middletown, DE
30 March 2020